Betty Schrampfer Azar

BASIC
ENGLISH GRAMMAR

Barbara Matthies, *Consulting Editor*

PRENTICE HALL REGENTS, Englewood Cliffs, NJ 07632

Library of Congress Cataloging in Publication Data

AZAR, BETTY SCHRAMPFER (date)
Basic English grammar.

Includes index.
1. English language—Text-books for foreign speakers.
2. English language—Grammar—1950–   . I. Matthies,
Barbara. II. Title.
PE1128.A96 1984   428.2'4   83-9768
ISBN 0-13-060434-8

Editorial/production supervision and
interior design: Barbara Alexander
Illustrations: Don Martinetti
Cover design: Ben Santora
Manufacturing buyer: Harry P. Baisley

© 1984 by Prentice-Hall, Inc., Englewood Cliffs, New Jersey 07632

Printed in the United States of America

20 19 18 17 16 15 14 13

ISBN 0-13-060434-8

PRENTICE-HALL INTERNATIONAL, INC., *London*
PRENTICE-HALL OF AUSTRALIA PTY. LIMITED, *Sydney*
EDITORA PRENTICE-HALL DO BRASIL, LTDA., *Rio de Janeiro*
PRENTICE-HALL CANADA INC., *Toronto*
PRENTICE-HALL OF INDIA PRIVATE LIMITED, *New Delhi*
PRENTICE-HALL OF JAPAN, INC., *Tokyo*
PRENTICE-HALL OF SOUTHEAST ASIA PTE. LTD., *Singapore*
WHITEHALL BOOKS LIMITED, *Wellington, New Zealand*

To DONALD

Contents

Page

Chapter 7
THE SIMPLE PAST TENSE 120

Chapter 8
EXPRESSING FUTURE TIME 150

Chapter 9
EXPRESSING ABILITY 178

Chapter 10
NOUNS AND PRONOUNS 203

Page

Chapter 11
MAKING COMPARISONS—PART I   230

Chapter 12
MAKING COMPARISONS—PART II   252

Appendix 1
NUMBERS   274

Appendix 2
DAYS OF THE WEEK AND MONTHS OF THE YEAR   276

Appendix 3
WAYS OF SAYING THE TIME   278

Appendix 4
IRREGULAR VERBS   279

INDEX   281

Preface

Basic English Grammar is a developmental skills text for students of English as a second language. It presents fundamental structures and vocabulary and provides ample opportunities for practice through extensive and varied exercises. While focusing on grammar, the text actively promotes the development of speaking, listening, and writing skills (and by extension reading skills) as well as situationally appropriate language use in everyday life in the United States and Canada.

ACKNOWLEDGMENTS

My thanks first of all go to Barbara Matthies, an experienced ESL teacher and administrator. She has—with perspicacity, frankness, and wit—contributed to every aspect of this text. An author can tend to think that every word is gold. Barbara easily and cheerfully cuts through such an illusion. Serving as a consultant from the inception of the text to the final manuscript, she has made me rethink, redirect, supplement, delete, enrich, and otherwise improve my presentations of material. Many of her insights have been incorporated in the text. In addition, she has been supportive as a friend throughout. I cannot thank her enough.

My thanks equally go to Donald Azar. His experiences in the teaching of ESL and in international education have provided many perspectives from which the text has benefited. He has helped me focus ideas, pursue options, and unsnarl snags. Throughout this project, he has shared and supported my enthusiasm.

My appreciation also goes to my students. It often seems to me that they have taught me more than I have ever taught them. They have provided the impetus for and determined the intentions of this text.

Special thanks also goes to Irene Juzkiw for her excellent critical review of the manuscript. Her suggestions were substantive and her criticisms right on the mark.

I also wish to express my thanks to the following teachers, colleagues, and friends for their contributions to the genesis, texture, and viability of this book: Ada Versteeg, Lilian Feinberg, Hazel Allen Lipa, Mary Ternoey, Carol Rivers, Alice Jennings, Charlotte Hanselman, Phyllis Mithin, John Schmidt, Michael Masyn, Liga Abolins, Michael Connelly, Harry Cargas, Jo Ann Ruckman, Peter Mahotka, David Keller, Thomas Edlun, Natalie Edlun, Nicki Herrington, Kathryn Moon Miller, Susan Warner Abbott, Kathryn Allahyari, and Charles Cox.

Finally I wish to express my appreciation to the following: to Marianne Russell, the ESL Editor at Prentice-Hall, for her encouragement and guidance; to Barbara Alexander, the production editor, for her expertise and patience; and to Don Martinetti, the illustrator, for his skill and humor.

Notes to the Teacher

LEVEL

Basic English Grammar seeks to meet the needs of lower-level ESL classes. While the introduction of structures and vocabulary is geared toward the low- or mid-beginner in the first parts of the text, the text can also, with appropriate pacing, be used with lower-intermediate students as a quick review and expansion of structure usage.

Basic English Grammar is the first in a series of three ESL grammar texts. The second in the series is *Fundamentals of English Grammar,* which is directed toward lower-intermediate and intermediate students. The third text, *Understanding and Using English Grammar,* is for intermediate through advanced students.

PRESENTATION OF GRAMMAR

In general, each unit is organized around a group of related structures and usages. The text is intended to be taught in the order in which it is presented; structures and vocabulary in earlier chapters serve as the basis for material in later chapters. However, if your class is lower-intermediate rather than beginning, you may wish to change the order of presentation somewhat to suit the needs of your students and your purposes.

Grammar receiving major emphasis is presented in charts consisting of examples accompanied by explanations. The examples are intended to be almost self-explanatory. The explanations are simplified as much as possible, with a minimum of terminology. Still, the students may not be able to grasp some parts of the charts by themselves at first. The intention is that you use the charts as a springboard in class. You may wish to discuss your own examples drawn from the immediate classroom context and relate them to the examples in the text as preparation for usage exercises. At times you may wish to delve into a usage exercise immediately, discuss form and meaning during the course of the exercise, and then return to a chart for the purpose of making certain generalizations.

The grammar charts serve various functions for various students. Some students devour the charts, while others pay them little or no mind, depending upon their learning strategies. Some students need to gain initial understanding from the charts before risking use, while others freely risk anything during usage exercises and refer to the charts only incidentally. In any case, the charts are not intended to be "learned" as an out-of-class homework assignment. A chart is only a starting point and a later reference source.

VOCABULARY

The text views vocabulary development as integral to the development of structure usage ability. Vocabulary is introduced and reinforced regularly. At times you will find it necessary to spend time in class discussing new vocabulary during exercises. The introduction of vocabulary is controlled so that it can easily be handled in the classroom and so that students should not have to spend a great deal of time at home looking up words in their dictionaries. Some exercises are specifically designed to enhance vocabulary acquisition while the students are practicing structure usage. Many of the illustrations are intended as aids for the teaching/learning of vocabulary.

EXERCISES

The goal in the exercises is to get the students talking about themselves—their activities, their ideas, their environment—as soon as possible, using the target structures. In general, the exercises in any given unit move from ones that focus almost entirely on manipulation of form and meaning to ones that demand more independent usage and involve a combination of skills.

Most of the exercises, those other than the oral exercises, are intended for out-of-class preparation and then in-class use. Typically, a teacher might discuss the grammar in a chart, have the students do the first three or four entries of an exercise in class, and then assign the rest of the exercise to be prepared for the next class. Usually students benefit more from preparing exercises at home than they do from going through exercises "cold" in class. Exercises that the students have prepared at home take less classtime to discuss and lead to more fruitful discussion.

Exercises specifically intended as written homework to be submitted to you are usually designated WRITTEN.

Some of the exercises are designated ORAL (BOOKS CLOSED). These exercises have various uses and purposes.

a) The students should be strongly encouraged to keep their books closed during these exercises. If an ORAL (BOOKS CLOSED) exercise is too difficult or too uncomfortable for your students, do the exercise first with books open and then later with books closed.

b) To initiate an ORAL (BOOKS CLOSED) exercise, it is usually sufficient simply to give the class an example or two of the intended pattern. The exercise examples can, of course, be supplemented by oral directions, and at times you may wish to write key words on the board to help the students focus on target structures or consider their options in their responses.

c) Once in a while you may wish to ask a student to assume the teacher role in some of the ORAL (BOOKS CLOSED) exercises; i.e., the student conducts the exercise by giving the cues and determining the appropriateness of the responses, while you retire to a corner of the room. Not all, but many, of the ORAL (BOOKS CLOSED) exercises are suitable for a "student-teacher." You may wish to designate a certain student as the "student-teacher" for a particular exercise for the next day's class and work with that student out of class in preparation for his/her role as teacher. Generally, a student-led oral exercise will take twice as much classtime as it would if teacher led, but if the time is available, it can be a valuable experience for the "student-teacher" and fun for the class as a whole.

d) Another use of the ORAL (BOOKS CLOSED) exercises is to divide the students into pairs or groups, with one student (book open) as the leader of the exercise.

e) Many of the ORAL (BOOKS CLOSED) exercises, especially those in which one student asks another a question, are meant to spur spontaneous discussion. Most of these exercises give a format (focusing on target structures) and topics that are intended to be used freely in the classroom. Encourage your students to expand upon their oral responses. Pursue interesting responses, grammar focus aside. Downplay correctness of form in favor of spontaneous communicative interaction. Allow for, even hope for, a modicum of mayhem as the students blurt out English in brief conversations with each other or with you in an easy, comfortable classroom.

f) Constant review is of course important, and the ORAL (BOOKS CLOSED) exercises provide a quick, easy way to review. Set aside five or ten minutes at the beginning or end of a class period to go over ORAL (BOOKS CLOSED) exercises from previous lessons. Besides benefiting from the reinforcement of structure usage and vocabulary, the students gain in self-confidence as they find their responses flowing more easily. Ask a "student-teacher" to conduct a review exercise if the time is available.

g) In the ORAL (BOOKS CLOSED) exercises, the symbol (. . .) indicates that you are to supply the name of a class member. Sometimes expressions of time and place are in parentheses, indicating that you are to supply an expression relevant to the people in your class. Delete entries that are irrelevant and make up your own entries to take advantage of the here-and-now classroom context and the particular situations of your students.

Exercises designated ORAL are intended to be done with books open but require no writing and no preparation.

TEACHER'S MANUAL

A teacher's manual is available. While primarily an answer key, it also contains a few additional oral exercises as well as some comments and suggestions.

I hope the text provides many enjoyable and profitable hours in class for both you and your students.

BETTY S. AZAR
Langley, Washington

chapter **1**

Using *Be* and *Have*

EXERCISE 1: Learn the names of your classmates. Write the names of your classmates in your book.

_____   _____

_____   _____

_____   _____

_____   _____

_____   _____

_____   _____

_____   _____

1–1 SUBJECT + *BE* + NOUN

SINGULAR	PLURAL	
		SINGULAR = one PLURAL = more than one (two or three or four or more)
SUBJECT + *BE* + NOUN	SUBJECT + *BE* + NOUN	
(a) I am a student.	(i) We are students.	I ⎫ you ⎪ he ⎬ = pronouns she ⎪ it ⎪ we ⎪ they ⎭
(b) You are a student.	(j) You are students.	
(c) John is a student.	(k) John and Mary are students.	
(d) He is a student.	(l) They are students.	
(e) Mary is a student.		
(f) She is a student.		John ⎫ Mary ⎪ rose ⎬ = nouns student ⎪ flower ⎭
(g) A rose is a flower.	(m) Roses are flowers.	
(h) It is a flower.	(n) They are flowers.	
		a student = singular noun **students** = plural noun
		NOTE: To make a noun plural, add **-s** to the noun.* Do not use **a** with a plural noun.
		be = a verb am ⎫ is ⎬ = forms of **be** are ⎭

* See 5–1 for more information about plural nouns.

EXERCISE 2: Complete the sentences. Use a verb: *am, is,* or *are.* Use a noun: *a student* or *students.*

1. We _____ are students. _____

2. I _____

3. John _____

4. He _____

5. Mary _____

6. She _____

7. John and Mary _____

8. They _____

9. We _____

10. You (*one person*) _____

11. You (*two persons*) _____

12. You and I _____

EXERCISE 3—ORAL (BOOKS CLOSED):

(To the teacher: Give the subject(s). The student is to complete the sentence with a form of **be** *+ a student/students while indicating the subject or subjects.)*

> *Example:*   (. . .)
> *Response:*   (. . .) is a student. *The responding student indicates* (. . .).

1. (. . .)
2. (. . .) and (. . .)
3. I
4. We
5. (. . .)
6. She
7. (. . .) and (. . .)

8. They
9. You
10. (. . .)
11. (. . .) and (. . .)
12. He
13. You and I
14. (. . .) and (. . .) and (. . .)

1-2 CONTRACTIONS WITH *BE*

	PRONOUN + **BE** = CONTRACTION		When people speak, they often push two words together. *A contraction = two words that are pushed together.*
AM	I + am = **I'm**	(a) **I'm** a student.	
IS	he + is = **he's** she + is = **she's** it + is = **it's**	(b) **He's** a student. (c) **She's** a student. (d) **It's** a flower.	Contractions of *a subject pronoun + be* are used in both speaking and writing.
ARE	you + are = **you're** we + are = **we're** they + are = **they're**	(e) **You're** a student. **You're** students. (f) **We're** students. (g) **They're** students.	PUNCTUATION: The mark in the middle of a contraction is called *an apostrophe.*

Note: Write an apostrophe above the line. Do not write an apostrophe on the line.

Right: *I'm a student.*
Wrong: *I͵m a student.*

EXERCISE 4:   Complete the sentences. Use contractions (*pronoun* + *be*).

1. *Mary* is a student. _____She's_____ in my class.

2. *John* is a student. _____ in my class.

3. I have *one brother.* _____ twenty years old.

4. I have *two sisters.* _____ students at the university.

5. I have *a dictionary*. _____ on my desk.

6. I like *my classmates*. _____ friendly.

7. I have *three books*. _____ on my desk.

8. *My brother* is twenty-six years old. _____ married.

9. *My sister* is twenty-one years old. _____ single.

10. *Mary and John* are students. _____ in my class.

11. I like *my books*. _____ interesting.

12. I like *grammar*. _____ easy.

13. *My brother and my sister* live at home. _____ students in high school.

14. *My brother and I* live in an apartment. _____ students at the university.

15. *Bob and I* live in a dormitory. _____ students.

16. I know *Mr. Smith*. _____ a teacher.

17. I know *Mrs. Smith*. _____ a teacher.

18. I know *Mr. and Mrs. Smith*. _____ teachers.

19. *Sue and I* live in an apartment. _____ roommates.

20. We live in *an apartment*. _____ on Pine Street.

21. *I* go to school. _____ a student.

22. I know *you*. _____ in my English class.

EXERCISE 5—ORAL: *Is* and *are* are also often contracted with nouns in spoken English. Listen to your teacher say the contractions in the following sentences and practice saying them yourself.

1. Grammar is easy. ("Grammar's easy.")
2. Mary is a student.
3. My book is on the table.
4. My books are on the table.
5. The weather is cold today.
6. My brother is twenty-one years old.
7. The window is open.
8. The windows are open.
9. My money is in my wallet.
10. Mr. Smith is a teacher.
11. John is at home now.
12. The sun is bright today.
13. My roommate is from Chicago.
14. My roommates are from Chicago.
15. My sister is a student in high school.

1-3   USING *HAVE* AND *HAS*

SINGULAR			PLURAL				
I	**have**	a pen.	**We**	**have**	pens.	*I* *you* *we* *they* } + *have*	
You	**have**	a pen.	**You**	**have**	pens.		
He	**has**	a pen.	**They**	**have**	pens.	*he* *she* *it* } + *has*	
She	**has**	a pen.					
It	**has**	blue ink.					

EXERCISE 6:   Complete the sentences. Use **have** or **has.**

1. I _____have_____ a dictionary.

2. We _____ grammar books.

3. Mary _____ a blue pen. She _____ a blue notebook too.

4. You _____ a pen in your pocket.

5. Bob _____ a notebook on his desk.

6. Mary and Bob _____ notebooks. They _____ pens too.

7. John is a student in our class. He _____ a red grammar book.

8. I _____ a grammar book. It _____ twelve chapters.

9. You and I are students. We _____ books on our desks.

10. John _____ a penny in his pocket. Mary _____ a dollar bill in her purse.

1-4   USING *MY, YOUR, HIS, HER, OUR, THEIR*

SINGULAR	PLURAL	SUBJECT — POSSESSIVE*
(a) **I** have a book. **My** book is red.	(e) **We** have books. **Our** books are red.	*I — my* *you — your* *he — his*
(b) **You** have a book. **Your** book is red.	(f) **You** have books. **Your** books are red.	*she — her* *we — our* *they — their*
(c) **He** has a book. **His** book is red.	(g) **They** have books. **Their** books are red.	
(d) **She** has a book. **Her** book is red.		

* *My, your, his, her, our,* and *their* are called possessive adjectives. They come in front of nouns.

EXERCISE 7: Complete the sentences. Use *my, your, his, her, our,* or *their.*

1. I have a pen._____My_____ pen is blue.

2. You have a pen. _____ pen is black.

3. Mary has a pen. _____ pen is green.

4. John has a pen. _____ pen is yellow.

5. John and I have pens. _____ pens are gray.

6. John and you have pens. _____ pens are red.

7. John and Mary have pens. _____ pens are orange.

8. I have a sister. _____ sister is twenty-one years old.

9. Mary has a car. _____ car is a Ford.

10. You have a pen. _____ pen is a ballpoint.

11. Jim and you have mustaches. _____ mustaches are dark.

12. Ann and Bob have a baby. _____ baby is eight months old.

13. Alice and I have notebooks. _____ notebooks are green.

14. Ann has a brother. _____ brother is in high school.

15. Jim has a coat. _____ coat is brown.

16. We have a dog. _____ dog is gray and white.

EXERCISE 8: Complete the sentences. Use *have* or *has.* Use *my, your, his, her, our,* or *their.*

1. I _____have_____ a book. _____My_____ book is interesting.

2. Bob _____ a bookbag. _____ bookbag is green.

3. You _____ a raincoat. _____ raincoat is brown.

4. She _____ a raincoat. _____ raincoat is red.

5. Ann and Bob are married. They _____ a

   baby. _____ baby is six months old.

6. Dick and Sue _____ a daughter. _____ daughter is
   ten years old.

7. Bob and I _____ a son. _____ son is seven years old.

8. I _____ a brother. _____ brother is sixteen.

9. We _____ grammar books. _____ grammar books are red.

10. Tom and you _____ bookbags. _____ bookbags are green.

11. Ann _____ a dictionary. _____ dictionary is red.

12. Tom _____ a car. _____ car is blue.

EXERCISE 9:   Complete the sentences with *my, your, his, her, our,* or *their.*

1. Alice is wearing a blouse. _____ blouse is light blue.

2. Tom is wearing a shirt. _____ shirt is yellow and brown.

3. I am wearing jeans. _____ jeans are blue.

4. Bob and Tom are wearing boots. _____ boots are brown.

5. Sue and you are wearing dresses. _____ dresses are red.

6. Ann and I are wearing sweaters. _____ sweaters are green.

7. You are wearing shoes. _____ shoes are dark brown.

8. Sue is wearing a skirt. _____ skirt is black.

9. John is wearing a belt. _____ belt is white.

10. Sue and Ann are wearing slacks. _____ slacks are dark gray.

11. Tom is wearing slacks. _____ slacks are dark blue.

12. I am wearing earrings. _____ earrings are gold.

EXERCISE 10—ORAL (BOOKS CLOSED):

(To the teacher: First ask the students to name all the colors and then all of the articles of clothing and jewelry they see in the room. Then indicate by gesture or words an article of clothing/jewelry and ask the students to describe its color using this pattern: possessive adjective + noun + **is/are** + color.*)*

Example: Look at Ali. Tell me about his shirt. What color is his shirt?
Response: His shirt is blue.

Example: Look at Rosa. What is this?
Response: A sweater.
Teacher: Tell me about her sweater. What color is it?
Response: Her sweater is red.

Example: Look at me. What am I touching?
Response: Your shoes.
Teacher: Tell me about the color.
Response: Your shoes are brown.

VOCABULARY CHECKLIST

COLORS	CLOTHES	JEWELRY
black	belt	bracelet
blue, dark blue, light blue	blouse	earrings
blue-green	boots	necklace
brown, dark brown, light brown	coat	ring
gray, dark gray, light gray	dress	watch/wristwatch
green, dark green, light green	gloves	
orange	hat	
pink	jacket	
purple	jeans	
red	pants	
tan, beige	sandals	
white	scarf	
yellow	shirt	
gold	shoes	
silver	skirt	
	slacks	
	suit	
	sweater	
	tie, necktie	
	T-shirt	

EXERCISE 11:   Complete the sentences in this composition by Carlos.

(1)   My name ___is___ Carlos. ___I am OR: I'm___ from Mexico.

(2)   _____ a student. _____ twenty years old.

(3)   My family lives in Mexico City. _____ father

(4)   _____ a businessman. _____ fifty-one years old.

(5)   _____ mother _____ a housewife.

(6)   _____ forty-nine years old.

(7)   I _____ two sisters and one brother. The names of my sisters

(8) _____ Rosa and Patricia. Rosa _____ a teacher.

(9) _____ twenty-eight years old. Patricia _____ a

(10) student. _____ eighteen years old. The name of

(11) _____ brother _____ Juan. _____ an

(12) engineer. He is married. He _____ two children.

(13)   I live in a dormitory. _____ a tall building. _____

(14) on Pine Street. My address _____ 3235 Pine St. I live with my

(15) roommate. _____ name is Bob. _____ from

(16) Chicago. _____ nineteen years old.

(17)   I like my classes. _____ interesting. I like _____

(18) classmates. _____ friendly.

EXERCISE 12: Write a composition by completing the sentences. (Use your own paper.) Note: A sentence begins with a capital letter (a big letter) and a sentence ends with a period (.).*

My name _____. I _____ from _____. _____ a student. _____ years old.

My family lives in _____. _____ father _____. _____ years old.

_____ mother _____. _____ old.

I have _____ sister(s) and _____ brother(s). The name(s) of my sister(s)

_____. _____ is a _____. _____ old. (*Write about each sister.*) The name(s)

of my brother(s) _____. _____ is a _____. _____ old. (*Write about each brother.*)

I live in (a dormitory, a house, an apartment). My address _____.

I live with _____. _____ name(s) _____.

I like _____ classes. _____ are _____. I like _____ classmates. They

_____.

_____

*In British English, a period is called a full stop.

1-5   USING *THIS* AND *THAT*

(a) I have a book in my hand. **This book** is red. (b) I see a book on your desk. **That book** is blue. (c) **This** is my book. (d) **That** is your book.	*this book* = the book is near me *that book* = the book is not near me

EXERCISE 13—ORAL (BOOKS CLOSED):   Use *this* and *that.* Touch and point.

> *Example:*   book
> *Response:*   This is my book. That is your book.

1. book	4. purse	7. coat	10. pencil
2. pen	5. dictionary	8. hat	sharpener
3. notebook	6. bookbag	9. pencil	11. watch
			12. nose

EXERCISE 14—ORAL (BOOKS CLOSED):   Use *this* and *that.* Touch and point to things in the classroom.

> *Example:*   red/yellow
> *Response:*   This (book) is red. That (shirt) is yellow.

1. red/blue	7. red/pink
2. red/green	8. dark blue/light blue
3. red/yellow	9. black/gray
4. blue/black	10. gold/silver
5. white/black	11. dark brown/tan
6. orange/green	12. purple/red

EXERCISE 15—ORAL: Talk about things and people in the classroom. Ask your classmates these questions:

1. What's this?
2. What's that?
3. Who's this?
4. Who's that?

1-6   USING *THESE* AND *THOSE*

	SINGULAR—PLURAL
(a) My books are on my desk. **These** are my books. (b) Your books are on your desk. **Those** are your books.	*this — these* *that — those*

EXERCISE 16—ORAL (BOOKS CLOSED):   Use *these* and *those*.

Example: books
Response: These are my books. Those are your books.

1. books
2. pens
3. shoes
4. earrings
5. jeans

6. matches
7. cigarettes
8. glasses/sunglasses
9. notebooks
10. hands

EXERCISE 17—ORAL (BOOKS CLOSED):   Use *this, that, these,* or *those*.

Example: book
Response: This is my book. That is your book.

Example: books
Response: These are my books. Those are your books.

1. book
2. books
3. dictionary
4. pens
5. pen

6. coat
7. shoes
8. wallet
9. purse
10. cigarettes

EXERCISE 18:   Complete the sentences. Use the words in parentheses.

1. (*This, These*)_____These_____books belong to me. (*That, Those*)

_____That_____ book belongs to Mary.

2. (*This, These*)_____ coat is black. (*That, Those*)_____
coats are tan.

3. (*This, These*) _____ earrings are gold. (*That, Those*)

_____ earrings are silver.

4. (*This, These*) _____ pencil belongs to Bob. (*That, Those*)

_____ pencil belongs to Alice.

5. (*This, These*) _____ sunglasses belong to me. (*That, Those*)

_____ sunglasses belong to you.

6. (*This, These*) _____ exercise is easy. (*That, Those*)

_____ exercises are hard.

7. Students are sitting in (*this, these*) _____ desks, but (*that, those*)

_____ desks are empty.

8. (*This, These*) _____ book is on my desk. (*That, Those*)

_____ books are on your desk.

1-7   *BE* + ADJECTIVE

SUBJECT + *BE* + ADJECTIVE			
(a)	A ball	**is**	**round.**
(b)	Balls	**are**	**round.**
(c)	Mary	**is**	**intelligent.**
(d)	Mary and John	**are**	**intelligent.**

round and **intelligent** = adjectives

Note: There is never a final **-s** on an adjective. An adjective does not have a plural form.

EXERCISE 19—ORAL (BOOKS CLOSED):   Use adjectives to describe objects.

(To the teacher: Bring to class some objects that the students can describe by using adjectives. Write the adjectives you want the students to use on the board; then produce objects to prompt descriptions. Discuss vocabulary as necessary.)

Suggestions:

1. round (a ball, a dime)
2. square (a box)
3. flat (a dime)
4. sweet (a candy bar)
5. sour (a lemon)
6. soft (a pillow)
7. hard (a rock)
8. sharp (a knife, a razor blade)
9. heavy (a rock)
10. light (a feather)

11. full (a glass with water)
12. empty (a glass)
13. wet (a wet handkerchief)
14. dry (a dry handkerchief)
15. dirty (a hand rubbed on the floor)
16. clean (a hand not rubbed on the floor)

17. long (a string)
18. short (a string)
19. loud (a tape recorder with volume turned up)
20. soft (a tape recorder with volume turned down)

EXERCISE 20: Make sentences by using *is* or *are* and an adjective from the following list. Use each adjective only one time.

bright	✔*hot*	*small/little*
cold	*important*	*soft*
flat	*large/big*	*sour*
funny	*round*	*square*
hard	*sharp*	*sweet*

1. Fire ____is hot._____

2. Balls and oranges _____

3. A box _____

4. Sugar _____

5. A lemon _____

6. Ice and snow _____

7. Rocks and metals _____

8. A pillow _____

9. A joke_____

10. Razor blades _____

11. The sun_____

12. Good health_____

13. A dime_____small, round, and

_____

14. An elephant_____, but

a mouse _____

EXERCISE 21—ORAL (BOOKS CLOSED):

    Example: round   Name something that is round.
    Response: (A ball, an orange, the world, my head, etc.) is round.

1. hot	7. flat	13. hard
2. square	8. little	14. soft
3. sweet	9. important	15. beautiful
4. sharp	10. cold	16. expensive
5. sour	11. funny	17. cheap
6. large	12. bright	18. free

1-8 NEGATIVE WITH *BE*

IS + NOT	(a) A ball **is not** square. A ball **isn't** square.	CONTRACTION: *is + not = isn't*
ARE + NOT	(b) Balls **are not** square. Balls **aren't** square.	CONTRACTION: *are + not = aren't*
AM + NOT	(c) I **am not** hungry.	*Am* and *not* are not contracted.

EXERCISE 22:   Complete the sentences. Use *is, isn't, are,* or *aren't.*

1. A ball _____isn't_____ square.

2. Balls _____are_____ round.

3. A mouse _____ big.

4. Lemons _____ yellow. Bananas _____ yellow too.

5. A lemon _____ sweet. It _____ sour.

6. A diamond _____ cheap.

7. Diamonds _____ expensive.

8. Apples _____ expensive.

9. The earth _____ flat. It _____ round.

10. My pen _____ heavy. It _____ light.

11. This room _____ dark. It _____ light.

12. A rock _____ hard. It _____ soft.

13. English grammar _____ hard. It _____ easy.

14. This exercise _____ difficult. It _____ easy.

15. My classmates _____ friendly.

16. A turtle _____ slow.

17. Airplanes _____ slow. They _____ fast.

18. The floor in the classroom _____ clean. It _____ dirty.

19. The weather _____ cold today.

20. The sun _____ bright today.

21. Ice cream and candy _____ sour. They _____ sweet.

22. My shoes _____ comfortable.

23. My desk _____ comfortable.

24. Flowers _____ ugly. They _____ beautiful.

25. Traffic at rush hour _____ noisy. It _____ quiet.

26. I'm in class right now. I _____ at home.

EXERCISE 23—ORAL (BOOKS CLOSED): Make sentences: Use *is/isn't* or *are/aren't.*

Example: A ball/round
Response: A ball is round.

Example: Balls/square
Response: Balls aren't square.

1. A box/square
2. A box/round
3. The earth/flat
4. The earth/round
5. Bananas/red
6. Bananas/yellow
7. A banana/soft
8. A banana/hard
9. A pillow/soft
10. Pillows/soft
11. Diamonds/expensive
12. Diamonds/cheap
13. Apples/expensive
14. Air/free
15. A pen/heavy
16. A pen/light

17. Flowers/ugly
18. A rose/beautiful
19. A turtle/fast
20. A turtle/slow
21. Airplanes/slow
22. Airplanes/fast
23. English grammar/difficult
24. English grammar/easy
25. This exercise/hard
26. The weather/hot today
27. The weather/cold today
28. Lemons/sweet
29. Ice cream and candy/sour
30. Traffic/noisy
31. Education/important
32. Good food/important
33. Good food and exercise/important
34. The students in this class/very intelligent

EXERCISE 24—ORAL: Do any of these words describe you?

Example: hungry?
Response: I'm hungry. OR: I'm not hungry.

1. hungry?
2. thirsty?
3. sleepy?
4. tired?
5. old?
6. young?

7. happy?
8. homesick?
9. married?
10. single?
11. angry?
12. nervous?

13. friendly?
14. lazy?
15. hardworking?
16. famous?
17. healthy?
18. sick?

chapter 2

Using *Be*

2-1 *BE* + PREPOSITIONAL PHRASE

***BE* + PREPOSITION + NOUN**				PREPOSITION + NOUN = PREPOSITIONAL PHRASE
(a)	Bob is	**at**	**the library.**	*at the library* = prepositional phrase
(b)	My books are	**on**	**that table.**	People often use ***be*** + *a prepositional phrase* to talk about *place.*
(c)	Mary is	**in**	**her room.**	Some common prepositions: ***around, at, between, in, on, under.***

EXERCISE 1—ORAL (BOOKS CLOSED):   Practice using place prepositions.

(To the teacher: Ask a student to perform an action and then to answer your question. If you wish, ask the class to perform the action together and to answer together.
Demonstrate the prepositional expressions of place as necessary. Reinforce any expressions that are difficult for your class by making up your own directions.)

Example: *under*   Put your hand under your chair. Where is your hand?
Response: My hand is/It's under my chair.

1. *on*   Put your pen on your book. Where is your pen?
2. *in*   Put your pen in your book. Where is your pen?

3. *under*   Put your pen under your book. Where is your pen?
4. *next to*   Put your pen next to your book. Where is your pen?
5. *on*   Put your hand on your ear. Where is your hand?
6. *next to*   Put your hand next to your ear. Where is your hand?
7. *around*   Put your hands around your neck. Where are your hands?
8. *next to*   Stand next to (. . .). Where are you?
9. *between*   Stand between (. . .) and (. . .). Where are you?

EXERCISE 2—ORAL (BOOKS CLOSED):   Same as the preceding exercise.

1. *in the front of*   Stand in the front of the room. Where are you?
2. *in the middle of*   Stand in the middle of the room. Where are you?
3. *in the back of*   Stand in the back of the room. Where are you?
4. *outside*   Go outside the room. Where are you?
5. *inside*   Come inside the room. Where are you?
6. *next to*   Stand next to (. . .). Where are you?
7. *in back of*   Stand in back of (. . .). Where are you?
8. *in front of*   Stand in front of (. . .). Where are you?

EXERCISE 3—ORAL (BOOKS CLOSED):

(To the teacher: Demonstrate the following prepositional expressions of place and ask the students to describe your position or the position of an object.)

>   *Example:*   (The teacher places a pen on a desk.) Where is my pen?
>   *Response:*   On the desk.

1. around	5. in the back of	9. inside	13. under
2. between	6. in front of	10. next to	
3. in	7. in the front of	11. on	
4. in back of	8. in the middle of	12. outside	

2-2 YES/NO QUESTIONS WITH *BE*

QUESTION	STATEMENT	
BE + SUBJECT	SUBJECT + **BE**	In a question, **be** comes in front of the subject.
(a) **Is** she a student?	**She** is a student.	*Punctuation:* A question ends with a question mark (?). A statement ends with a period (.).
(b) **Are** they at home?	**They** are at home.	

QUESTION	SHORT ANSWER (+ LONG ANSWER)*	
(c) **Is** she a student?	Yes, **she is.** (She's a student.) No, **she's not.** (She's not a student.) No, **she isn't.** (She isn't a student.)	Notice in the short answers: After *yes,* **be** is not contracted with the pronoun subject. After *no,* two contractions are possible with no difference in meaning.
(d) **Are** they at home?	Yes, **they are.** (They're at home.) No, **they're not.** (They're not at home.) No, **they aren't.** (They aren't at home.)	

* When people answer a question, they usually give only a "short answer," but sometimes they give a "long answer" too.

EXERCISE 4:   Make questions and give short answers.

1. A: _____Are you tired?_____

   B: _____No, I'm not._____ (I'm not tired.)

2. A: _____Is Mary in your class?_____

   B: _____Yes, she is._____ (Mary is in my class.)

3. A: _____

   B. _____ (I'm not homesick.)

4. A: _____

   B: _____ (Bob is homesick.)

5. A: _____

   B: _____ (My sister is a student.)

6. A: _____

   B: _____ (My pen is in my pocket.)

7. A: _____

    B: _____ (Sue isn't here today.)

8. A: _____

    B. _____ (My brother isn't in the United States.)

9. A: _____

    B: _____ (I'm from Canada.)

10. A: _____

    B: _____ (The students in this class are intelligent.)

11. A: _____

    B: _____ (The chairs in this room aren't comfortable.)

12. A: _____

    B: _____ (I'm not married.)

13. A: _____

    B: Of course not! Elephants aren't pink. Are you crazy?

EXERCISE 5—ORAL (BOOKS CLOSED):   Ask a classmate a question. Use *Are you . . . ?*

> *Example:*   hungry
> *Student A:*   (. . .), are you hungry?
> *Student B:*   Yes, I am. OR: No, I'm not.

1. hungry	12. a teacher
2. sleepy	13. a doctor
3. thirsty	14. in the middle of the room
4. married	15. in the back of the room
5. single	16. in the front of the room
6. tired	17. in class
7. homesick	18. in bed
8. lazy	19. at the library
9. cold	20. at home
10. comfortable	21. in (*name of this city*)
11. a student	22. in (*name of another city*)

23. in Canada
24. in the United States
25. from the United States
26. in high school
27. a high school student

28. a student at (*name of school*)
29. a university student/a college student
30. from (*name of country*)

EXERCISE 6—ORAL (BOOKS CLOSED): Ask a classmate a question.

Example: a ball/round
Student A: (. . .), is a ball round?
Student B: Yes, it is.

Example: a ball/square.
Student A: (. . .), is a ball square?
Student B: No, it isn't/it's not.

1. a mouse/big
2. sugar/sweet
3. lemons/sweet
4. ice cream and candy/sour
5. the world/flat
6. the world/round
7. your desk/comfortable
8. your shoes/comfortable
9. your eyes/brown
10. the sun/bright today
11. the weather/cold today

12. your pen/heavy
13. apples/expensive
14. diamonds/cheap
15. English grammar/easy
16. the floor in this room/clean
17. elephants/pink
18. turtles/intelligent
19. your dictionary/under your desk
20. your books/on your desk
21. your desk/in the middle of the room
22. your pen/in your pocket

2-3   QUESTIONS WITH *BE:* USING *WHERE*

QUESTION				SHORT ANSWER (+ LONG ANSWER)	
(a)	**Is**	**the book**	on the table?	**Yes, it is.** (The book is on the table)	***Where*** asks about *place.*
(b) **Where**	**is**	**the book?**		**On the table.** (The book is on the table.)	
(c)	**Are**	**the books**	on the table?	**Yes, they are.** (The books are on the table.)	
(d) **Where**	**are**	**the books?**		**On the table.** (The books are on the table.)	

EXERCISE 7: Make questions.

1. A: _____ Is Mary at home? _____
   B: Yes, she is. (Mary is at home.)

2. A: _____ Where is Mary? _____
   B: At home. (Mary is at home.)

3. A: _____ Where is my book? _____
   B: On the desk. (Your book is on the desk.)

4. A: _____
   B: Yes, it is. (Your notebook is on the table.)

5. A: _____
   B: On the desk. (Your dictionary is on the desk.)

6. A: _____
   B: In my pocket. (My wallet is in my pocket.)

7. A: _____
   B: On Main Street. (The post office is on Main Street.)

8. A: _____
   B: Yes, it is. (The train station is on Grand Avenue.)

9. A: _____
   B: Over there. (The bus stop is over there.)

10. A: _____
    B: At the library. (Tom is at the library.)

11. A: _____
    B: Yes, she is. (Ann is in class today.)

12. A: _____
    B: Yes, they are. (The students are in class today.)

13. A: _____
    B: In my bookbag. (My books are in my bookbag.)

14. A: _____
    B: At the zoo. (Sue and Dick are at the zoo today.)

15. A: _____
    B: At the park. (Jean is at the park.)

16. A: _____

    B: In California. (Los Angeles is in California.)

17. A: _____

    B: Yes, it is. (Miami is in Florida.)

18. A: _____

    B: In Ontario. (Toronto is in Ontario.)

EXERCISE 8—ORAL (BOOKS CLOSED): Ask a classmate a question. Use *where.*

> *Example:*   your pen
> *Student A:*   Where is your pen?
> *Student B:*   (*free response*)

1. your grammar book
2. your dictionary
3. your money
4. your books
5. (. . .)
6. (. . .) and (. . .)

7. your sunglasses
8. your pen
9. your apartment
10. your parents
11. the post office
12. (*the name of a place in this city: a store, landmark, restaurant, etc.*)

EXERCISE 9—ORAL (BOOKS CLOSED): Ask a classmate a question. Use *where.*

(To the teacher: Draw or provide a map of the United States and/or Canada. Put place names on slips of paper that you hand out to the class. Student A is to ask a where *question about the word(s) on his/her slip of paper. A volunteer Student B is to answer the question by pointing to the place on the map and saying:* It's (They're) here. *OR:* It's (They're) there.*)*

Suggestions:

1. New York City
2. Los Angeles
3. Montreal
4. Washington, D.C.
5. Toronto

6. Miami
7. the Great Lakes
8. the Rocky Mountains
9. Texas
10. the Mississippi River

2-4   USING *BE:* PAST TIME

PRESENT TIME	PAST TIME	
(a) I **am** in class **today**. (b) Alice **is** at the library **today**. (c) My friends **are** at home **today**.	I **was** in class **yesterday**. Alice **was** at the library **yesterday**. My friends **were** at home **yesterday**.	Past forms of **be** = **was** and **were**.
SIMPLE PAST TENSE OF **BE:** I was we were you were you were he was they were she was it was		$\left.\begin{array}{l}I\\he\\she\\it\end{array}\right\}$ + **was** $\left.\begin{array}{l}we\\you\\they\end{array}\right\}$ + **were**

EXERCISE 10:   Change the sentences to the past.

PRESENT TIME

PAST TIME

1. Bob is in class today.   He was in class yesterday too.

2. I'm in class today.   I was in class yesterday too.

3. Mary is at the library
   today.   She

4. We're in class today.

5. Jim and Ann are at home
   today.

6. You're busy today.

7. I'm tired today.

8. It's cold today.

9. The classroom is hot
   today.

10. Ann is in her office today.

11. Tom is in his office today.

12. Ann and Tom are in their
    offices today.

EXERCISE 11—ORAL (BOOKS CLOSED):   Talk about today and yesterday.

> *Example:*   I'm in class.
> *Response:*   I'm in class today. I was in class yesterday too.
>
> *Example:*   (. . .) is in class.
> *Response:*   (. . .) is in class today. He/She was in class yesterday too.

1. We're in class.
2. I'm in class.
3. (. . .) is in class.
4. (. . .) and (. . .) are in class.
5. (. . .) is in class.
6. (. . .) and (. . .) and (. . .) are in class today.
7. (. . .) is here.
8. (. . .) is absent.
9. I'm tired today.
10. (. . .) and (. . .) are (in the front row).
11. The window is open/closed.
12. It's hot/cold.

EXERCISE 12—ORAL (BOOKS CLOSED):   Use *be* (present and past) and prepositional expressions of place.

> *To Student A:*   Put your book on the floor. Where's your book?
> *Student A:*   It's on the floor.
> *To Student A:*   Now put it back on your desk.
> *To Student B:*   Where was (. . .)'s book?
> *Student B:*   It was on the floor.

1. *on top of*   Put your hand on top of your head. Where's your hand?
   Now put it (back on your desk). Where was (. . .)'s hand?
2. *in*   Put your pen in your purse/pocket.
3. *beside*   Put your pen beside your book.
4. *on*   Put your wallet on your desk.
5. *around*   Put your hands around your neck.
6. *under*   Put your book under your desk.
7. *on top of*   Put your right hand on top of your head.
8. *above*   Put your right hand above your head.
9. *between*   Stand between (. . .) and (. . .).
10. *in the middle of*   Stand in the middle of the room.
11. *in front of*   Put your book in front of your face.
12. *in the front of*   Put your book in the front of the room.

13. *in the back of*   Put your book in the back of the room.
14. *in back of*   Put your hand in back of your head.
15. *behind*   Put your hand behind your head.
16. *next to*   Stand next to (. . .).
17. *beside*   Stand beside (. . .).
18. *against*   Put your chair/desk against the wall.

VOCABULARY CHECKLIST: SOME PREPOSITIONAL EXPRESSIONS OF PLACE

above	in	inside
against	in back of	next to
around	in the back of	on
behind	in front of	on top of
beside	in the front of	outside
between	in the middle of	under

2-5   PAST OF *BE:* NEGATIVE

(a) I **was not** in class yesterday. (b) I **wasn't** in class yesterday. (c) They **were not** at home last night. (d) They **weren't** at home last night.	Negative contractions: *was + not = wasn't* *were + not = weren't* $\left.\begin{array}{l} I \\ he \\ she \\ it \end{array}\right\} + wasn't$ $\left.\begin{array}{l} we \\ you \\ they \end{array}\right\} + weren't$

EXERCISE 13:   Study the time expressions.

PRESENT	PAST
today	**yesterday**
this morning	**yesterday morning**
this afternoon	**yesterday afternoon**
tonight	**last night**
this week *	**last week**

Complete the sentences. Use ***wasn't*** or ***weren't.*** Use a past time expression.

1. Bob is here today, but _____ he wasn't here yesterday.

---

* See 8–3 for more information about the use of *today, this morning, this afternoon, tonight, this week.*

2. I'm at home tonight, but_____I wasn't at home last night._____

3. Alice is busy today, but _____

4. We're in class this morning, but _____

5. Tom is at the library tonight, but _____

6. It's cold this week, but_____

7. Dick and Janet are at work this morning, but _____

8. Tom is absent from class today, but _____

9. I'm busy this week, but _____

10. Mr. and Mrs. Jones are at home tonight, but _____

11. Ms. Anderson is downtown this afternoon, but _____

12. Miss Kelly is at home this morning, but _____

13. You're in class today, but _____

14. Dr. Ruckman is in her office this afternoon, but_____

15. The dentist is in his office this afternoon, but _____

2-6 PAST OF *BE:* YES/NO QUESTIONS

BE + SUBJECT			SHORT ANSWER (+ LONG ANSWER)
(a) **Were**	**you**	in class yesterday?	Yes, **I was.** (I was in class yesterday.) No, **I wasn't.** (I wasn't in class yesterday.)
(b) **Was**	**Bob**	at home last night?	Yes, **he was.** (He was at home last night.) No, **he wasn't.** (He wasn't at home last night.)

EXERCISE 14:   Make questions and give short answers.

1. (*you / at home / last night*)

   A:___Were you at home last night?_____

   B: Yes, _____I was._____

2. (*Dick / in class / yesterday*)

   A:___Was Dick in class yesterday?_____

   B: No, _____he wasn't._____

3. (*Dick / absent from class / yesterday*)

   A: _____

   B: Yes, _____

4. (*Dick and Sue / at home / last night*)

   A: _____

   B: Yes, _____

5. (*you / nervous / the first day of class*)

   A: _____

   B: No, _____

6. (*Ann / at the library / last night*)

   A: _____

   B: Yes, _____

7. (*you / in the United States / last year*)

   A: _____

   B: No, _____

8. (*you and your wife / in Canada / last year*)

   A: _____

   B: No, _____

9. (*you and your husband / at home / yesterday morning*)

   A: _____

   B: Yes, _____

10. (*the weather in Chicago / good / last winter*)

    A: _____

    B: No, _____   It was terrible.

EXERCISE 15:   Make questions and give short answers.

1. (*you / in class / yesterday*)

   A: _____Were you in class yesterday?_____

   B: Yes, _____I was._____

2. (*Ann / in class / today*)

    A: _____ Is Ann in class today? _____

    B: No, _____ she isn't. _____ She's absent.

3. (*Sue and Bob / here / yesterday afternoon*)

    A: _____

    B: Yes, _____

4. (*Dick / at the party / last night*)

    A: _____

    B: No, _____ He was at the library.

5. (*Mary / absent / today*)

    A: _____

    B: Yes, _____ She's at home. She has a cold.

6. (*you / tired / last night*)

    A: _____

    B: Yes, _____ I went to bed early.

7. (*you / hungry / right now*)

    A: _____

    B: No, _____ But I'm thirsty.

8. (*Jason and Marcus / late for class / yesterday morning*)

    A: _____

    B: Yes, _____ They're always late for class.

9. (*Mr. Johnson / at the meeting / last night*)

    A: _____

    B: Yes, _____ He was there.

10. (*Ms. Robertson / in her office / this week*)

    A: _____

    B: No, _____ She's out of town.

11. (*the weather / cold / today*)

    A: _____

    B: No, _____ It's warm.

12. (*the weather / cold in Florida / in the summer*)

    A: _____

    B: No, _____ It's hot.

13. (*the weather / cold in Alaska / in the winter*)

    A: _____

    B: Yes, _____ It's very cold.

14. (*the weather / hot in New York City / last summer*)

    A: _____

    B: Yes, _____ It was very hot.

15. (*the students in this class / intelligent*)

    A: _____

    B: Of course, _____! They are very intelligent!

EXERCISE 16—ORAL (BOOKS CLOSED): Ask your classmates questions.

> *Example:*   in class/now
> *Student A:*   (. . .), are you in class now?
> *Student B:*   Yes, I am.

> *Example:*   at the library/last night
> *Student A:*   (. . .), were you at the library last night?
> *Student B:*   No, I wasn't.
> *Student A:*   Where were you?
> *Student B:*   I was (at home/in my room/at a party, etc.)

(*To the teacher: If Student B answers* yes, *the exercise item is finished. If Student B answers* no, *Student A should follow with a* where *question.*)

1. at home/now
2. at home/yesterday morning
3. at home/last night
4. in class/yesterday
5. in Chicago/now
6. in the United States/now
7. in the United States/last week
8. at the library/last night
9. in Canada/last year
10. (*etc., using the names of stores, restaurants, parks, and the like in this city*)

2-7 USING *IT* TO TALK ABOUT THE WEATHER

(a) It's cold today. (b) It's sunny today. (c) It was cloudy yesterday. (d) It's hot and humid today. (e) It's raining today. (f) It's snowing today.	In English, people usually use *it* when they talk about the weather.

EXERCISE 17—ORAL: How's the weather today? Use these words to talk about the weather today.

> *Example:*   hot
> *Response:*   It's hot today. OR: It isn't/It's not hot today.

1. hot	6. sunny	11. gloomy
2. warm	7. cloudy	12. humid
3. cool	8. partly cloudy	13. muggy
4. chilly	9. windy	14. raining
5. cold	10. foggy	15. snowing

EXERCISE 18: Make sentences from the information. Use *but* in your sentences.

1. *today:* warm — *yesterday:* cold

   It's warm today, but it was cold yesterday.

2. *today:* not cold — *yesterday:* cold

   It's not cold today, but it was (cold) yesterday.*

3. *today:* not hot — *yesterday:* hot

4. *today:* hot — *yesterday:* cold

5. *today:* hot — *yesterday:* not hot

---

* In the second part of the sentence (after *but*), it is not necessary to repeat the adjective: *It's not cold today, but it was yesterday.*

6. *today:* sunny — *yesterday:* cloudy

_____

7. *today:* not sunny — *yesterday:* sunny

_____

8. *today:* foggy — *yesterday:* sunny

_____

9. *today:* windy — *yesterday:* not windy

_____

10. *today:* cool — *yesterday:* hot and humid

_____

2-8 USING *IT* TO TALK ABOUT TIME

QUESTION	ANSWER	
(a) What day is it?	It's Monday.	In English, people use *it* to express (to talk about) time.
(b) What month is it?	It's September.	
(c) What year is it?	It's 19____.	Look at Appendixes 1 and 2 in the back of the book for lists of days, months, and numbers.
(d) What's the date today?	It's September 15th. It's the 15th of September.	
(e) What time is it?	It's 9:00.*	Look at Appendix 3 in the back of the book for ways of saying the time.
	It's nine. It's nine o'clock. It's nine (o'clock) a.m.	

* Use a colon (two dots) between the hour and the minutes.

EXERCISE 19: Make questions. Use *what* in your questions.

1. A: _____What day is it?_____
   B: It's Tuesday.

2. A: _____
   B: It's March 14th.

3. A: _____
   B: Ten-thirty.

4. A: _____

   B: March.

5. A: _____

   B: It's six-fifteen.

6. A: _____

   B: The 1st of April.

7. A: _____

   B: Wednesday.

8. A: _____

   B: July 3rd.

9. A: _____

   B: It's 6:05.

10. A: _____

    B: 10:55.

2-9 PREPOSITIONS OF TIME

at	(a) We have class **at one o'clock.** (b) I have an appointment with the doctor **at 3:00.** (c) We sleep **at night.**	***at*** + a specific time on the clock ***at*** + *night*
in	(d) My birthday is **in October.** (e) I was born **in 1960.** (f) We have class **in the morning.** (g) Bob has class **in the afternoon.** (h) I study **in the evening.**	***in*** + month ***in*** + year ***in*** + *the morning* ***in*** + *the afternoon* ***in*** + *the evening*
on	(i) I have class **on Monday.** (j) I was born **on October 31, 1960.**	***on*** + day of the week ***on*** + date
from ... to	(k) We have class **from 1:00 to 2:00.**	***from*** (a specific time) ***to*** (a specific time)

EXERCISE 20: Complete the sentences with prepositions of time.

1. We have class _____ at _____ ten o'clock.

2. We have class _____ ten _____ eleven.

3. I have class _____ the morning.

4. I work _____ the afternoon.

5. I study _____ the evening.

6. I sleep _____ night.

7. I was born _____ May.

8. I was born _____ 1959.

9. I was born _____ May 25.*

10. I was born _____ May 25, 1959.

11. The post office isn't open _____ Sunday.

12. The post office is open _____ 8:00 a.m. _____ 5:00 p.m. _____ Monday.

13. The post office closes _____ 5:00 p.m.

EXERCISE 21: Complete the sentences with prepositions of time.

1. Jane has an appointment with the dentist _____ ten-thirty.

2. We go to class _____ the morning.

3. The bank is open _____ Friday, but it isn't open _____ Saturday.

4. My birthday is _____ February.

5. I was born _____ February 14, 1963.

6. I watch television _____ the evening.

7. I go to bed _____ night.

8. The bank is open _____ 9:00 a.m. _____ 3:00 p.m.

9. I was in high school _____ 1978.

10. New Year's Day is _____ January 1.

11. I study at the library _____ the afternoon.

12. We have Christmas vacation _____ December.

_____

*See Appendix 2 for the usual spoken forms of dates.

chapter 3

Be + -Ing

3-1 BE + -ING: USING THE PRESENT PROGRESSIVE TENSE*

(a) *am* + *-ing*	I **am sitting** in class right now.	In (a): When I say this sentence, I am in class. I am sitting; I am not standing. The action (*sitting*) is happening right now, and I am saying the sentence at the same time.
(b) *is* + *-ing*	Mary **is sitting** in class right now.	
(c) *are* + *-ing*	You **are sitting** in class right now.	
		am, is, are = helping verbs **sitting** = the main verb
		am, is, are + **-ing** = the present progressive tense

* The present progressive is also called the present continuous or the continuous present.

EXERCISE 1—ORAL (BOOKS CLOSED): Practice using the present progressive.

(To the teacher: Give the students directions in order to prompt responses using the present progressive. The actor should sustain the action until the description is completed. Demonstrate vocabulary as necessary.)

> *Example:* Smile. (. . .), please smile. What are you doing?
> *Response:* I'm smiling.

Example: Smile. (. . .) and (. . .), please smile. What are you doing?
Response: We're smiling.

Example: Smile. (. . .), please smile. What is he/she doing?
Response: He/She is smiling.

1. Stand in the middle of the room.
2. Sit in the middle of the room.
3. Stand in the back of the room.
4. Smile.
5. Stand between (. . .) and (. . .).
6. Touch the floor.
7. Touch the ceiling.
8. Touch your toes.
9. Open/Close the door/window.
10. Close/Open the door/window.
11. Shake hands with (. . .).
12. Smile at (. . .).
13. Stand up and turn around in a circle.
14. Hold your book above your head.
15. Hold up your right hand.
16. Hold up your left hand.
17. Touch your right ear with your left hand.
18. Stand up.
19. Sit down.
20. Clap your hands.

EXERCISE 2—ORAL (BOOKS CLOSED):   Practice using the present progressive.

(To the teacher: All responses in the exercise should include be + wearing.
First ask three or four students what they are wearing today. Next ask three or four students what another student is wearing. Then name an article of clothing or jewelry and ask one student to identify by name another student who is wearing such. Alternate singular and plural. Work on placement of the adjective (color) before the noun if necessary. Emphasize a *and* –s *in your cues.)*

Example: a blue shirt
Response: (. . .) is wearing a blue shirt.

Example: blue shirts
Response: (. . .) and (. . .) are wearing blue shirts.

Suggestions:

1. gold earrings
2. blue jeans
3. a blouse
4. a red blouse
5. gray slacks
6. brown boots
7. a black belt
8. a necklace
9. running shoes
10. *etc.*

EXERCISE 3—ORAL (BOOKS CLOSED):   Practice using the present progressive.

(To the teacher: Use the words in the list to prompt usage of the present progressive.

1. First act out the words in the list yourself and ask the students to tell you what you are doing. Discuss vocabulary as necessary.)

> *Example:*   *(You pantomime drinking.)* What am I doing?
> *Response:*   You're drinking.

(2. After going through the list with yourself as the pantomimist, go through the list again with the students as the pantomimists.)

> *Example:*   drive *(The student pantomimes driving.)* What are you doing?
> *Response:*   I'm driving.
> *Teacher:*   What is (. . .) doing?
> *Response:*   He/She's driving.

(The pantomimist should sustain the action until the oral description is completed.)

1. drink	9. fly	17. pull
2. eat	10. smile	18. clap
3. drive	11. laugh	19. kick
4. read	12. cry	20. count
5. sleep	13. dance	21. stand in back of (. . .)
6. write	14. wave	22. touch (. . .)
7. walk	15. smoke	23. shake hands with (. . .)
8. run	16. push	24. sit on the floor

3-2   THE PRESENT PROGRESSIVE: YES/NO QUESTIONS

QUESTION				SHORT ANSWER (+ LONG ANSWER)
BE + SUBJECT + *-ING*				
(a)	**Is**	Mary	**sleeping?**	**Yes, she is.** (She's sleeping.) **No, she's not.** (She's not sleeping.) **No, she isn't.** (She isn't sleeping.)
(b)	**Are**	you	**watching** TV?	**Yes, I am.** (I'm watching TV.) **No, I'm not.** (I'm not watching TV.)

EXERCISE 4: Make questions. Give short answers.

1. A: _____ Is Mary reading a book? _____

   B: No, _she isn't/she's not_ . (Mary isn't reading a book.)

2. A: _____ Are you writing a letter? _____

   B: Yes, _____. (I'm writing a letter.)

3. A: _____

   B: Yes, _____. (Dick is drinking a cup of coffee.)

4. A: _____

   B: No, _____. (Mary isn't eating lunch.)

5. A: _____

   B: Yes, _____. (The baby is crying.)

6. A: _____

   B: No, _____. (I'm not studying.)

7. A: _____

   B: Yes, _____. (Liz and Jack are dancing.)

8. A: _____

   B: No, _____. (The girls aren't playing in the street.)

9. A: _____

   B: Yes, _____. (The airplane is flying to Chicago.)

10. A: _____

    B: Yes, _____. (The students are writing in their books.)

11. A: _____

    B: Yes, _____. (My brother is talking to his girlfriend on the phone.)

12. A: _____

    B: No, _____. (My coat isn't hanging in the closet.)

EXERCISE 5—ORAL (BOOKS CLOSED):

(To the teacher: On slips of paper, write the words in Exercise 3. Hand the slips out to the class. Each student is to pantomime the word on his/her slip to prompt another student to ask a yes/no question using the present progressive. The student doing the pantomime should give a short response.)

> *Example:* drive *(on a slip of paper)*
> *Student A:* *(Student A pantomimes driving.)*
> *Student B:* Are you driving?
> *Student A:* Yes, I am.

(Collect and redistribute the slips of paper. As Student A performs his/her pantomime, Students B and C are to talk about it.)

> *Example:* drive *(on a slip of paper)*
> *Student A:* *(Student A pantomimes driving.)*
> *Student B:* (. . .), is (. . .) driving?
> *Student C:* Yes, he/she is.

(Note: If you wish, encourage the students to ask questions that would be answered no *as a variation.)*

EXERCISE 6: Below are some pictures of John and Mary.

PICTURE 1

A. VOCABULARY CHECKLIST

eat dinner	a bowl	meat
hold a knife and a fork	a bowl of salad	a piece of meat
cut a piece of meat	a candle	a plate
have a steak for dinner	a cup	a restaurant
burn	a cup of coffee	a saucer
	a fork	a spoon
	a glass	a steak
	a glass of water	a table
	a knife	a waiter

B. ANSWER THE QUESTIONS

1. What is Mary doing?
2. What do you see on the table?
3. What is Mary holding in her right hand? In her left hand?
4. What is in the bowl?
5. What is on the plate?
6. What is in the cup?
7. What is burning?
8. Is Mary eating breakfast?
9. Is Mary at home? Where is she?
10. What is she cutting?

C. COMPLETE THE SENTENCES

11. Mary is sitting _____ a table.

12. There is a candle _____ the table.

13. There is coffee _____ the cup.

14. Mary _____ holding a knife _____ her right hand.

15. She's _____ a restaurant.

16. She _____ at home.

17. She _____ eating breakfast.

PICTURE 2

A. VOCABULARY CHECKLIST

study at the library
read a book
take notes

the circulation desk
a librarian
a shelf (*singular*)
　　shelves (*plural*)*

B. ANSWER THE QUESTIONS

1. What is John doing?
2. What do you see in the picture?
3. Is John at home? Where is he?

4. Is John reading a newspaper?
5. Where is the librarian standing?
6. Is John right-handed or left-handed?

C. COMPLETE THE SENTENCES

7. John is studying _____ the library.

8. He is sitting _____ a table.

9. He is sitting _____ a chair.

10. His legs are _____ the table.

11. There are books _____ the shelves.

12. John is writing _____ a piece of paper.

13. He's taking notes _____ a piece of paper.

14. He _____ reading a newspaper.

15. The librarian _____ standing _____ the circulation desk.

16. Another student is sitting _____ John.

---

*See 5–2 for information about nouns with irregular plural forms.

PICTURE 3

```
MARY S. JONES                                    212
3471 TREE ST.
CHICAGO, IL 60565                     May 3, 19 82
PAY TO THE
ORDER OF        Cash                          $ 25 00
    Twenty five and 00/100                     DOLLARS

FIRST NATIONAL BANK
605 MICHIGAN AVE.
CHICAGO, IL 60503                     Mary S. Jones
1:021 20091: 438"200
```

A. VOCABULARY CHECKLIST

write a check   a bank   name and address
sign a check   cash   first name/given name
sign her name   a check   middle initial
                        the date   last name/family name/
                                               surname

B. ANSWER THE QUESTIONS

1. What is Mary doing?
2. What is Mary's address?
3. What is Mary's full name?
4. What is Mary's middle initial?
5. What is Mary's last name?

6. How much money does Mary want?
7. What is in the upper left corner of the check?
8. What is in the lower left corner of the check?
9. What is the name of the bank?

C. COMPLETE THE SENTENCES

10. Mary is writing a _____.

11. She is signing _____ name.

12. The name _____ the bank is First National Bank.

13. Mary lives _____ 3471 Tree Street.*

14. Mary lives _____ Chicago, Illinois.*

15. Mary's name and address is _____ the upper left corner

    _____ the check.

---

* Prepositions of place:

    at + address
    on + street
    in + city, state/province, country

I live **at 2563 Hill Street.**
I live **on Hill Street**
I live **in Chicago.**
I live **in Illinois.**
I live **in the United States.**

16. Mary is signing her name _____ the lower right corner

_____ the check.

PICTURE 4

A. VOCABULARY CHECKLIST

cash a check   a bank teller   a man (*singular*)

stand in line   a counter   men (*plural*)*

                 a line   a woman (*singular*)

                                      women (*plural*)*

                                      people (*plural*)*

B. ANSWER THE QUESTIONS

1. What is Mary doing?
2. Is Mary at a store? Where is she?
3. What do you see in the picture?
4. Who is standing behind Mary, a man or a woman?
5. Who is standing at the end of the line, a man or a woman?
6. How many men are there in the picture?
7. How many women are there in the picture?
8. How many people are there in the picture?
9. How many people are standing in line?

C. COMPLETE THE SENTENCES

10. Mary is _____ a bank.

11. Four people are standing _____ line.

12. Mary is standing _____ the counter.

13. The bank teller is standing _____ the counter.

---

* See 5–2 for information about nouns with irregular plural forms.

14. There are five people _____ the picture.

15. Mary is cashing a _____.

16. A woman _____ standing _____ Mary.

17. Mary _____ standing _____ a woman.

18. A man _____ standing _____ _____ the end

    _____ the line.

19. A businessman _____ standing _____ the woman
    with the big hat and the young man in jeans.

PICTURE 5

A. VOCABULARY CHECKLIST

cook	a kitchen	bread
cook dinner	a list/a grocery list	coffee
make dinner	a pot	an egg
taste (*food*)	a refrigerator	margarine
	a stove	milk
		pepper
	a salt shaker	salt
	a pepper shaker	a TV dinner

B. ANSWER THE QUESTIONS

1. What is John doing?
2. What do you see in the picture?
3. Where is John?
4. Is John tasting his dinner?
5. Is John a good cook?

6. Where is the refrigerator?
7. What is on the refrigerator?
8. Is the food on the stove hot or cold?
9. Is the food in the refrigerator hot or cold?

C. COMPLETE THE SENTENCES

10. John is making dinner. He's _____ the kitchen.

11. There is a pot _____ the stove.

12. The stove is _____ the refrigerator.

13. There is a grocery list _____ the refrigerator door.

14. A salt shaker and a pepper shaker are _____ the stove.

15. There is hot food _____ top _____ the stove.

16. There is cold food _____ the refrigerator.

PICTURE 6

A. VOCABULARY CHECKLIST

watch TV/watch
   television
sit on a sofa
sing
sleep
swim

a cat
a dog
a fish
a fish bowl
a floor
a lamp

a living room
a rug
a singer
a sofa
a TV set/a television set

B. ANSWER THE QUESTIONS

1. What are John and Mary doing?
2. What do you see in the picture?
3. Are Mary and John in a kitchen? Where are they?
4. Where is the lamp?
5. Where is the rug?
6. Where is the dog?

7. Where is the cat?
8. Is the cat walking? What is the cat doing?
9. What is the dog doing?
10. What is on top of the TV set?
11. Is the fish watching TV?
12. What is on the TV screen? What are John and Mary watching?

C. ANSWER THE QUESTIONS

13. John and Mary _____ watching TV.

14. They _____ sitting _____ a sofa.

15. They _____ sleeping.

16. There is a rug_____ the floor.

17. A dog _____ sleeping _____ the rug.

18. A cat _____ sleeping _____ the sofa.

PICTURE 7

A. VOCABULARY CHECKLIST

talk to (*someone*)	an arrow	a piece of paper
talk on the phone	a calendar	a telephone book
talk to each other	a heart	a wall
smile	a phone/a telephone	
draw a picture	a picture	
	a picture of a mountain	

B. ANSWER THE QUESTIONS

1. What are John and Mary doing?
2. What do you see in the picture?
3. Is John happy? Is Mary happy? Are John and Mary smiling?
4. Are they sad?
5. Who is standing? Who is sitting?
6. Is John is his bedroom? Where is John?

7. What is Mary drawing?
8. What is on Mary's table?
9. What is above Mary's table?
10. What is on the wall next to the refrigerator?
11. Where is the clock?
12. What time is it?
13. What is on the wall above the table?

C. COMPLETE THE SENTENCES

14. John and Mary _____ talking _____ the phone.

15. John _____ talking _____ Mary. Mary

    _____ talking _____ John. They _____

    talking to _____ other.

16. John is _____ the kitchen. He's standing _____ the
    refrigerator.

17. There is a calendar _____ the wall next to the refrigerator.

18. Mary _____ sitting _____ a table. She's

    _____ a picture.

19. There is a telephone book _____ the table.

20. There is a picture _____ a mountain _____ the table.

PICTURE 8

A. VOCABULARY CHECKLIST

sleep   a bed
dream   a dream
dream about (*someone/something*)   a head
                                         a pillow

B. ANSWER THE QUESTIONS

1. What is Mary doing?
2. What is John doing?
3. What are Mary and John doing?
4. What do you see in the picture?
5. Is Mary in her bedroom?

6. Is John in class? Where is he?
7. Is John standing or lying down?
8. Is Mary dreaming?
9. Are Mary and John dreaming about each other?
10. Are John and Mary in love?

C. COMPLETE THE SENTENCES

11. John and Mary _____ sleeping. They are _____ bed.

12. John _____ dreaming _____ Mary. Mary

    _____ dreaming _____ John. They

    _____ dreaming _____ each _____.

13. Mary's head is _____ a pillow.

14. John and Mary _____ in the living room.

15. They _____ asleep. They _____ awake.

16. John and Mary love each other. They are _____ love.

3-3 THE PAST PROGRESSIVE TENSE

PRESENT PROGRESSIVE	right now	(a) It's 10:00. **I am sitting** in class.
PAST PROGRESSIVE	yesterday	(b) It was 10:00. **I was sitting** in class.

EXERCISE 7: Complete the sentences. Use a form of *be* + *sitting*.

1. I ____am sitting____ in class right now.

2. I ____was sitting____ in class yesterday too.

3. You _____ in class right now.

4. You _____ in class yesterday too.

5. John _____ in class right now.

6. He _____ in class yesterday too.

7. We _____ in class today.

8. We _____ yesterday too.

9. Mary _____ in class now.

10. She _____ in class yesterday too.

11. John and Mary _____ in class today.

12. They _____ in class yesterday too.

EXERCISE 8: Look at the pictures in Exercise 6. Describe what Mary and John were doing yesterday.

EXERCISE 9—WRITTEN (BOOKS CLOSED): This is a spelling test.

(To the teacher: Use this exercise as a pretest and have the students check their own answers as you discuss chart 3–4.)

Example:	Standing. I am standing in the front row of the room. Standing.
Written response:	standing

1. smile + *–ing*	5. read + *–ing*
2. write + *–ing*	6. rain + *–ing*
3. sit + *–ing*	7. stand + *–ing*
4. run + *–ing*	8. push + *–ing*

3-4 SPELLING OF *-ING*

END OF VERB	-ING FORM	vowels = *a, e, i, o, u*
Rule 1: A CONSONANT + **-E**	DROP THE **-E**, ADD **-ING**	consonants = *b, c, d, f, g, h, j, k, l, m, n, p, q, r, s, t, v, w, x, y, z,*
smile **write**	**smiling** **writing**	
Rule 2: ONE VOWEL + ONE CONSONANT	DOUBLE THE CONSONANT, ADD **-ING**	Exception to Rule 2: Do not double *w, x,* and *y.*
sit **run**	**sitting** **running**	*snow — snowing* *fix —fixing* *say — saying*
Rule 3: TWO VOWELS + ONE CONSONANT	ADD **-ING;** DO NOT DOUBLE THE CONSONANT	
read **rain**	**reading** **raining**	
Rule 4: TWO CONSONANTS	ADD **-ING;** DO NOT DOUBLE THE CONSONANT	
stand **push**	**standing** **pushing**	

EXERCISE 10:   Write the *-ing* forms for the following words.

1. stand_____standing_____

2. smile_____

3. run_____

4. rain_____

5. sleep_____

6. step _____

7. eat _____

8. count _____

9. sit_____

10. wear_____

11. ride_____

12. cut _____

13. dance _____

14. put _____

15. look _____

16. smoke_____

17. snow_____

18. fix_____

19. say _____

20. cry _____

EXERCISE 11:   Write the *-ing* forms for the following words.

1. dream_____

2. shine_____

3. clap _____

4. bite_____

5. hit _____

6. throw_____

7. catch _____

8. draw_____

9. break _____

10. sneeze_____

11. cough_____

12. laugh _____

13. drop_____

14. sign_____

15. fly_____

16. study_____

17. erase_____

18. get _____

EXERCISE 12—ORAL (BOOKS CLOSED):

(To the teacher: Ask Student A to act out your directions while Student B describes this action using the present progressive. Student A should sustain the action until the description is completed.)

   Example: erase the board
   Student A: *(Student A sustains the action of erasing the board.)*
   Student B: (. . .)/He/She is erasing the board.

1. erase the board
2. draw a picture on the board
3. sneeze
4. cough
5. wave at your friends
6. sign your name on the board
7. clap your hands
8. sing
9. count your fingers
10. bite your finger
11. hit your desk

12. drop your pen
13. tear a piece of paper
14. break a piece of chalk
15. fall down
16. fall asleep
17. sleep
18. snore
19. chew gum
20. *two students:* throw and catch (*something in the room*)
21. hold your grammar book between your feet
22. carry your book on the top of your head to the front of the room

EXERCISE 13—WRITTEN (BOOKS CLOSED): Practice spelling -*ing*.

(To the teacher: Perform some or all of the actions in Exercise 12 to prompt written responses.)

> *Example:* Act out erasing the board and ask, "What am I doing?"
> *Response:* You're erasing the board. (*written*)

chapter 4

The Simple Present Tense

4-1 FORM AND BASIC MEANING OF THE SIMPLE PRESENT TENSE

	SINGULAR	PLURAL	
1st PERSON	I talk	we talk	Notice: The verb after **he, she, it** (3rd person singular) has a final **-s.**
2nd PERSON	you talk	you talk	
3rd PERSON	he talks she talks it rains	they talk	

(a) I **eat** breakfast **every morning.**	The simple present tense expresses habits.
(b) Ann **speaks** English **every day.**	In (a): **every morning** = Monday morning, Tuesday morning, Wednesday morning, Thursday morning, Friday morning, Saturday morning, and Sunday morning.
(c) We **sleep every night.**	
(d) They **go** to the beach **every weekend.**	Eating breakfast is a habit, a usual activity.

EXERCISE 1:   What do you do every morning? On the left, there is a list of habits. On the right, make a list of your habits every morning in order. What do you do first, second, third, etc.?*

HABITS

  (a) eat breakfast

  (b) go to class

  (c) put on my clothes

  (d) drink a cup of coffee/
       tea

  (e) shave

  (f) put on my make-up

  (g) take a shower/bath

  (h) get up

  (i) pick up my books

  (j) walk to the bathroom

  (k) watch TV

  (l) look in the mirror

✔(m) turn off the alarm
       clock

  (n) go to the kitchen/the
       cafeteria

  (o) brush/comb my hair

  (p) say good-bye to my
       roommate/wife/
       husband

  (q) brush my teeth

  (r) do exercises
  (s) smoke a cigarette
  (t) wash my face
  (u) stretch, yawn, and rub
       my eyes

MY HABITS EVERY MORNING

The alarm clock rings.

1. I turn off the alarm clock

2. I

3.

4.

5.

---

* To the teacher: Discuss the vocabulary in the habits column, then tell each student to make his/her own list of activities in order of time. When the lists are completed, discuss a few of them with books open. Then with books closed, ask the students to describe their everyday morning activities orally.

4-2   USING FREQUENCY ADVERBS: *ALWAYS, USUALLY, OFTEN, SOMETIMES, SELDOM, RARELY, NEVER*

always	usually	often	sometimes	seldom	rarely	never
100%	99-90%	90-75%	75-25%	25-10%	10-1%	0%

(a) **Bob always comes** to class.	***Always, usually, often, sometimes, seldom, rarely,*** and ***never*** are called *frequency adverbs.*
(b) **Mary usually comes** to class.	
(c) **We often watch** TV at night.	Frequency adverbs come between the subject and the simple present verb:*
(d) **I sometimes drink** tea with dinner.	
(e) **I seldom go** to movies.	SUBJECT + {ALWAYS / USUALLY / OFTEN / SOMETIMES / SELDOM / RARELY / NEVER} + VERB
(f) **Anna rarely makes** a mistake.	
(g) **I never eat** paper.	

* Frequency adverbs sometimes come at either the beginning or at the end of a sentence. For example:
   Sometimes I get up at 7:00.
   I **sometimes** get up at 7:00.
   I get up at 7:00 **sometimes.**
Also: See 4-3 for the use of frequency adverbs with *be.*

EXERCISE 2—ORAL: Add the frequency adverbs in parentheses to the sentences.

1. (*always*)   I eat breakfast. (*I always eat breakfast.*)
2. (*usually*)   I get up at 7:00.
3. (*often*)   I drink two cups of coffee in the morning.
4. (*never*)   I eat bacon.
5. (*seldom*)   I watch TV in the morning.
6. (*sometimes*) I have tea with dinner.
7. (*usually*)   Bob eats lunch at the cafeteria.
8. (*rarely*)   Ann drinks tea.
9. (*always*)   I do my homework.
10. (*often*)   We listen to music after dinner.
11. (*never*)   John and Sue watch TV in the afternoon.
12. (*always*)   The students speak English in the classroom.

EXERCISE 3—ORAL: Use *always, usually, often, sometimes, seldom, rarely,* and *never* to talk about your activities (your habits) after 5:00 p.m. every day.

1. eat dinner
2. eat dinner at six o'clock
3. eat dinner at eight o'clock
4. watch TV
5. listen to music
6. go to a movie
7. go shopping
8. go dancing
9. go swimming
10. spend time with my friends
11. talk on the phone
12. speak English
13. write a letter
14. read a newspaper
15. study
16. study English grammar
17. drink beer
18. play with my children
19. kiss my husband/wife
20. have a snack
21. go to bed
22. go to bed at eleven o'clock
23. go to bed after midnight
24. go to bed early
25. go to bed late
26. turn off the light
27. dream
28. dream in English

4-3 USING FREQUENCY ADVERBS WITH *BE*

SUBJECT + *BE* + FREQUENCY ADVERB	Frequency adverbs follow *be.*
I am { always usually often sometimes seldom rarely never } late for class.	

EXERCISE 4: Add the frequency adverb in parentheses to the sentence.

1. Ann is on time for class. (*always*) ___Ann is always on time for class.___

2. Ann comes to class on time. (*always*) ___Ann always comes to class on time.___

3. Sue is late for class (*often*) _____

4. Sue comes to class late. (*often*) _____

5. Ron is happy. (*never*) _____

6. Ron smiles. (*never*)_____

7. Bob is at home in the evening. (*usually*)_____

8. Bob stays at home in the evening. (*usually*) _____

9. It snows in October. (*sometimes*) _____

10. It is cold in October. (*sometimes*)_____

11. Tom studies at the library in the evening. (*seldom*) _____

12. Tom is at the library in the evening. (*seldom*)_____

13. I eat breakfast. (*rarely*)_____

14. I take the bus to school. (*often*) _____

15. The bus is on time. (*usually*) _____

16. The weather is hot in July. (*always*) _____

17. Sue drinks coffee. (*never*) _____

18. She drinks tea. (*sometimes*)_____

EXERCISE 5—WRITTEN: Describe a typical day in your life, from the time you get up in the morning until you go to bed.

Use the following words to show the order of your activities: *then, next, at . . . o'clock, after that, later.*

Example: I usually get up at seven-thirty. I shave, brush my teeth, and take a shower. Then I put on my clothes and go to the student cafeteria for breakfast. After that I go back to my room. Sometimes I smoke a cigarette. At 8:15 I leave the dormitory. I go to class. My class begins at 8:30. I'm in class from 8:30 to 11:30. After that I eat lunch. I usually have a sandwich and a glass of milk for lunch. (Continue until you complete your day.)

EXERCISE 6: Practice voiced and voiceless sounds.

VOICED		VOICELESS	
/b/	I rub	*/p/*	I sleep
/d/	I ride	*/t/*	I write
/v/	I drive	*/f/*	I laugh

/b/ + /z/	he rubs*		/p/ + /s/	he sleeps
/d/ + /z/	he rides		/t/ + /s/	he writes
/v/ + /z/	he drives		/f/ + /s/	he laughs

EXERCISE 7:   The final sounds of the verbs in these sentences are *voiced.* Final **-s** is pronounced **/z/.**
    Find the verb in each sentence. Pronounce it. Then read the sentence aloud.

1. Cindy rides the bus to school.
2. The teacher often stands in the front of the room.

3. Jack usually drives his car to school.
4. George lives in the dormitory.

5. Rain falls.
6. Jean rarely smiles.

7. Sally often dreams about her boyfriend.
8. Sam always comes to class on time.

9. Sometimes Dick runs to class.
10. It rains a lot in Seattle.

11. Mary wears blue jeans every day.
12. Jack always remembers his wife's birthday.

13. Ann always pays her bills on time.
14. It snows in New York City in the winter.

EXERCISE 8:   The final sounds of the verbs in these sentences are *voiceless.* Final **-s** is pronounced **/s/.**
    Find the verb in each sentence. Pronounce it. Then read the sentence aloud.

1. Bob sleeps for eight hours every night.
2. My child often claps her hands.
3. Our teacher always helps us.

---

*Reminder: Add –s to a simple present verb when the subject is *he/she/it* or *a singular noun.*

4. Jack writes a letter to his girlfriend every day.
5. Cindy always bites her pencil in class.
6. Mary usually gets up at 7:30.

7. Dick never laughs.
8. Sue coughs because she smokes.

9. Bob always talks in class.
10. Sue usually drinks a cup of coffee in the morning.
11. Dick walks to school every day.
12. Jean asks a lot of questions in class.

EXERCISE 9: Notice the examples. Use the words in parentheses to complete the sentences.

(a) *cry* + **-s** = **cries**	End of verb: consonant + **-y** Spelling: change **y** to **i**, add **-es**
(b) *pay* + **-s** = **pays**	End of verb: vowel + **-y** Spelling: add **-s**

1. (*pay, always*)   John ____always pays____ his bills on time.

2. (*cry, seldom*)   Our baby _____ at night.

3. (*study, every day*)   Paul _____ at the library

_____.

4. (*stay, usually*)   Jean _____ home at night.

5. (*fly*)   Bob is a pilot. He _____ a plane.

6. (*carry, always*)   Carol _____ her books to class.

7. (*pray, every day*)   Jack _____.

8. (*buy, seldom*)   Ann _____ new clothes.

9. (*worry, often*)   Cindy is a good student, but she _____ about her grades.

10. (*enjoy*)   Don _____ good food.

EXERCISE ___ ... ___ e verbs in parentheses to completing ...

(a) **-sh** +	erb: **-sh, -ch, -ss, -x**
(b) **-ch** +	ing: add **-es**
(c) **-ss** +	tion: /əz/
(d) **-x** +	

1. (*brush*) Ann _____ her hair every morning.

2. (*teach*) Alex _____ English.

3. (*fix*) A mechanic _____ cars.

4. (*study*) Dick _____ at the university.

5. (*drink*) Sally _____ tea every afternoon.

6. (*wear*) Carol usually _____ a skirt and blouse
to class.

7. (*watch*) Tom often _____ television at night.

8. (*kiss*) Mary always _____ her husband
good-bye in the morning.

9. (*wash*) Bob seldom _____ dishes.

10. (*stretch*) When Don gets up in the morning, he

    (*yawn*) _____ and

    _____ .

11. (*stay*) Sometimes Jack _____ in bed in the
morning.

12. (*carry*) Sue _____ her books in her bookbag.

EXERCISE 11:   Notice the examples. Use the verbs in parentheses to complete the sentence.

(a) **I have** a book. (b) **He has** a book.	**have:** he she } has it
(c) **I do** my work. (d) **She does** her work.	**do:** he she } does /dəz/ it
(e) **They go** to school. (f) **She goes** to school.	**go:** he she } goes it
(g) He **says** hello.	Pronounciation of **says:** /sez/

1. (*do*)   Bob always _____ does _____ his homework.

2. (*do*)   We always _____ do _____ our homework.

3. (*have*)   Bob and Tom _____ their books.

4. (*have*)   Sally _____ a car.

5. (*go*)   Bill _____ to school every day.

6. (*go*)   My friends often _____ to the beach.

7. (*say*)   The teacher always _____ good morning
              to the class.

8. (*say*)   The students always _____ good morning
              to the teacher.

9. (*do*)   Anna seldom _____ her homework.

10. (*do*)   We _____ exercises in class every day.

11. (*go*)   Dick _____ downtown every weekend.

     (*go*)   He _____ shopping.

12. (*have*) Alice _____ a snack every evening around
              9:00.

4-4   SUMMARY: SPELLING AND PRONUNCIATION OF -S AND -ES

(a) rub — rubs ride — rides smile — smiles	To make a simple present verb 3rd person singular, you usually add only **-s**, as in (a) and (b).

dream — dreams run — runs wear — wears drive — drives pay — pays snow — snows	In (a): **-s** is pronounced /z/. The final sounds in (a) are *voiced*.
(b) drink — drinks sleep — sleeps write — writes laugh — laughs	In (b): **-s** is pronounced /s/. The final sounds in (b) are *voiceless*.
(c) study — studies cry — cries	End of verb: consonant + **-y** Spelling: change **y** to **i**, add **-es** Pronunciation: /z/
(d) pay — pays buy — buys	End of verb: vowel + **-y** Spelling: add **-s** Pronunciation: /z/
(e) push — pushes wash — washes teach — teaches watch — watches kiss — kisses fix — fixes	End of verb: **-sh, -ch, -ss, -x** Spelling: add **-es** Pronunciation: /əz/
(f) have — **has** go — **goes** do — **does**	The 3rd person singular forms of **have, go,** and **do** are irregular.

EXERCISE 12—ORAL (BOOKS CLOSED): Talk about everyday activities using the given verb.

Example: eat
Student A: I eat breakfast every morning.
Teacher: What does (. . .) do every morning?
Student B: He/She eats breakfast.

Example: eat
Student A: I always eat dinner at the student cafeteria.
Teacher: What does (. . .) always do?
Student B: He/She always eats dinner at the student cafeteria.

1. eat	6. study	11. listen to
2. go	7. get up	12. have
3. drink	8. watch	13. wash
4. brush	9. walk	14. put on
5. speak	10. do	15. carry
		16. kiss

EXERCISE 13: Complete the sentences. Use the words in parentheses. Use *the simple present tense.* Pay special attention to singular and plural and to spelling.

1. The students (*ask, often*)_____ often ask _____ questions in class.

2. Ron (*study, usually*) _____ at the library every evening.

3. Jane (*bite*) _____ her fingernails when she is nervous.

4. Don (*wash, usually*) _____ the dishes after dinner.

5. Sometimes I (*worry*) _____ about my grades at school.

   Mary (*worry, never*) _____ about her grades. She

   (*study*) _____ hard.

6. Ms. Jones (*teach*) _____ math at the local high

   school. Mr. Anderson (*teach*) _____ English.

7. Birds (*fly*) _____. They (*have*)

   _____ wings.

8. A bird (*fly*) _____. It (*have*)

   _____ wings.

9. A mechanic (*fix*) _____ cars. A bartender (*mix*)

   _____ drinks.

10. Dick (*say, always*) _____ hello to his neighbor in the morning.

11. Mary (*pay, always*) _____ attention in class. She

    (*answer*) _____ questions. She (*listen*)

_____ to the teacher. She (*ask*)

_____ questions.

12. Betty and Tom (*pay, always*) _____ their bills on time.

13. Jerry (*do, always*) _____ his homework. He (*go, never*) _____ to bed until his homework is finished.

14. Jean and Fred (*jog*) _____ in the park every day. They (*enjoy*) _____ jogging.

15. John (*enjoy*) _____ cooking. He (*try, often*) _____ to make a delicious new recipe.

EXERCISE 14: Complete the sentences. Use the words in parentheses. Use *the simple present tense* or *the present progressive tense.*

1. I (*sit*) ____am sitting_____ in class right now. I (*sit, always*) ____always sit_____ in the same seat every day.

2. Ali (*speak*) _____ Arabic, but right now he (*speak*) _____ English.

3. Right now we (*do*) _____ an exercise in class. We (*do*) _____ exercises in class every day.

4. Bob (*wear*) _____ blue jeans today. He (*wear*) _____ blue jeans every day.

5. I (*study*) _____ English every day. I'm in class now. I (*study*) _____ English.

6. I'm in class now. I (*look*) _____ at my classmates. Kim (*write*) _____ in his book. Francisco (*look*) _____ out the window. Yoko (*bite*) _____ her pencil. Abdullah (*smile*) _____. Maria (*sleep*) _____. Jung-Po (*chew*) _____ gum.

7. The person on the bench in the picture above is Barbara. She's an accountant. She (*work*) _____ for the government. She (*have*)

_____ an hour for lunch every day. She (*eat, often*)

_____ lunch in the park. She (*bring, usually*)

_____ a sandwich and some fruit with her to the park.

She (*sit, usually*) _____ on a bench, but sometimes she

(*sit*) _____ on the grass. While she's at the park, she

(*watch*) _____ people and animals. She (*watch*)

_____ joggers and squirrels. She (*relax*)

_____ when she eats at the park.

8. Right now I (*look*) _____ at a picture of Barbara. She

(*be, not*) _____ at home in the picture. She (*be*)

_____ at the park. She (*sit*)

_____ on a bench. She (*eat*)

_____ her lunch. Some joggers (*run*)

_____ on a path through the park. A squirrel (*sit*)

_____ on the ground in front of Barbara. The squirrel

(*eat*) _____ a nut. Barbara (*watch*)

_____ the squirrel. She (*watch, always*)

_____ squirrels when she eats lunch in the park. Some

ducks (*swim*) _____ in the pond in the picture, and

some birds (*fly*) _____ in the sky. A police officer

(*ride*) _____ a horse. He (*ride*)

_____ a horse through the park every day. Near

Barbara, a family (*have*) _____ a picnic. They (*go*)

_____ on a picnic every week.

4-5 THE SIMPLE PRESENT: NEGATIVE

(a)	**I**	**do not**	drink coffee.
	We	**do not**	drink coffee.
	You	**do not**	drink coffee.
	They	**do not**	drink coffee.

Negative: **I**, **we**, **you**, **they** } + ***do not*** + *main verb*

(b)	**He**	**does not**	drink coffee.
	She	**does not**	drink coffee.
	It	**does not**	rain every day.

he, **she**, **it** } + ***does not*** + *main verb*

Do and ***does*** are called *helping verbs.*

Notice: In 3rd person singular, there is no **-s** on the main verb. The final **-s** is part of ***does***.

(c) I **don't** drink tea. They **don't** have a car.	Contractions: ***do not = don't*** ***does not = doesn't***
(d) He **doesn't** drink tea. Mary **doesn't** have a car.	People usually use contractions when they speak. People often use contractions when they write.

EXERCISE 15: Use verbs from the list to complete the sentences. Make all of the sentences NEGATIVE by using ***does + not/do + not.***

carry	*make*
do	*put on*
drink	*shave*
eat	*smoke*
go	*speak*

1. Bob ____doesn't go____ to school every day.

2. My roommates _____ Spanish.

3. Fred has a beard. He _____ in the morning.

4. Sue has a briefcase. She _____ a bookbag to class.

5. We _____ to class on Sunday.

6. Sally takes care of her health. She _____ cigarettes.

7. Jane and Alex always have lunch at home. They _____ at the cafeteria.

8. Sometimes I _____ my homework.

9. Jack is a careful writer. He _____ mistakes in spelling when he writes.

10. My sister _____ coffee.

11. Sometimes Ann _____ her make-up.

12. I am lazy. I _____ exercises in the morning.

EXERCISE 16—ORAL: Change the sentences. Make the sentences negative.

> *Example:* I like tea.
> *Response:* I don't like tea.

1. Bob likes tea.
2. We have class every day.
3. Mary knows Jim
4. I speak French.
5. He sits in the front row.
6. You need your umbrella today.
7. It snows in this city in the winter.
8. I live with my family.
9. I'm hungry.
10. I understand that sentence.
11. Dick is at home.
12. Dick lives in the dorm.
13. They're busy.
14. They work hard.
15. We have a homework assignment.
16. We're in class.
17. It's cold today.
18. It's raining today.
19. It rains every day.
20. This city has nice weather in the summer.

EXERCISE 17: Complete the sentences. Use the words in parentheses. Use the simple present tense.

1. Bob (*like*)____likes_____ tea, but he (*like, not*)

   ____doesn't like_____ coffee.

2. Mary (*know*) _____ Ali, but she (*know, not*)

   _____ Hiroshi.

3. Pablo and Maria (*want*) _____ to stay home tonight. They

   (*want, not*) _____ to go to the movie.

4. Dick (*be, not*) _____ hungry. He (*want, not*)

   _____ a sandwich.

5. Mr. Smith (*drink, not*) _____ coffee, but Mr. Jones

   (*drink*) _____ twelve cups every day.

6. I (*be, not*) _____ rich. I (*have, not*)

   _____ a lot of money.

7. This pen (*belong, not*) _____ to me. It (*belong*)

   _____ to Pierre.

8. My friends (*live, not*) _____ in the dorm. They (*have*)

   _____ an apartment.

9. It (*be*) _____ a nice day today. It (*be, not*)

   _____ cold. You (*need, not*) _____

   your coat.

10. Today (*be*) _____ a holiday. We (*have, not*)

    _____ class today.

EXERCISE 18—ORAL (BOOKS CLOSED): Use *not*.

> *Teacher:*   eat breakfast every day
> *Student A:* I don't eat breakfast every day.
> *Teacher:*   Tell me about (Student A).
> *Student B:* He/She doesn't eat breakfast every day.

1. walk to school every day
2. shave every day
3. read a newspaper every day
4. go shopping every day
5. study grammar every day
6. watch TV every day
7. write a letter every day
8. go dancing every day
9. drink coffee every day
10. eat lunch every day
11. listen to music every day
12. come to class every day

4-6 THE SIMPLE PRESENT: YES/NO QUESTIONS

QUESTION				SHORT ANSWER (+ LONG ANSWER)	*Do I* *Do you* *Do we* *Do they* } + main verb (simple form)
DO/DOES + SUBJECT + MAIN VERB					
(a) **Do**	**you**	**like**	coffee?	Yes, **I do.** (I like coffee.) No, **I don't.** (I don't like coffee.)	*Does he* *Does she* *Does it* } + main verb (simple form)
(b) **Does**	**Bob**	**like**	coffee?	Yes, **he does.** (He likes coffee.) No, **he doesn't.** (He doesn't like coffee.)	Notice in (b): The main verb in the question (*like*) does not have a final *-s*. The final *-s* is part of *does*.

EXERCISE 19—ORAL (BOOKS CLOSED): Ask classmates questions.

Teacher: walk to school every day
Student A: Do you walk to school every day?
Student B: Yes, I do. OR: No, I don't.
Student A: Does (Student B) walk to school every day?
Student C: Yes, he/she does. OR: No, he/she doesn't.

1. walk to school every day
2. watch TV every day
3. eat breakfast every day
4. speak English every day
5. come to class every day
6. get up at 7 o'clock every day
7. talk on the phone every day
8. go to the bank every day
9. wear blue jeans every day
10. have a car
11. have a bicycle
12. like ice cream
13. like (*name of city*)
14. live in (*name of a dormitory*)
15. live in an apartment
16. go shopping every day

EXERCISE 20: Make questions. Give short answers.

1. A: ___Do you like tea?_____

   B: ___Yes, I do._____ (I like tea.)

2. A: ___Do you like coffee?_____

    B: ___No, I don't._____ (I don't like coffee.)

3. A: _____

    B: _____ (I don't speak Japanese.)

4. A: _____

    B: _____ (Ann speaks French.)

5. A: _____

    B: _____ (Ann and Tom don't speak Arabic.)

6. A: _____

    B: _____ (I do exercises every morning.)

7. A: _____

    B: _____ (I don't have a Spanish-English dictionary.)

8. A: _____

    B: _____ (Sue has a cold.)

9. A: _____

    B: _____ (The teacher comes to class every day.)

10. A: _____

    B: _____ (Jim and Sue don't do their homework every
        day.)

11. A: _____

    B: _____ (It rains a lot in April.)

12. A: _____

    B: _____ (My parents live in Bangkok.)

EXERCISE 21: Make questions. Give short answers. Use the names of
your classmates in the questions.

1. A: ___Does (Carlos) speak English?_____

    B: ___Yes, he does._____ (He speaks English.)

2. A: _____ Does (Yoko) speak Spanish? _____

   B: _____ No, she doesn't. _____ (She doesn't speak Spanish.)

3. A: _____ Is (Ali) in class today? _____

   B: _____ No, he isn't. _____ (He isn't in class today.)

4. A: _____

   B: _____ (He comes to class every day.)

5. A: _____

   B: _____ (They're in class today.)

6. A: _____

   B: _____ (She sits in the same seat every day.)

7. A: _____

   B: _____ (He has a mustache.)

8. A: _____

   B: _____ (She doesn't have a bicycle.)

9. A: _____

   B: _____ (He's wearing blue jeans today.)

10. A: _____

    B: _____ (He wears blue jeans every day.)

11. A: _____

    B: _____ (They aren't from Indonesia.)

12. A: _____

    B: _____ (They don't have dictionaries on their desks.)

13. A: _____

    B: _____ (She's writing in her book right now.)

14. A: _____

    B: _____ (She studies hard.)

15. A: _____

    B: _____ (They speak English.)

4-7   THE SIMPLE PRESENT: ASKING QUESTIONS WITH *WHERE*

QUESTION					SHORT ANSWER (+ LONG ANSWER)
(*WHERE*) + *DOES/DO* + SUBJECT +			MAIN VERB		
(a)	Does	Mary	live	**in Chicago?**	Yes, she does. (Mary lives in Chicago.) No, she doesn't. (Mary doesn't live in Chicago.)
(b) **Where**	does	Mary	live?		**In Chicago.** (Mary lives in Chicago.)
(c)	Do	they	study	**at the library?**	Yes, they do. (They study at the library.) No, they don't. (They don't study at the library.)
(d) **Where**	do	they	study?		**At the library.** (They study at the library.)

EXERCISE 22:   Make questions.

1. A: ___Does Jean eat lunch at the cafeteria every day?___

   B: Yes, she does. (Jean eats lunch at the cafeteria every day.)

2. A: ___Where does Jean eat lunch every day?___

   B: At the cafeteria. (Jean eats lunch at the cafeteria every day.)

3. A: _____

   B: Yes, they do. (Mr. and Mrs. Powell live in San Francisco.)

4. A: _____

   B: In San Francisco. (Mr. and Mrs. Powell live in San Francisco.)

5. A: _____

   B: Yes, he does. (Peter works at the post office.)

6. A: _____

   B: At the post office. (Peter works at the post office.)

7. A: _____

   B: Yes, I do. (I live in the dormitory.)

8. A: _____
   B: In the dormitory. (I live in the dormitory.)

9. A: _____
   B: At a department store. (I buy my clothes at a department store.)

10. A: _____
    B: At a restaurant. (Bill eats dinner at a restaurant every day.)

11. A: _____
    B: In the front row. (I sit in the front row during class.)

12. A: _____
    B: At the University of Wisconsin. (Barbara goes to school at the University of Wisconsin.)

Use either *is/are* or *does/do* in your questions:

13. A: _____
    B: On my desk. (My book is on my desk.)

14. A: _____
    B: To class. (I go to class every morning.)

15. A: _____
    B: In class. (The students are in class right now.)

16. A: _____
    B: In Canada. (Montreal is in Canada.)

17. A: _____
    B: In Canada. (My uncle lives in Canada.)

18. A: _____
    B: To the park. (I go to the park on weekends.)

EXERCISE 23—ORAL (BOOKS CLOSED): Ask a classmate a question. Use *where.*

> *Example:* live
> *Student A:* Where do you live?
> *Student B:* (free response)

1. live
2. eat lunch every day

3. sit during class
4. study at night

5. go to school
6. buy your clothes
7. buy your groceries
8. go on weekends
9. go after class
10. eat dinner

4-8 THE SIMPLE PRESENT: ASKING QUESTIONS WITH *WHEN* AND *WHAT TIME*

QUESTION					SHORT ANSWER (+ LONG ANSWER)
QUESTION WORD + ***DOES/DO*** + SUBJECT +			MAIN VERB		
(***WHEN/WHAT TIME***)					
(a) **When**	do	you	go	to class?	**At nine o'clock.** (I go to class at nine o'clock.)
(b) **What time**	do	you	go	to class?	**At nine o'clock.** (I go to class at nine o'clock.)
(c) **When**	does	Mary	eat	dinner?	**At six p.m.** (Mary eats dinner at six p.m.)
(d) **What time**	does	Mary	eat	dinner?	**At six p.m.** (Mary eats dinner at six p.m.)

EXERCISE 24: Make questions.

1. A: _____ When/What time do you eat breakfast? _____
   B: At 7:30. (I eat breakfast at 7:30 in the morning.)

2. A: _____ When/What time do you usually eat breakfast? * _____
   B: At 7:30. (I usually eat breakfast at 7:30.)

3. A: _____
   B: At 7:00. (I get up at 7:00.)

4. A: _____
   B: At 7:00. (I usually get up at 7:00.)

5. A: _____
   B: At 8:15. (The movie starts at 8:15.)

6. A: _____
   B: At half-past twelve. (I usually eat lunch at half-past twelve.)

_____

* Notice the position of ***usually:***
   QUESTION WORD + ***DOES/DO*** + SUBJECT + ***USUALLY*** + MAIN VERB

7. A: _____

    B: At 9:05. (The train leaves at 9:05.)

8. A: _____

    B: At 5:30. (The restaurant opens at 5:30.)

9. A: _____

    B: Around 11:00. (I usually go to bed around 11:00.)

10. A: _____

    B: Between 6:30 and 8:00. (I usually eat dinner between 6:30 and 8:00.)

11. A: _____

    B: At 10:00 p.m. (The library closes at 10:00 p.m. on Saturday.)

12. A: _____

    B: At a quarter past eight. (My classes begin at a quarter past eight.)

EXERCISE 25—ORAL (BOOKS CLOSED): Ask a classmate a question. Use *when* or *what time.*

    Example: eat breakfast
    Student A: When/What time do you eat breakfast?
    Student B: (*free response*)

1. get up
2. usually get up
3. eat breakfast
4. leave home in the morning
5. usually get to class
6. eat lunch
7. go back home
8. get home
9. have dinner
10. usually study in the evening
11. go to bed

EXERCISE 26—ORAL/WRITTEN: Interview someone (a friend, a roommate, a classmate, etc.) about his/her daily schedule. Use the information from the interview to write a composition.

Some questions you might want to ask during the interview:

What do you do every morning?
What do you do every afternoon?
What do you do every evening?

What time do you . . . ?
When do you . . . ?
Where do you . . . ?

chapter 5

Nouns

EXERCISE 1: Name things that belong to each category. Make a list. All of the words you use in this exercise are called *nouns.*

Make one list at a time, working individually or in groups, and then compare your list with your classmates' lists.

1. Name clothing you see in this room. (*shirt . . .*)
2. Name kinds of fruit. (*apple . . .*)
3. Name things you drink. (*coffee . . .*)
4. Name parts of the body. (*head . . .*)
5. Name kinds of animals. (*horse . . .*)
6. Name cities in the United States and Canada. (*New York City, Montreal . . .*)
   Note: The names of cities begin with capital letters.
7. Name languages. (*English . . .*)
   Note: The names of languages begin with capital letters.
8. Name school subjects. (*history . . .*)

5-1 NOUNS: SINGULAR AND PLURAL

SINGULAR	PLURAL	
(a) one pen one apple one cup one elephant	two pens three apples four cups five elephants	To make the plural form of most nouns: add **-s**

(b) **baby** **city**	**babies** **cities**	End of noun: *consonant* + *-y* Plural form: change **y** to **i,** add *-es*
(c) **boy** **key**	**boys** **keys**	End of noun: *vowel* + *-y* Plural form: add *-s*
(d) **wife** **thief**	**wives** **thieves**	End of noun: *-fe* or *-f* Plural form: change **f** to **v,** add *-es*
(e) **dish** **match** **class** **box**	**dishes** **matches** **classes** **boxes**	End of noun: *-sh, -ch, -ss, -x* Plural form: add *-es* Pronunciation: */əz/*
(f) **tomato** **potato**	**tomatoes** **potatoes**	End of noun: *consonant* + *o* Plural form: add *-es*
zoo **radio**	**zoos** **radios**	End of noun: *vowel* + *o* Plural form: add *-s*

EXERCISE 2:   Complete the sentences. Use the plural form of the words in the lists. Use each word only one time.

LIST A:

baby	*dictionary*
✔ *boy*	*key*
city	*lady*
country	*party*
cowboy	*tray*

1. Mr. and Mrs. Parker have one daughter and two sons. They have one girl and two _____boys_____ .

2. The students in my class come from many _____.

3. Women give birth to _____.

4. My money and my _____ are in my pocket.

5. I know the names of many _____ in the U.S. and Canada.

6. I like to go to _____ because I like to meet and talk to people.

7. People carry their food on _____ at a cafeteria.

8. We always use our _____ when we write compositions.

9. Good evening, _____ and gentlemen.

10. _____ ride horses.

LIST B:

knife   *thief*
leaf   *wife*
life

11. Please put the _____, forks, and spoons on the table.

12. Sue and Ann are married. They are _____. They have husbands.

13. We all have some problems in our _____.

14. Police officers catch _____.

15. It is fall. The _____ are falling from the trees.

LIST C:

bush	*glass*	*sandwich*	*tomato*
class	*match*	*sex*	*zoo*
dish	*potato*	*tax*	

16. Bob drinks eight _____ of water every day.

17. There are two _____: male and female.

18. Please put the _____ and the silverware on the table.

19. All citizens pay money to the government every year. They pay their

_____.

20. I can see trees and _____ outside the window.

21. I want to light the candles. I need some _____.

22. When I make a salad, I use lettuce and _____.

23. Sometimes Sue has a hamburger and French-fried _____ for dinner.

24. Some animals live all of their lives in _____.

25. Dick is a student. He likes his _____.

26. We often eat _____ for lunch.

EXERCISE 3: Practice the pronunciation of *-s/-es.*

GROUP A: Final *-s* is pronounced /z/ after voiced sounds.

1. taxicabs	7. years
2. beds	8. lives
3. dogs	9. trees
4. balls	10. cities
5. rooms	11. boys
6. coins	12. days

GROUP B: Final **-s** is pronounced **/s/** after voiceless sounds.

13. books
14. desks
15. cups

16. groups
17. cats
18. students

GROUP C: Final **-s/-es** is pronounced **/əz/**

after ''s'' sounds:
19. classes
20. glasses
21. horses
22. places
23. sentences
24. faces
25. offices
26. pieces
27. boxes
28. sexes

after ''z'' sounds:
29. sizes
30. exercises
31. roses
32. noises

after ''sh'' sounds:
33. dishes
34. bushes

after ''ch'' sounds:
35. matches
36. sandwiches

after ''ge/dge'' sounds:
37. pages
38. ages
39. oranges
40. bridges
41. edges

EXERCISE 4:   Practice the pronunciation of **-s/-es.**
    Find the plural noun(s) in each sentence. Pronounce the noun(s). Then read the sentence aloud.

1. There are twenty desks in the room.
2. Oranges are usually sweet.
3. Roses are beautiful flowers. Rose bushes are beautiful.

4. We are reading sentences aloud.
5. I like to visit new places.
6. Pennies, nickels, dimes, and quarters are coins.
7. We do exercises in class.
8. I need two pieces of paper.
9. Don wants three sandwiches for lunch.
10. At the zoo you can see tigers, monkeys, birds, elephants, bears, and snakes.
11. Department stores sell many sizes of clothes.
12. The students are carrying books and bookbags.

13. The weather is terrible. It's raining cats and dogs.
14. The teachers have their offices in this building.
15. Engineers build bridges.
16. People have two ears, two eyes, two arms, two hands, two legs, and two feet.
17. Square tables and rectangular tables have four edges.
18. My dictionary has 350 pages.
19. I like apples, bananas, strawberries, and peaches.
20. There are three junior colleges in this city.

21. My apartment has cockroaches in the kitchen.

5-2 NOUNS: IRREGULAR PLURAL FORMS

SINGULAR	PLURAL	EXAMPLES
(a) **child**	**children**	Mr. and Mrs. Smith have *one child.* Mr. and Mrs. Jones have *two children.*
(b) **foot**	**feet**	I have *a right foot* and *a left foot.* I have *two feet.*
(c) **man**	**men**	I see *a man* on the street. I see *two men* on the street.
(d) **mouse**	**mice**	My cat sees *a mouse.* Cats like to catch *mice.*
(e) **tooth**	**teeth**	*My tooth* hurts. *My teeth* are white.
(f) **woman**	**women**	There is *one woman* in our class. There are *ten women* in your class.
(g) **fish**	**fish**	Bob has an aquarium. He has *one fish.* Sue has an aquarium. She has *seven fish.*
(h) **—**	**people**	There are *fifteen people* in this room. (Notice: **people** does not have a final **-s.**)

EXERCISE 5—ORAL (BOOKS CLOSED): Use *two* and the plural form of the noun.

> *Example:* one child
> *Response:* two children

1. one child
2. one woman
3. one tooth
4. one foot
5. one man
6. one mouse
7. one fish
8. one page
9. one place
10. one banana
11. one child
12. one desk

13. one sentence
14. one man
15. one orange
16. one foot
17. one knife
18. one sex

19. one girl
20. one exercise
21. one tooth
22. one woman
23. one boy
24. one mouse

Example: one man and one woman
Response: two people

25. one man and one boy
26. one woman and one man
27. one child and one adult
28. one girl and one woman
29. one girl and one boy

5-3   NOUNS: COUNT AND NONCOUNT

	SINGULAR	PLURAL	
COUNT NOUN	**a book** **one book**	**books** **two books** **some books** **a lot of books** **many books** **a few books**	**A COUNT NOUN:** SINGULAR: *a* + *noun* **one** + *noun* PLURAL: *noun* + **-s**
NONCOUNT NOUN	**money** **some money** **a lot of money** **much money** **a little money**		**A NONCOUNT NOUN:** SINGULAR: do not use *a* do not use **one** PLURAL: A noncount noun does not have a plural form.

COMMON NONCOUNT NOUNS

advice	money	bread
furniture	music	butter
help	paper	cheese
homework	traffic	coffee
information	weather	food
mail	work	fruit

meat	sugar	beef
milk	tea	chicken*
pepper	water	fish
rice	wine	ham
salt		lamb
soup	bacon	pork

EXERCISE 6—ORAL: Most nouns are count nouns. Complete the following by naming things you see in the classroom.

1. I see a _____. I see a _____. I see a _____

   and a _____.

2. I see two _____.

3. I see three/four/five/six/*etc.* _____.

4. I see some _____.

5. I see a lot of _____.

6. I see many _____.

EXERCISE 7:   Study the examples.

(a) A dog is **an animal.**	Use **an** in front of a word that begins with a vowel (*a, e, i, o, u*) or a vowel sound:
(b) Mr. Lee is **an old man.**	
(c) I need **an hour** to finish my work.	an animal an hour † an elephant an idea an ocean an uncle

Complete the sentences. Use **a** or **an.**

1. Bob is eating _____ apple.

2. Tom is eating _____ banana.

---

*Some nouns can be used either as a count noun or as a noncount noun. For example:
   Count: There is a chicken in the farmer's yard.
Noncount: I like chicken. I often have some chicken with rice for dinner.

†Compare: *an hour,* but *a horse, a hotel, a house*

3. Alice works in _____ office.

4. I have _____ idea.

5. I have _____ good idea.

6. Sue is talking to _____ man.

7. Sue is talking to _____ old man.

8. I need to see _____ doctor.

9. Cuba is _____ island.

10. Mary is reading_____ article in the newspaper.

11. Bill is _____ uncle. He has _____ niece and _____ nephew.

12. _____ hour has sixty minutes.

13. Miss Anderson has _____ job.

14. She has _____ unusual job.

15. I go to _____ university.*

EXERCISE 8: Use *a/an* or *some.* All of the nouns are count nouns in this exercise.

1. Bob has ____a____ book on his desk.

2. Bob has ____some____ books on his desk.

3. I see _____ desk in this room.

4. I see _____ desks in this room.

5. Are _____ students standing in the front of the room?

6. Is _____ student standing in the middle of the room?

7. I'm hungry. I would like _____ apple.

8. The children are hungry. They would like _____ apples.

9. _____ children are playing in the street.

10. _____ child is playing in the street.

11. We are doing _____ exercise in class.

12. We are doing _____ exercises in class.

---

*Use *a* in front of *university* because it does not begin with a vowel sound.

EXERCISE 9: Use **some** + *the word in parentheses* to complete the sentence. Add **-s** to a count noun (or give the irregular plural form). Do not add **-s** to a noncount noun.

1. (*money*)   I need ____some money____ .

2. (*desk*)   I see ____some desks____ in this room.

3. (*man*)   ____Some men____ are working in the street.

4. (*music*)   I want to listen to _____.

5. (*flower*)   Don wants to buy _____ for his girlfriend.

6. (*information*)   I need _____.

7. (*help*)   Fred needs _____.

8. (*furniture*)   We need to buy _____.

9. (*chair*)   We need to buy _____.

10. (*child*)   _____ are playing in the park.

11. (*homework*)   I can't go to the movie because I have

_____ to do.

12. (*water*)   I'm thirsty. I would like _____.

13. (*food*)   I'm hungry. I would like _____.

14. (*sandwich*)   The children are hungry. They want to make

_____.

15. (*banana*)   The monkeys are hungry. They would like

_____.

16. (*fruit*)   I'm hungry. I would like _____.

17. (*letter*)   I have _____ in my mailbox.

18. (*mail*)   I have _____ in my mailbox.

EXERCISE 10: Use *a/an* or *some*.

1. I need _____ money.

2. I need _____ dollar.

3. Alice has _____ mail in her mailbox.

4. Alice has _____ letter in her mailbox.

5. We have _____ table, _____ sofa, and _____ chairs in our living room.

6. We have _____ furniture in our living room.

7. Sue has a stereo. She is listening to _____ record. She is listening to _____ music.

8. I'm busy. I have _____ homework to do.

9. Jane is very busy. She has _____ work to do.

10. Jane has _____ job. She is _____ secretary.

11. I'm hungry. I would like _____ orange.

12. The children are hungry. They would like _____ oranges. They would like _____ fruit.

13. I need _____ information about the bus schedule.

14. This box is heavy. I need _____ help.

15. I'm confused. I need _____ advice.

16. I want to write _____ letter. I need _____ paper.

17. Dick wants to write _____ letter. He needs _____ piece of paper.

18. I'm looking out the window. I see _____ cars, _____ bus, and _____ trucks on the street. I see _____ traffic.

EXERCISE 11—ORAL (BOOKS CLOSED): Use **a, an,** or **some** with the given word.

Example: book   *Example:* books   *Example:* money
Response: a book   *Response:* some books   *Response:* some money

1. desk	14. apple	27. window	40. bread
2. desks	15. man	28. horse	41. office
3. animal	16. old man	29. hour	42. food
4. animals	17. men	30. dishes	43. table
5. chair	18. bananas	31. women	44. cheese
6. chairs	19. banana	32. oranges	45. matches
7. furniture	20. fruit	33. orange	46. exercise
8. child	21. island	34. place	47. advice
9. children	22. help	35. places	48. house
10. music	23. university	36. homework	49. people
11. homework	24. uncle	37. mail	50. potatoes
12. flower	25. rice	38. letter	51. baked potato
13. information	26. boys	39. letters	52. sugar

EXERCISE 12: Use **a/an** or **some.**

1. I'm hungry. I would like _____ fruit. I would like

   _____ apple.

2. Jane is hungry. She would like _____ food. She would like

   _____ sandwich.

3. I'm thirsty. I'd like _____ water. I'd like _____ glass

   of water. Ann would like _____ milk.

4. I'm having _____ meat for dinner. I'm having _____

   roast beef.

5. I need _____ sugar for my coffee. Please hand me the sugar. Thank

   you.

6. I want to make _____ sandwich. I need _____ bread

   and _____ cheese. I'd like to have _____ soup with

   my sandwich.

7. Bob is having _____ beans, _____ meat, and
_____ bowl of soup for dinner.

8. There are _____ bananas, apples, and oranges on the table. There
is _____ fruit on the table.

9. There is _____ chicken in the farmer's yard.

10. Would you like _____ chicken for dinner tonight?

11. There is _____ pig in the farmer's yard.

12. I had _____ pork for dinner last night.

13. There is _____ cow in the farmer's yard.

14. I would like _____ roast beef for dinner tonight. Bob would like
_____ steak.*

15. There is _____ lamb in the farmer's yard.

16. We had _____ lamb for dinner last night.

17. _____ fish is swimming in the pond.

18. I had _____ fish for lunch yesterday.

—————————

Steak can be either count or noncount:
  I had a steak for dinner. (I had a whole steak.)
  I had some steak for dinner last night. (I had a part of a steak.)

EXERCISE 13: Complete the following. Use: *a piece of*
a cup of
a glass of
a bowl of

John is hungry and thirsty. He would like:

1. <u>a cup of/a glass of</u> tea.

2. _____ bread.

3. _____ water.

4. _____ coffee.

5. _____ cheese.

6. _____ soup.

7. _____ meat.

8. _____ wine.

9. _____ fruit.

10. _____ rice.

EXERCISE 14—ORAL (BOOKS CLOSED): Use *I would like.*

> *Example:*   coffee
> *Response:* I would like some coffee. OR: I would like a cup of coffee.

> *Example:*   new pen
> *Response:* I would like a new pen.

1. coffee
2. money
3. dollar
4. paper
5. new book
6. new books
7. fruit
8. banana
9. apple
10. oranges
11. water
12. new pencil
13. information
14. help
15. advice
16. food
17. sandwich
18. meat
19. roast beef
20. soup
21. salt
22. sugar
23. new shirt/
    blouse
24. new shoes
25. new
    furniture
26. new car
27. tea
28. cheese
29. rice
30. bread
31. chicken
32. fish

EXERCISE 15: Change *a lot of* to *many* or *much* in the following sentences. Use *many* with count nouns. Use *much* with noncount nouns.*

1. I don't have a lot of money. (*I don't have much money.*)
2. Tom has a lot of problems.

---

* Much is usually used only in negative sentences and in questions. *Much* is rarely used in statements.

3. I want to visit a lot of cities in the United States and Canada.

4. I don't put a lot of sugar in my coffee.

5. I have a lot of questions to ask you.

6. Sue and John have a small apartment. They don't have a lot of furniture.

7. You can see a lot of people at the zoo on Sunday.

8. Dick doesn't get a lot of mail because he doesn't write a lot of letters.

9. Chicago has a lot of skyscrapers. Montreal has a lot of tall buildings too.

10. Mary is lazy. She doesn't do a lot of work.

11. I don't drink a lot of coffee.

12. Don is a friendly person. He has a lot of friends.

13. Do you usually buy a lot of fruit at the market?

14. Does Don drink a lot of coffee?

15. Do you write a lot of letters?

EXERCISE 16—ORAL: Change *some* to *a few* or *a little.* Use *a few* with count nouns. Use *a little* with noncount nouns.

1. I need some paper. (*I need a little paper.*)

2. I usually add some salt to my food.

3. I have some questions to ask you.

4. Bob needs some help. He has some problems. He needs some advice.

5. I need to buy some clothes.

6. I have some homework to do tonight.

7. I usually get some mail every day.

8. I usually get some letters every day.

9. When I'm hungry in the evening, I usually eat some cheese.

10. We usually do some oral exercises in class every day.

EXERCISE 17: Use these words in the sentences. Use the plural form if necessary.

bush	*foot*	*information*	*page*
child	*fruit*	*knife*	*paper*
city	*furniture*	✔*match*	*piece*
country	*help*	*money*	*sex*
edge	*homework*	*monkey*	*traffic*

1. I want to smoke a cigarette. I need some___   matches   .

2. I have a lot of _____ in my wallet. I'm rich.

3. There are two _____: male and female.

4. I would like to visit many _____ in the United States. I'd like to visit Chicago, Los Angeles, Dallas, Miami, and some others.

5. There are some _____, forks, and spoons on the table.

6. I want to take the bus downtown, but I don't know the bus schedule. I need

some _____ about the bus schedule.

7. I want to write a letter. I have a pen, but I need some _____.

8. There are three _____ in North America: Canada, the United States, and Mexico.

9. There are a lot of trees and _____ in the park.

10. Bob is studying. He has a lot of _____ to do.

11. I like to go to the zoo. I like to watch animals. I like to watch elephants, tigers,

and _____.

12. There is a lot of _____ on the street during rush hour.

13. My dictionary has 437 _____.

14. My notebook has 150 _____ of paper.

15. Susie and Bobby are seven years old. They aren't adults. They're

_____.

16. A piece of paper has four _____.

17. We need a new bed, a new sofa, and some new chairs. We need some new

_____.

18. People wear shoes on their _____.

19. I like apples, oranges, and bananas. I eat a lot of _____.

20. Barbara has four suitcases. She can't carry all of them. She needs some

_____.

EXERCISE 18: Use these words in the sentences. Use the plural form if necessary.

advice	*glass*	*penny*	*thief*
centimeter	*horse*	*potato*	*tray*
dish	*inch*	*sentence*	*weather*
fish	*leaf*	*size*	*woman*
foot	*man*	*strawberry*	*work*

1. _____ fall from the trees in autumn.

2. Sometimes I have a steak, a salad, and French-fried _____ for dinner.

3. When the temperature is around 77°F (25°C), I'm comfortable. But I don't like very hot _____.

4. Cowboys ride _____.

5. Plates and bowls are called _____.

6. Married _____ are called wives.

7. _____ steal things: money, jewelry, cars, etc.

8. Five _____ equal one nickel.

9. People carry their food on _____ at a cafeteria.

10. I'm not busy today. I don't have much _____ to do.

11. Sweaters in a store often have four _____: small, medium, large, and extra large.

12. I have a problem. I need your help. I need some _____ from you.

13. Some _____ have mustaches.

14. _____ are small, red, sweet, and delicious.

15. Ann has five _____ in her aquarium.

16. In some countries, people don't use cups for their tea. Instead, they use

_____.

17. There are 100 _____ in a meter.

18. There are 12 _____ in a foot.*

19. There are 3 _____ in a yard.**

20. There are twenty-five _____ in this exercise.

_____

*1 inch = 2.54 centimeters.   1 foot = 30.48 centimeters.
**1 yard = 0.91 meters.

5-4 USING *SOME* AND *ANY*

STATEMENT:	(a) Alice has **some money.**	Use **some** in a statement.
NEGATIVE:	(b) Alice doesn't have **any money.**	Use **any** in a negative sentence.
QUESTION:	(c) Does Alice have **any money?** (d) Does Alice have **some money?**	Use either **some** or **any** in a question.
(e) I don't have **any money.** (*noncount noun*) (f) I don't have **any matches.** (*plural count noun*)		**Any** is used with noncount nouns and plural count nouns.

EXERCISE 19: Use **some** or **any** to complete the sentences.

1. I have _____some_____ money.

2. I don't have _____any_____ money.

3. Do you have _____some/any_____ money?

4. Do you need _____ help?

5. No, thank you. I don't need _____ help.

6. Bob needs _____ help.

7. Mary usually doesn't get _____ mail.

8. We don't have _____ fruit in the apartment. We don't have

   _____ apples, _____ bananas, or _____

   oranges.

9. The house is empty. There aren't _____ people in the house.

10. I need _____ paper. Do you have _____ paper?

11. Ann can't write a letter because she doesn't have _____ paper.

12. Steve is getting along fine. He doesn't have _____ problems.

13. I need to go to the grocery store. I need to buy _____ food. Do you

    need to buy _____ groceries?

14. I'm not busy tonight. I don't have _____ homework to do.

15. Dick can't use the pay phone because he doesn't have _____ dimes.

EXERCISE 20—ORAL (BOOKS CLOSED): Use *some* and *any*. Ask a classmate a question about what he or she sees in this room.

> *Example:*   desks
> *Student A:*   Do you see any (some) desks in this room?
> *Student B:*   Yes, I do. I see some desks/a lot of desks/twenty desks.
>
> *Example:*   monkeys
> *Student A:*   Do you see any (some) monkeys in this room?
> *Student B:*   No, I don't. I don't see any monkeys.

1. books
2. flowers
3. dictionaries
4. birds
5. furniture
6. food
7. curtains
8. paper
9. bookbags
10. children
11. hats
12. signs on the wall
13. bicycles
14. erasers
15. pillows
16. red sweaters
17. dogs or cats
18. bookshelves
19. women
20. light bulbs

EXERCISE 21:   Use *any* or *a*. Use *any* with noncount nouns and plural count nouns. Use *a* with singular count nouns.

1. I don't have _____any_____ money.

2. I don't have _____a_____ pen.

3. I don't have _____any_____ brothers or sisters.

4. We don't need to buy _____ new furniture.

5. Mr. and Mrs. Kelly don't have _____ children.

6. I can't make _____ coffee. There isn't _____ coffee in the house.

7. Ann doesn't want _____ cup of coffee.

8. I don't like this room because there aren't _____ windows.

9. Sue is very unhappy because she doesn't have _____ friends.

10. I don't need _____ help. I can finish my homework by myself.

11. I don't have _____ television set in my dormitory room.

12. I can't make a sandwich because there isn't _____ bread in the house.

13. Iowa is an agricultural state. The land is flat and rich. There aren't

_____ mountains in Iowa.

14. I'm getting along fine. I don't have _____ problems.

15. Dick doesn't have _____ car, so he has to take the bus to school.

16. I don't have _____ homework to do tonight.

17. I don't need _____ new clothes.*

18. I don't need _____ new suit.

5-5 POSSESSIVE NOUNS

	SINGULAR NOUN	POSSESSIVE FORM	
(a) Sue and Ann have coats. **Sue's coat** is black. **Ann's coat** is blue.	Sue Ann	Sue's Ann's	To show that a person possesses something, add an apostrophe (') and **-s** to a singular noun.
(b) My mother has a name. My **mother's name** is Fran.	mother	mother's	POSSESSIVE NOUN, SINGULAR: *noun + apostrophe (') + -s*
(c) My friend has an apartment. My **friend's apartment** is small.	friend	friend's	
(d) The student has a book. The **student's book** is red.	student	student's	
	PLURAL NOUN	POSSESSIVE FORM	
(e) The students have books. The **students' books** are red.	students	students'	Add an apostrophe (') at the end of a plural noun (after the **-s**).
(f) My friends have an apartment. My **friends' apartment** is small.	friends	friends'	POSSESSIVE NOUN, PLURAL: *noun + -s + apostrophe (')*
(g) My parents have names. My **parents' names** are Fran and Bill.	parents	parents'	

_____

* *Clothes* = always plural. The word *clothes* does not have a singular form.

EXERCISE 22: Use the information below to make sentences with possessive nouns.

1. Bob has a cat.   Bob's cat likes to sleep on the sofa in the living room.

2. Mary has a mother.   Do you know Mary's mother?

3. My friends have an apartment. _____

4. My friend has an apartment. _____

5. My parents have a telephone number. _____

6. My mother has a name. _____

7. My father has a name. _____

8. John has a sister. _____

9. The students have books. _____

10. The student has books. _____

11. Barbara has a dormitory room. _____

12. My teachers have names. _____

EXERCISE 23—WRITTEN:

Write sentences about things your classmates possess. For example:

Kim's dictionary is on his desk.
Anna's purse is brown.
Carlos's shirt is green.*

_____

*A singular noun that ends in -s (e.g., Carlos) has two possible possessive forms:
Carlos's shirt
Carlos' shirt
It is not necessary to add a final -s if the noun already ends in -s.

5-6 POSSESSIVE: IRREGULAR PLURAL NOUNS

(a) The **children's toys** are on the floor.	Irregular plural nouns (*children, men, women, people*) have an irregular plural possessive form. The apostrophe (') comes <u>before</u> the final **-s**.
(b) That store sells **men's clothing**.	
(c) That store sells **women's clothing**.	General rule: If a plural noun ends in **-s**, add the apostrophe (') after the **-s**. If a plural noun does not end in **-s**, add an apostrophe (') and a final **-s**.
(d) Biographies are the stories of **people's lives**.	
	REGULAR PLURAL POSSESSIVE NOUN: *the students' books* IRREGULAR PLURAL POSSESSIVE NOUN: *the women's books*

EXERCISE 24: Complete the sentences by using the correct possessive form of the nouns in parentheses.

1. (*children*)   That store sells ____children's____ books.

2. (*girl*)   Mary is a _____ name.

3. (*girls*)   Mary and Sue are _____ names.

4. (*women*)   Mary and Sue are _____ names.

5. (*uncle*)   Dick is living at his _____ house.

6. (*person*)   A biography is the story of a _____ life.

7. (*people*)   Biographies are the stories of _____ lives.

8. (*students*)   _____ lives are busy.

9. (*brother*)   Do you know my _____ wife?

10. (*brothers*)   Do you know my _____ wives?

11. (*wife*)   My _____ parents live in California.

12. (*dog*)   My _____ name is Fido.

13. (*dogs*)   My _____ names are Fido and Rover.

14. (*men*)   Are Jim and Tom _____ names?

15. (*man, woman*)   Chris can be a _____ nickname or a _____ nickname.

16. (*children*)   Our _____ school is near our house.

EXERCISE 25: Complete the sentences.

1. My husband's ____brother____ is my brother-in-law.

2. My father's _____ is my uncle.

3. My mother's _____ is my grandmother.

4. My sister's _____ are my nieces and nephews.

5. My aunt's _____ is my mother.

6. My wife's _____ is my mother-in-law.

7. My brother's _____ is my sister-in-law.

8. My father's _____ and _____ are my grandparents.

9. My niece is my brother's _____.

10. My nephew is my sister's _____.

EXERCISE 26:   This is a game. The object of the game is to fill in each list with nouns. Write one noun that begins with each letter of the alphabet, if possible. The nouns must belong to the category of the list. When you finish one list, count the number of nouns in your list. That is your score.*
     Look at list 1. It is an example.

LIST 1 *things in nature*	LIST 2 *things you eat or drink*	LIST 3 *animals or insects*	LIST 4 *things you can buy at a department store*
A air	A _____	A _____	A _____
B bush	B _____	B _____	B _____
C _____	C _____	C _____	C _____
D dew	D _____	D _____	D _____
E earth	E _____	E _____	E _____
F fish	F _____	F _____	F _____
G grass	G _____	G _____	G _____

_____

* *To the teacher:* The game can be done with a time limit in class (3–5 minutes per list) or at home. It can be played with the students filling out the lists individually or in groups.

LIST 1 *things in nature*	LIST 2 *things you eat or drink*	LIST 3 *animals or insects*	LIST 4 *things you can buy at a department store*
H _____	H _____	H _____	H _____
I ___ice___	I _____	I _____	I _____
J _____	J _____	J _____	J _____
K _____	K _____	K _____	K _____
L ___leaf___	L _____	L _____	L _____
M ___moon___	M _____	M _____	M _____
N _____	N _____	N _____	N _____
O ___ocean___	O _____	O _____	O _____
P ___plant___	P _____	P _____	P _____
Q _____	Q _____	Q _____	Q _____
R ___rain___	R _____	R _____	R _____
S ___star___	S _____	S _____	S _____
T ___tree___	T _____	T _____	T _____
U _____	U _____	U _____	U _____
V _____	V _____	V _____	V _____
W ___water___	W _____	W _____	W _____
X _____	X _____	X _____	X _____
Y _____	Y _____	Y _____	Y _____
Z _____	Z _____	Z _____	Z _____
Score: ___15___	Score: _____	Score: _____	Score: _____

chapter 6

Some Special Verbs and Expressions

6-1 USING *NEED* AND *WANT;* USING INFINITIVES

	VERB + NOUN	VERB + INFINITIVE		***Need*** is stronger than ***want. Need*** gives the idea that something is *very important.*
(a) People **need**	**food.**	People **need**	**to eat.**	
(b) I **want**	**a sandwich.**	I **want**	**to eat** a sandwich.	***Need*** and ***want*** are followed by a noun or by an infinitive.
				An infinitive = ***to*** + *the simple form of a verb.* *

*The simple form of a verb means a verb without *-s, -ed,* or *-ing.*
Examples of the simple form of a verb: *come, help, answer, write.*
Examples of infinitives: *to come, to help, to answer, to write.*

EXERCISE 1: Use the words in the list or your own words to complete the sentences. Use an infintive (***to*** + *verb*) in each sentence.

buy	*do*	*listen to*	*play*	*walk*
call	*get*	*marry*	*take*	*wash*
cash	*go*	*pay*	*talk to*	*watch*

1. Anna is sleepy. She wants _____to go_____ to bed.

2. I want _____ downtown today because I need _____ a new coat.

3. Mike wants _____ TV tonight. There's a good program on Channel 5.

4. Do you want _____ soccer with us at the park this afternoon?

5. I need _____ Margaret on the phone.

6. I want _____ to the bank because I need _____ a check.

7. Dick doesn't want _____ his homework tonight.

8. My clothes are dirty. I need _____ them.

9. John loves Mary. He wants _____ her.

10. It's the end of the month. I need _____ my bills.

11. It's a nice day. I don't want _____ the bus home today. I want _____ home instead.

12. Do you want _____ some music on the radio?

13. Helen needs _____ an English course.

14. Where do you want _____ for lunch?

15. What time do you need _____ to the bus station?

EXERCISE 2: Here are twelve short conversations. Complete the sentences. Use the words in parentheses and other necessary words.

1. A: (*you/want/go*)   A: _____Do you want to go_____
                                downtown this afternoon?

   B: (*I/need/buy*)   B: Yes, I do. ____I need to buy____
                                a winter coat.

2. A: (*you/want/go*)   A: Where_____
                                for dinner tonight?
                             B: Rossini's Restaurant.

3. A: (*you/need/be*)   A: What time _____
                            at the airport?
                         B: Around six. My plane leaves at seven.

4. A: (*Jean/not/want/go*)   A: _____
                                 to the baseball game.
                              B: Why not?

   A: (*she/need/study*)   A: Because _____
                               for a test.

5. A: (*I/want/take*)   A: I'm getting tired. _____
                            a break for a few minutes.
                         B: Okay. Let's take a break. We can finish the
                            work later.

6. A: (*Peter/want/go back*)   A: _____
                                   to his apartment.
                                B: Why?

   A: (*he/want/change*)   A: Because _____
                               his clothes before he goes to the party.

7. A: (*you/want/get up*)   A: What time _____
                                in the morning?

   B: (*I/want/leave*)   B: 5:30. _____
                             for Chicago at 6:00. It will take me seven
                             hours to drive there, so I want to get an early
                             start.

8. A: (*we/not/need/come*)   A: _____
                                 to class on Friday.
                              B: Why not?
                              A: It's a holiday.

9. A: (*you/want/go*)   A: Where _____
                            for your vacation?

   B: (*I/want/visit*)   B: _____
                             Niagara Falls, New York City, and
                             Washington, D.C.

10. A: (*I/need/look up*)   A: May I see your dictionary? _____
a word.
B: Of course. Here it is.
A: Thanks.

11. A: (*I/need/talk to*)   A: _____
the Foreign Student Advisor.
B: Why?

    A: (*I/need/renew*)   A: _____
my visa.

12. A: (*you/want/come*)   A: _____
with us to the park?

    B: (*I/need/get*)   B: Sure. Thanks. _____
some exercise.

6-2 USING *HAVE + INFINITIVE (HAS TO/HAVE TO)*

(a) People **need to eat** food.	(a) and (b) have basically the same meaning. (c) and (d) have basically the same meaning.
(b) People **have to eat** food.	***Have*** + *infinitive* has a special meaning: it expresses the same idea as ***need.***
(c) Jack **needs to study** for his test.	Usual pronunciation:
(d) Jack **has to study** for his test.	**have to = "hafta" has to = "hasta"**

EXERCISE 3—ORAL: Change the sentences by using ***have to*** or ***has to.***

1. Do you need to go downtown this afternoon? (*Do you have to go downtown this afternoon?*)
2. I need to go to the grocery store.
3. Does Kate need to study tonight?
4. She needs to study for a test.
5. What time does Jim need to leave for the airport?
6. He needs to be at the airport at 7:00.
7. Ann doesn't need to find a new apartment.
8. We don't need to go to class tomorrow.

9. I need to go downtown because I need to buy some new clothes.
10. Do you need to see* the Foreign Student Advisor?

EXERCISE 4: Complete the sentences. Use the words in parentheses. Use **has/have** + *infinitive* in all the sentences.

1. A: (*Sue/leave for*)   A: What time _____ does Sue have to leave for**
                               the airport?

    B: (*she/be*)   B: Around 5:00. _____ She has to be _____
                               at the airport at 6:15.

2. A: (*I/go*)   A: _____ to the
                               grocery store.
                           B: Why?

    A: (*I/get*)   A: Because _____
                               some milk and bread.

3. A: (*Kate/stay*)   A: _____ home
                               tonight.
                           B: Why?

    A: (*She/study*)   A: Because _____
                               for a test.

4. A: (*you/be*)   A: What time _____
                               at the dentist's office?
                           B: 3:00. I have a three o'clock appointment.

5. A: (*Tom/find*)   A: _____ a new
                               apartment?
                           B: Yes, he does.

6. A: (*Yoko/not/take*)   A: _____
                               another English course. Her English is very good.

    B: (*you/take*)   B: _____
                               another English course?
                           A: Yes, I do. I need to study more English.

_____

see = meet with, talk to
  Examples: *I have to see a doctor. I have to see a dentist.*
**leave for = begin a trip to a place*

7. A: (*Steve/go*)   A: _____
                             downtown this afternoon.
                          B: Why?

   A: (*he/buy*)   A: _____ a
                             winter coat.

8. A: (*I/see*)   A: _____ the
                             Foreign Student Advisor.
                          B: Is she in her office now?
                          A: Yes. Do you want to come with me?

   B: (*I/talk*)   B: Yes. _____ to
                             her about my visa.

9. A: (*I/go*)   A: _____ to the
                             bank this afternoon.
                          B: Why?

   A: (*I/cash*)   A: Because _____
                             a check. I need some money.

EXERCISE 5—ORAL (BOOKS CLOSED):   Use *have to/has to.* Use *because.*

   Example: go downtown/buy some new shoes
   Student A: I have to go downtown because I have to buy some new shoes.
   Teacher: Why does (Student A) have to go downtown?
   Student B: (Student A) has to go downtown because he/she has to buy some
                  new shoes.

1. go to the drugstore/buy some toothpaste
2. go the the grocery store/get some milk
3. go shopping/get a new coat
4. go to the post office/mail a package
5. stay home tonight/study grammar
6. go to the hospital/visit a friend
7. go to the bank/cash a check
8. go to downtown/go to the immigration office
9. go to the bookstore/buy a notebook
10. go to (*name of a store in the city*)/buy (*a particular thing at that store*)

EXERCISE 6—ORAL (BOOKS CLOSED): Answer the questions.

1. What do you want to do today?*
2. What do you have to do today?
3. What do you want to do tomorrow?
4. What do you have to do tomorrow?
5. What does a student need to do?

6. Who has to go shopping? Why?
7. Who has to go to the post office? Why?
8. Who has to go to the bank? Why?
9. Where do you have to go today? Why?
10. Where do you want to go tomorrow? Why?

6-3 USING *WOULD LIKE*

(a) I'm thirsty. I want a glass of water.	**would like = want**
(b) I'm thirsty. I **would like** a glass of water.	(a) and (b) have the same meaning, but **would like** is often more polite than **want**. **I would like** is a nice way of saying **I want**.

(c)   **I would like**
  You would like
  He would like
 She would like   a glass of water.
  We would like
They would like
	Notice in (c):
	There is not a final **-s** on **would**.
	There is not a final **-s** on **like**.

(d) **I would like** a sandwich.
(e) **I'd**   like a sandwich.
	CONTRACTIONS: I'd = I would
	    you'd = you would
	    he'd = he would
	    she'd = she would
	    we'd = we would
	    they'd = they would

WANT + INFINITIVE (f) I want to eat a sandwich. *WOULD LIKE* + INFINITIVE (g) I **would like** **to eat** a sandwich.	Notice in (g): **would like** can be followed by an infinitive.

EXERCISE 7—ORAL: Change the sentences by using **would like.**

1. I want to meet your parents. (*I would like/I'd like to meet your parents.*)
2. Ann wants to go to the beach on Sunday.

---

* *What do you want to* is often pronounced "whaddayuh wanna."

3. I want to go downtown this afternoon.
4. Mr. Hill wants another cup of coffee.
5. Bob wants to visit Yellowstone Park in Wyoming.
6. Steve and his girlfriend want to go shopping this afternoon.
7. I want to listen to some music after dinner tonight.
8. Marcia wants some fruit because she's hungry.
9. We want to leave for the airport at 4:30.
10. Mrs. Martin wants some apple pie for dessert.

EXERCISE 8—ORAL (BOOKS CLOSED):   Answer the questions.

1. Who's hungry right now? (. . .), are you hungry? What would you like?
2. Who's thirsty? (. . .), are you thirsty? What would you like?
3. Who's sleepy? What would you like to do?
4. What would you like to do this weekend? What do you have to do this weekend?
5. What do you have to do after class today? What would you like to do?
6. What cities would you like to visit in the United States and Canada?
7. What countries would you like to visit?
8. What do you want to do tonight? What do you have to do tonight?
9. What languages would you like to learn? What language(s) do you have to learn?
10. What would you like to have for dinner tonight?

6-4   USING *WOULD YOU LIKE*

(a) A: **Would you like** some coffee? B: **Yes, I would.** Thank you.	***would you like = do you want***
(b) A: **Would you like** to come with us to the movie? B: **Yes, I would.** I'd like to see that movie.	
(c) A: **Would you like** a can of beer? B: **Sure.** Thanks.	In (c): ***sure*** = an informal way of saying yes. ***thanks*** = an informal way of saying ***thank you.***
(d) A: **Would you like** some tea? B: **No thank you.**	Notice in (d): A polite negative response is ***No thank you.***
(e) A: **Would you like** a can of beer? B: **No thanks.** I have to drive.	In (e): ***no thanks*** = an informal way of saying ***no thank you.***

EXERCISE 9—ORAL:* Ask a classmate a question. Use *would you like.*

> *Example:*   some coffee
> *Student A:*   Would you like some coffee?
> *Student B:*   _____ (*Answer the question*).

1. an apple
2. something to eat
3. some fruit
4. a Coke/Pepsi/7-Up/Orange Crush/ etc.
5. to go to the zoo tomorrow
6. to go out for dinner tomorrow night
7. to come to my party
8. to go downtown with me this afternoon

9. some tea
10. a can of beer
11. something to drink
12. to come to my apartment for dinner Thursday night
13. to go shopping with me
14. a cigarette
15. a piece of candy
16. to go on a picnic this weekend

6-5 WOULD LIKE VS. LIKE

(a) **I would like to go** to the zoo.	In (a): *I would like to go the zoo* means *I want to go to the zoo.*
(b) **I like to go** to the zoo.	In (b): *I like to go to the zoo* means *I enjoy the zoo.*
	Would like indicates that I want to do something now or in the future.
	Like indicates that I always, usually, or often enjoy something.

EXERCISE 10—ORAL: Answer the questions.

1. Do you like to go the zoo?
2. Would you like to go to the zoo with me this afternoon?
3. Do you like apples?
4. Would you like an apple right now?
5. Do you like dogs?
6. Would you like to have a dog as a pet?

---

* *To the teacher:* Encourage Student A to look at the text only briefly and then to look directly at Student B when he/she asks the question. Do the exercise with books closed if your students can handle the longer entries. Encourage a variety of responses to the questions and discuss the appropriateness of informal usage.

7. What do you like to do when you have free time?

8. What do you want to do this evening?

9. What would you like to do tomorrow?

10. What do you have to do every day?

EXERCISE 11—WRITTEN: Complete the sentences with your own words.
(Use your own paper.)

1. I have to _____ every day.

2. I like to _____ every day.

3. I want to _____ today.

4. I have to _____ and _____ today.

5. I would like to _____ today.

6. I don't have to _____ every day.

7. I don't like to _____ every day.

8. I don't want to _____ today.

9. I would like to _____ tomorrow.

10. Do you like to _____?

11. Would you like to _____?

12. Do you have to _____?

REMINDER:

SIMPLE PRESENT (*HABIT*)	PRESENT PROGRESSIVE (*RIGHT NOW*)	
(a) I **study** grammar **every day**.	(b) I am in class **right now**. I am **studying** grammar.	The simple present expresses habits and usual activities. The present progressive describes actions that are happening right now, at the time the speaker is talking.
(c) I **read** this book **every day**.	(d) I **am reading** this book **right now**.	

6-6   VERBS NOT USED IN THE PRESENT PROGRESSIVE

(a) I'm hungry **right now**. I **want** an apple.	Some verbs are not used in the present progressive.
(b) I **hear** a siren. **Do** you **hear** it too?	CORRECT: I want an apple. INCORRECT: I am wanting an apple.

THESE VERBS ARE USUALLY NOT OR NEVER USED IN THE PRESENT PROGRESSIVE:

want	hear	understand
need	see	know
like	smell	believe
love	taste	think (*meaning believe*) *
hate		

* Sometimes *think* is used in progressive tenses. See 6–7 for a discussion of **think that** and **think about**.

EXERCISE 12:   Use the words in parentheses to complete the sentences. Use *the simple present* or *the present progressive*.

1. Alice is in her room right now. She (*read*)___is reading___ a book.

   She (*like*) ___likes___ the book.

2. It (*snow*) _____ right now. It's beautiful! I (*like*)

   _____ this weather.

3. I (*know*) _____ Mary Jones. She's in my class.

4. The teacher (*talk*) _____ to us right now. I (*understand*)

   _____ everything she's saying.

5. Don is at a restaurant right now. He (*eat*) _____ dinner.

   He (*like*) _____ the food. It (*taste*)_____

   _____ good.

6. Sniff-sniff. I (*smell*) _____ gas. (*smell, you*) _____

   _____ it too?

7. John (*tell*) _____ us a story right now. I (*believe*) _____

   his story. I (*think*) _____ that his story is true.

8. Ugh! That cigar (*smell*) _____ terrible.

9. Look at the picture. Jane (*sit*) _____ in a chair. A cat (*sit*)

   _____ on her lap. Jane (*hate*) _____
   the cat.

10. Look at the picture. Mr. Allen (*hold*) _____ a cat. He

(*love*) _____ the cat. The cat (*lick*) _____

_____ Mr. Allen's face.

EXERCISE 13—ORAL: Discuss the examples. Then answer the questions.

SEE, LOOK AT, AND WATCH:*

(a) I **see** many things in this room.
(b) I**'m looking at** the clock. I want to know the time.
(c) Bob **is watching** TV.

HEAR AND LISTEN TO:**

(d) I'm in my apartment. I'm trying to study. I **hear** music from the next apartment. The music is loud.
(e) I'm in my apartment. I'm studying. I have a tape recorder. **I'm listening to** music. I like to listen to music when I study.

QUESTIONS:

1. What do you see in this room?
   Now look at something. What are you looking at?
2. Turn to page 85 in this book. What do you see?
   Now look at one thing on that page. What are you looking at?
3. Look at the floor. What do you see?
4. Look at the board. What do you see?
5. What programs do you like to watch on TV?
6. What sports do you like to watch?
7. What animals do you like to watch when you go to the zoo?
8. What do you hear right now?
9. What do you hear when you walk down the street?
10. What do you hear at night in the place where you live?
11. What do you listen to when you go to a concert?
12. What do you listen to when you go to a language laboratory?

---

* *See* = an unplanned act; it happens because my eyes are open.
Look at = a planned act; it happens for a reason.
Watch = a planned act; I watch something for a long time but I look at something for a short time.

** *Hear* = an unplanned act.
Listen to = a planned act.

6-7 USING *THINK ABOUT* **AND** *THINK THAT*

	***THINK* + *ABOUT* + A NOUN**		
(a) I think	about	my family every day.	In (a): Ideas about my family are in my mind every day.
(b) I am thinking	about	grammar right now.	In (b): My mind is busy now. Ideas about grammar are in my mind right now.
	***THINK* + *THAT* + A STATEMENT**		
(c) I	think	that	Sue is lazy.	In (c): In my opinion, Sue is lazy. I believe that Sue is lazy.
(d) Sue	thinks	that	I am lazy.	People use ***think that*** when they want to say (to state) their opinions, their beliefs.
(e) I	think	that	the weather is nice.	The present progressive is often used with ***think about.*** The present progressive is not used with ***think that.***
(f) I think that John is nice. (g) I think John is nice.			(f) and (g) have the same meaning. People often omit ***that*** after ***think,*** especially in speaking.

EXERCISE 14:   Make sentences. Use *I think (that)* to give your opinion.

1. English grammar is easy/hard/fun/interesting.

    _____ I think (that) English grammar is _____

2. The food at the school cafeteria is delicious/terrible/good/excellent/awful.

    _____

3. Baseball is interesting/boring/confusing.

    _____

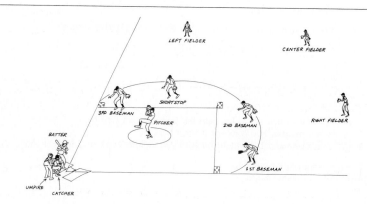

4. People in this city are friendly/unfriendly/kind/cold.

_____

EXERCISE 15:   Complete the sentences.

1. I think that the weather today is _____

2. I think my classmates are _____

3. Right now I'm thinking about _____

4. In my opinion, English grammar is _____

5. In my opinion, soccer is _____

6. I think that my parents are _____

7. I think North American food is _____

8. I think about _____

9. I think that _____

10. In my opinion, _____

EXERCISE 16:   Look at the picture of this family. Their last name is Smith.

the baby = Bobby
the daughter = Ellen
the son = Paul
the mother = Mrs. Smith
the father = Mr. Smith
the cat = Pussycat
the bird = Tweetie
the mouse = ????

Complete the sentences. Use the words in parentheses. Use the _Simple Present_ or the _Present Progressive._ Use an infinitive where necessary.

(1)   The Smiths are at home. It is evening. Paul (_sit_) _____

(2) on the sofa. He (_read_) _____ a newspaper. Ellen (_sit_)

(3) _____ at the desk. She (_study_) _____

(4) _____. While she is studying, she (*listen to*) _____

(5) _____ music on her radio. Paul (*hear*)_____

(6) _____ the music, but he (*listen to, not*) _____

(7) _____ it right now. He (*concentrate*)_____

(8) _____ on the weather report in the newspaper. He (*think*

(9) *about*) _____ the weather report.

(10)   Ellen (*study*) _____ her chemistry text. She (*like*)

(11) _____ chemistry. She (*think*)_____

(12) that chemistry is easy. She (*think about*) _____ chemical

(13) formulas. She (*understand*) _____ the formulas. She

(14) (*like*) _____ her chemistry course, but she (*like, not*)

(15) _____ her history course.

(16)   Mrs. Smith is in the kitchen. She (*cook*) _____ dinner.

(17) She (*cut*) _____ vegetables for a salad. Steam (*rise*)

(18) _____ from the pot on the stove. Mrs. Smith (*like, not*)

(19) _____ to cook, but she (*know*) _____

(20) _____ that her family has to eat good food. While she

(21) (*make*) _____ dinner, Mrs. Smith (*think about*)

(22) _____ a vacation on the beach. Sometimes Mrs. Smith

(23) (*get*) _____ tired of cooking all the time, but she (*love*)

(24) _____ her family very much and (*want*)_____

(25) _____ to take care of their health.

(26)   Mr. Smith (*stand*) _____ near the front door. He (*take*

(27) *off*) _____ his coat. Under his coat, he (*wear*)_____

(28) _____ a suit. Mr. Smith is happy to be home. He (*think*

(29) *about*) _____ dinner. After dinner, he (*want*)_____

(30) _____ (*watch*) _____ television. He

(31) (*need*) _____ (*go*) _____ to bed

(32) early tonight because he has a busy day at work tomorrow.

(33)   In the corner of the living room, a mouse (*eat*) _____ a

(34) piece of cheese. The mouse thinks that the cheese (*taste*) _____

(35) _____ good.

(36)   Pussycat (*see, not*) _____ the mouse. She (*smell, not*)

(37) _____ the mouse. Pussycat (*sleep*) _____

(38) _____ . She (*dream about*) _____ a

(39) mouse.

(40)   Bobby is in the middle of the living room. He (*play with*) _____

(41) _____ a toy train. He (*see, not*)_____

(42) _____ the mouse because he (*look at*) _____

(43) _____ his toy train. The bird, Tweetie, (*sing*) _____

(44) _____ . Bobby (*listen to, not*) _____

(45) the bird. Bobby is busy with his toy train. But Mrs. Smith can hear the bird. She

(46) (*like*) _____ (*listen to*) _____

(47) Tweetie sing.

6-8   THERE + BE

THERE + BE + SUBJECT *+ (PLACE)*	

(a) **There**   **is**   **a bird**   in the tree.
 	
(b) **There**   **are**   **four birds**   in the tree.
	There + be is used to say that something exists in a particular place.
	
	Notice: The subject follows *be:*
	
	    there + is + singular noun
	    there + are + plural noun

(c) **There's** a bird in the tree.
 	
(d) **There're** four birds in the tree.
	Contractions:
	    there + is = there's
	    there + are = there're

EXERCISE 17:   Make sentences with *there is* or *there are.* Use the phrases (groups of words) in italics in your sentences.

1. *on my desk*
   a book

   There is (There's) a book on my desk.

2. *some books*
   on John's desk

   There are (There're) some books on John's desk.

3. *on the wall*
   a map

4. *some pictures*
   on the wall

5. *in this room*
   three windows

6. *fifteen students*
   in this room

7. *in the refrigerator*
   some milk

8. *a bus stop*
   at the corner of Main
   Street and 2nd
   Avenue

9. *in Canada*
   ten provinces

10. *on television tonight*
    a good program

EXERCISE 18—ORAL: Everybody should put one or two objects (e.g., a dime, some matches, a pen, a dictionary) on a table in the classroom. Then describe the items on the table by using *there is* and *there are.*

Examples: There are three dictionaries on the table.
There are some keys on the table.
There is a pencil sharpener on the table.

6-9 *THERE + BE:* YES/NO QUESTIONS

	QUESTION		SHORT ANSWER
	BE + **THERE** + SUBJECT		
(a)	**Is** **there** **any milk** in the refrigerator?		Yes, **there is.** No, **there isn't.**
(b)	**Are** **there** **any eggs** in the refrigerator?		Yes, **there are.** No, **there aren't.**

EXERCISE 19—ORAL: Ask a classmate a question about the contents of the refrigerator in the picture. Use the nouns in the list in your questions. Use "Is there . . . ?" or "Are there . . . ?"

Examples—Student A: Is there any (some) milk in the refrigerator?
    Student B: Yes, there is.

    Student A: Are there any (some) onions in the refrigerator?
    Student B: No, there aren't.

1. milk
2. onions
3. cheese
4. butter
5. eggs
6. bread
7. apples
8. potatoes

9. orange juice
10. strawberries
11. oranges
12. fruit
13. hamburger
14. hamburgers*
15. meat
16. roses

---

* *some hamburger* (noncount) = meat
a hamburger (count) = a sandwich with hamburger inside

EXERCISE 20—ORAL:

Student A: Ask a classmate questions about this city. Use "Is there ...?" or "Are there...?" Your book is open.

Student B: Answer the questions. Your book is closed.

Example—Student A: Is there a zoo in (*name of this city*)?

Student B: Yes, there is. OR: No, there isn't. OR: I don't know.

1. a zoo
2. an airport
3. an aquarium
4. any lakes
5. any good restaurants
6. a good (Vietnamese) restaurant

7. a train station
8. a subway
9. a botanical garden
10. any swimming pools
11. an art museum
12. a good public transportation system

6-10   *THERE + BE:* ASKING QUESTIONS WITH *HOW MANY*

QUESTION						SHORT ANSWER (+ LONG ANSWER)
HOW MANY + SUBJECT +		*ARE* + *THERE* + (PLACE)				
(a) **How many**	**chapters**	**are**	**there**	in this book?		Twelve. (There are twelve chapters in this book.)
(b) **How many**	**provinces**	**are**	**there**	in Canada?		Ten. (There are ten provinces in Canada.)

* See 10-11 for more information about *how many* and *how much.*

EXERCISE 21—ORAL (BOOKS CLOSED): Ask a classmate a question. Use *how many.*

Example: chapters in this book

Student A: How many chapters are there in this book?

Student B: Twelve.

1. pages in this book
2. states in the United States
3. provinces in Canada

4. windows in this room
5. people in this room
6. women in this room

7. men in this room
8. floors in this building
9. letters in the English alphabet

10. countries in North America
11. people in your family
12. continents in the world

EXERCISE 22—ORAL: Complete the sentences.

1. I need . . . because . . . .
2. I want . . . because . . . .
3. I would like . . . .
4. Would you like . . . ?
5. Do you like . . . ?
6. I have to . . . because . . . .
7. There is . . . .
8. There are . . . .

9. I'm listening to . . . , but I also hear . . . .
10. I'm looking at . . . , but I also see . . . .
11. I'm thinking about . . . .
12. I think that . . . .
13. In my opinion, ...
14. How many . . . are there . . . ?
15. Is there . . . ?
16. What time do you have to . . . ?

EXERCISE 23—ORAL: Bring to class one or two pictures of your country (or any interesting picture). Ask your classmates to describe the picture(s).

EXERCISE 24—WRITTEN: Choose one of the pictures your classmates brought to class. Describe the picture in a composition.

chapter 7

The Simple Past Tense

7-1 PAST TIME WORDS

YESTERDAY	LAST	AGO
(a) Bob was here **yesterday. yesterday morning. yesterday afternoon. yesterday evening.**	(b) Sue was here **last night. last week. last month. last year. last spring. last summer. last fall. last winter.** **last Monday. last Tuesday. last Wednesday.** *etc.*	(c) Tom was here **five minutes ago. two hours ago. three days ago. a (one) week ago. six months ago. a (one) year ago.**

EXERCISE 1: Use *yesterday* or *last.*

1. Tom wasn't in class _____last_____ week.

2. I was downtown _____ morning.

3. Two students were absent _____ Friday.

4. Ann wa

5. Ann wa

6. I visite   month.

7. I drean

8. Juan w

9. My sist

10. We wa

11. Ali played with his children _____

12. Yoko arrived in Los Angeles _____ summer.

13. I visited my aunt and uncle _____ fall.

EXERCISE 2: Complete the sentences. Use **ago** in your completion.

1. I'm in class now, but I was at home   <u>ten minutes ago/two hours ago/etc.</u>   .

2. I'm in class today, but I was absent from class _____.

3. I'm in this country now, but I was in my country _____.

4. I was in high school _____.

5. I was in elementary school _____.

6. I arrived in this city _____.

7. There is a nice park in this city. I was at the park _____.

8. We finished EXERCISE 1 _____.

9. I was home in bed _____.

10. It rained in this city _____.

7-2 THE SIMPLE PAST TENSE: USING -ED

simple present: (a) I **walk** to school **every day.** *simple past:* (b) I **walked** to school **yesterday.**	*verb* + **-ed** = the simple past tense
simple present: (c) Ann **walks** to school **every day.** *simple past:* (d) Ann **walked** to school **yesterday.**	*I* *you* *he* *she* } + **walked** (*verb* + **-ed**) *it* *we* *they*

EXERCISE 3:   Complete the sentences. Use the words in the list; use the *Simple Present* or the *Simple Past*.

ask	✔ rain	wait
cook	shave	walk
dream	smile	watch
erase	stay	work

1. It often _____rains_____ in the morning. It _____rained_____ yesterday morning.

2. I _____ to school every morning. I _____ to school yesterday morning.

3. Sue often _____ questions. She _____ a question in class yesterday.

4. Dick doesn't have a beard anymore. He _____ three days ago.

5. Mike _____ his own dinner yesterday evening. He _____ his own dinner every evening.

6. I usually _____ home at night because I have to study. I _____ home last night.

7. I have a job at the library. I _____ at the library every evening. I _____ there yesterday evening.

8. When I am asleep, I often _____. I _____ about my family last night.

9. Mary usually _____ for the bus at a bus stop in front of her apartment building. She _____ for the bus there yesterday morning.

10. The teacher _____ some words from the board a couple of minutes ago. He used his hand instead of an eraser.

11. Our teacher is a warm, friendly person. She often _____ when she is talking to us.

12. I _____ a movie on television last night. I usually _____ TV in the evening because I want to improve my English.

EXERCISE 4:   Read the words aloud. Then use the words to complete the sentences.

GROUP A: Final *-ed* is pronounced */t/* after voiceless sounds:

1. walked	✔ 5. watched	9. kissed	13. laughed
2. worked	6. touched	10. erased	14. coughed
3. cooked	7. washed	11. helped	
4. asked	8. finished	12. stopped	

15. I _____watched_____ TV last night.

16. Mary _____ to class yesterday instead of taking the bus.

17. I _____ the dirty dishes after dinner last night.

18. Bob _____ the board with an eraser.

19. John loves his daughter. He _____ her on the forehead.

20. The joke was funny. We _____ at the funny story.

21. The rain _____ a few minutes ago. The sky is clear now.

22. I worked for three hours last night. I _____ my homework about nine o'clock.

23. Steve _____ my shoulder with his hand to get my attention.

24. Mr. Wilson _____ in his garden yesterday morning.

25. Judy _____ because she was sick. She had the flu.

26. Don is a good cook. He _____ some delicious food last night.

27. Linda _____ a question in class yesterday.

28. I had a problem with my visa. The Foreign Student Advisor _____ me with my problem.

GROUP B: Final *-ed* is pronounced */d/* after voiced sounds:

1. rained	5. smiled	9. remembered
2. signed	6. killed	10. played
3. shaved	7. sneezed	11. enjoyed
4. arrived	8. closed	12. snowed

13. It's winter. The ground is white because it _____ yesterday.

14. Linda _____ in the United States three weeks ago. She

    _____ at the airport on September 3rd.*

15. The girls and boys _____ baseball after school yesterday.

16. Al _____ a contract to buy a washer and dryer yesterday. He

    _____ his name on the bottom line of the contract.

17. Bob used to have a beard, but now he doesn't. He _____ this morning.

18. The students' test papers were very good. The teacher, Mr. Jackson, was very

    pleased. He _____ when he returned the test papers to his students.

19. I have my books with me. I didn't forget them today. I _____ to bring them to class.

20. Mrs. Lane was going crazy because there was a fly in the room. The fly was

    buzzing all around the room. Finally, she _____ it with a rolled up newspaper.

21. I _____ the party last night. It was fun. I had a good time.

22. The window was open. Martha _____ it because it was cold outside.

23. The streets were wet this morning because it _____ last night.

24. "Achoo!" When Judy _____, Bob said, "Bless you." Dick said, "Gesundheit!"

_____

*Notice preposition usage after *arrive:*
  I arrive *in* a country or *in* a city.
  I arrive *at* a particular place (a building, an airport, a house, an apartment, a party, *etc.*)
Arrive is followed by either *in* or *at*. *Arrive* is not followed by *to*.

GROUP C: Final *-ed* is pronounced /əd/ after /t/ and /d/:

1. waited
2. wanted
3. counted
4. visited
5. invited

6. needed
7. added
8. folded

9. The children _____ some candy after dinner.

10. Mr. Miller _____ to stay in the hospital for two weeks after he had an operation.

11. I _____ the number of students in the room.

12. Mr. and Mrs. Johnson _____ us to come to their house last Sunday.

13. Last Sunday we _____ the Johnsons.

14. I _____ the letter before I put it in the envelope.

15. Jerry _____ for the bus at the corner of 5th Avenue and Main Street.

16. The children _____ the numbers on the blackboard in arithmetic class yesterday.

EXERCISE 5—ORAL (BOOKS CLOSED): Practice pronouncing *-ed.*

Example: walk to the front of the room
Student A: (Student A walks to the front of the room.)
Teacher: What did (. . .) do?
Student B: He/She walked to the front of the room.
Teacher: What did you do?
Student A: I walked to the front of the room.

1. smile
2. laugh
3. cough
4. sneeze
5. shave (*pantomime*)
6. erase the board
7. sign your name
8. open the door
9. close the door
10. ask a question

11. wash your hands (*pantomime*)
12. touch the floor
13. point at the door
14. fold a piece of paper
15. count your fingers
16. push (*something in the room*)
17. pull (*something in the room*)
18. yawn
19. pick up your pen
20. add two and two on the board

7-3 SPELLING OF *-ED* VERBS

END OF VERB	-ED FORM
Rule 1: A CONSONANT + *-E* **smile** **erase**	ADD *-D* **smiled** **erased**
Rule 2: ONE VOWEL + ONE CONSONANT * **stop** **rub**	DOUBLE THE CONSONANT, ADD *-ED* **stopped** **rubbed**
Rule 3: TWO VOWELS + ONE CONSONANT **rain** **need**	ADD *-ED:* DO NOT DOUBLE THE CONSONANT **rained** **needed**
Rule 4: TWO CONSONANTS **count** **help**	ADD *-ED:* DO NOT DOUBLE THE CONSONANT **counted** **helped**
Rule 5: CONSONANT + *-Y* **study** **carry**	CHANGE *-Y* TO *-I*, ADD *-ED* **studied** **carried**
Rule 6: VOWEL + *-Y* **play** **enjoy**	ADD *-ED:* DO NOT CHANGE *-Y* TO *-I* **played** **enjoyed**

* Do not double **x** (*fix* + *-ed* = *fixed*).
Do not double **w** (*snow* + *-ed* = *snowed*).

The consonant is not doubled in some two-syllable verbs: *opened, listened, visited, answered.*
For two-syllable verbs that end in a vowel and a consonant, the consonant is not doubled if the stress is on the first syllable (*visited, opened*), but the consonant is doubled if the stress is on the second syllable (*occurred, preferred*).

EXERCISE 6:   Give the **-ed** and **-ing** forms of these words.*

	–ED	–ING
1. count	counted	counting
2. stop		
3. smile		
4. rain		
5. help		
6. dream		
7. clap		
8. erase		
9. rub		
10. yawn		
11. study		
12. stay		
13. worry		
14. enjoy		

EXERCISE 7:   Use the correct form of the words in the list to complete the sentences.

carry	✔ *finish*	*stay*
clap	*learn*	*stop*
cry	*rub*	*taste*
enjoy	*smile*	*wait*
fail		

1. I ____finished____ my homework at nine last night.

2. We _____ some new vocabulary yesterday.

3. I _____ the soup before dinner last night. It was delicious.

4. Linda _____ for the bus at the corner yesterday.

5. The bus _____ at the corner. It was on time.

_____

* See 3–4 for the spelling of *-ing* forms.

6. We _____ the play at the theater last night. It was very good.

7. At the theater last night, the audience _____ when the play was over.

8. Ann _____ her suitcases to the bus station yesterday. They weren't heavy.

9. The baby _____ her eyes because she was sleepy.

10. I _____ home and watched a sad movie on TV last night. I

    _____ at the end of the movie.

11. Bob _____ his examination last week. His grade was "F".

12. Jane _____ at the children. She was happy to see them.

EXERCISE 8: Complete the sentences. Use the words in parentheses. Use the *simple present, present progressive,* or *simple past.* Pay attention to spelling and pronunciation.

1. I (*walk*) ____walked_____ to school yesterday.

2. I (*sit*) ____am sitting_____ in class right now.

3. I usually (*go*) ____go_____ to bed at eleven o'clock every night.

4. Sally (*finish*) _____ her homework at ten o'clock last night.

5. I (*study*) _____ at the library yesterday.

6. I (*study*) _____ English every day.

7. I am in class right now. I (*study*) _____ English.

8. I need an umbrella because it (*rain*) _____ right now.

9. It (*rain*) _____ yesterday morning.

10. My roommate (*help*) _____ me with my homework last night.

11. We can go outside now. The rain (*stop*) _____ a few minutes ago.

12. The children are in the park. They (*play*) _____ baseball.

13. I (*play*) _____ soccer last week.

14. Yesterday morning I (*brush*) _____ my teeth, (*wash*)

    _____ my face, and (*shave*) _____.

15. Ann is in her living room right now. She (*watch*) _____ television.

16. Ann usually (*watch*) _____ TV in the evening.

17. She (*watch*) _____ a good program on TV last night.

18. We (*do*) _____ an exercise in class right now. We (*use*) _____ verb tenses in sentences.

19. I (*arrive*) _____ in the United States a month ago.

20. Tom's airplane (*arrive*) _____ at the airport at 6:05 p.m. yesterday.

EXERCISE 9: Study the examples. Notice the spelling of these two-syllable verbs: The final consonant is not doubled.

SIMPLE FORM	PAST FORM
answer	answered
happen	happened
listen	listened
open	opened
visit	visited

Use these verbs in the following sentences:

1. We _____ to some music after dinner last night.

2. Yesterday I _____ my aunt and uncle at their home.

3. The teacher _____ a question for me in class.

4. I _____ the window because the room was hot.

5. A car accident _____ at the corner of 5th Street and Main yesterday.

EXERCISE 10: This is a spelling test. Give the **-ed** form of each word.

(To the teacher: Use this exercise as a spelling bee or for written practice.)

1. stop	6. rain	11. carry	16. need
2. wait	7. cry	12. open	17. stay
3. study	8. listen	13. fold	18. help
4. smile	9. rub	14. taste	19. drop
5. enjoy	10. visit	15. happen	20. count

7-4 THE SIMPLE PAST: IRREGULAR VERBS*

<table>
<tr><td>

IRREGULAR VERBS

PRESENT   PAST

come – came
do – did
eat – ate
get – got
go – went
have – had
see – saw
sit – sat
sleep – slept
stand – stood
write – wrote

</td><td>

(a) I **come** to class **every day.**
(b) I **came** to class **yesterday.**

(c) I **do** my homework **every day.**
(d) I **did** my homework **yesterday.**

(e) Ann **eats** breakfast **every morning.**
(f) Ann **ate** breakfast **yesterday morning.**

</td><td>

Some verbs do not have **-ed** forms. The past form is irregular.

</td></tr>
</table>

* See Appendix 4 for a list of irregular verbs.

EXERCISE 11:   Change the sentences to the past.

1. Tom gets some mail every day.   Tom got some mail yesterday.

2. They go downtown every day. _____

3. We have lunch every day._____

4. I see my friends every day. _____

5. Hamid sits in the front row every day. _____

6. I sleep for eight hours every night._____

7. The students stand in line at the cafeteria. _____

8. I write a letter to my parents every week. _____

9. Kate comes to class late every day. _____

10. We do exercises in class every day. _____

11. I eat breakfast every morning. _____

12. I get up at seven every day._____

EXERCISE 12—ORAL (BOOKS CLOSED):   Change the sentences to the past.

Example: I come to class every day.
Response: I came to class yesterday.

1. I eat lunch every day.
2. I see you every day.
3. I sit in class every day.
4. I write a letter every day.
5. I do my homework every day.
6. I have breakfast every day.

7. I go downtown every day.
8. I get up at eight every day.
9. I stand at the bus stop every day.
10. I sleep for eight hours every night.
11. I come to school every day.

EXERCISE 13: Complete the sentences. Use the words in parentheses. Use *simple present, present progressive,* or *simple past.* Pay attention to spelling and pronunciation.

1. I (*get*) _____ up at eight o'clock yesterday morning.

2. Mary (*talk*) _____ to John on the phone last night.

3. Mary (*talk*) _____ to John on the phone right now.

4. Mary (*talk*) _____ to John on the phone every day.

5. Jim and I (*eat*) _____ lunch at the cafeteria two hours ago.

6. We (*eat*) _____ lunch at the cafeteria every day.

7. I (*go*) _____ to bed early last night.

8. My roommate (*study*) _____ Spanish last year.

9. Sue (*write*) _____ a letter to her parents yesterday.

10. She (*write*) _____ a letter to her parents every week.

11. Sue is in her room right now. She (*sit*) _____ at her desk.

    She (*write*) _____ a letter to her boyfriend.

12. Marianne (*do*) _____ her homework last night.

13. Yesterday I (*see*) _____ Dick at the library.

14. I (*have*) _____ a dream last night. I (*dream*)

    _____ about my friends. I (*sleep*)

    _____ for eight hours.

15. Alice (*smoke*) _____ a cigarette after class yesterday.

16. My wife (*come*) _____ home around five every day.

17. Yesterday she (*come*) _____ home at 5:15.

18. Our teacher (*stand*) _____ in the middle of the room right now.

19. Our teacher (*stand*) _____ in the front of the room yesterday.

20. John usually (*sit*) _____ in the back of the room, but

   yesterday he (*sit*) _____ in the front row. Today he (*be*)

   _____ absent. He (*be*) _____ absent
   two days ago too.

7-5   THE SIMPLE PAST: NEGATIVE

SUBJECT + *DID* + *NOT* + MAIN VERB					*I* *you* *he* *she* ⎬ + *did not* + main verb *it* *we* *they*
(a) I	**did**	**not**	**walk**	to school yesterday.	
(b) You	**did**	**not**	**walk**	to school yesterday.	+ *did not* + main verb (simple form)
(c) Tom	**did**	**not**	**eat**	lunch yesterday.	
(d) They	**did**	**not**	**come**	to class yesterday.	
(e) I **didn't walk** to school yesterday. (f) They **didn't come** to class yesterday.					Negative contraction: *did* + *not* = *didn't*

EXERCISE 14—ORAL (BOOKS CLOSED):   Use *I don't* and *I didn't*.

Example: walk to school
Response: I don't walk to school every day. I didn't walk to school yesterday.

1. eat breakfast
2. watch TV
3. go shopping
4. read the newspaper
5. study

6. go to the library
7. visit my friends
8. see (. . .)
9. do my homework
10. shave

(To the teacher: Repeat the exercise entries, but include a Student B who will use **he/she doesn't** *and* **he/she didn't**.*)*

Example: walk to school
Student A: I don't walk to school every day. I didn't walk to school yesterday.
Teacher: Tell me about (Student A).
Student B: He/She doesn't walk to school every day. He/She didn't walk to school yesterday.

EXERCISE 15:   Complete the sentences. Use the words in parentheses. Use *simple present, simple past,* or *present progressive.*

1. I (*go, not*) _____ didn't go _____ to a movie last night. I (*stay*)

   _____ stayed _____ home.

2. Fred (*come, not*) _____ doesn't come _____ to class every day.

3. Sue (*read*) _____ is reading _____ a book right now. She (*watch, not*)

   _____ isn't watching _____ TV.

4. I (*finish, not*) _____ my homework last night. I (*go*)

   _____ to bed early.

5. Jane (*stand, not*) _____ up right now. She (*sit*)

   _____ down.

6. It (*rain, not*) _____ right now. The rain (*stop*)

   _____ a few minutes ago.

7. The weather (*be, not*) _____ cold today, but it (*be*)

   _____ cold yesterday.

8. Mary and I (*go, not*) _____ shopping yesterday. We (*go*)

   _____ shopping last Monday.

9. I (*go*) _____ to a movie last night, but I (*enjoy, not*)

   _____ it.

10. I (*write*) _____ a letter to my girlfriend yesterday, but I

    (*write, not*) _____ a letter to her last week.

11. My husband (*come, not*) _____ home for dinner last night.

    He (*stay*) _____ at his office.

12. The children (*go*) _____ to bed a half an hour ago. They

    (*sleep*) _____ now.

13. We (*be*) _____ late for the movie last night. The movie

    (*start*) _____ at 7:00, but we (*arrive, not*)

    _____ until 7:15.

14. Mary (*ask*) _____ Bob a question a few minutes ago, but

   he (*answer, not*) _____ her question.

15. I (*eat, not*) _____ lunch every day because I (*want*)

   _____ to lose some weight. I (*eat, not*)

   _____ lunch yesterday either.

7-6   THE SIMPLE PAST: YES/NO QUESTIONS

DID + SUBJECT + MAIN VERB				SHORT ANSWER	(+ LONG ANSWER)
(a) **Did**	**Mary**	**walk**	to school?	**Yes, she did.** **No, she didn't.**	(She walked to school.) (She didn't walk to school.)
(b) **Did**	**you**	**come**	to class?	**Yes, I did.** **No, I didn't.**	(I came to class.) (I didn't come to class.)

EXERCISE 16:   Make questions. Give short answers.

1. A: _____Did you walk downtown yesterday?_____

   B: Yes, _____I did._____ (I walked downtown yesterday.)

2. A: _____Did it rain last week?_____

   B: No, _____it didn't._____ (It didn't rain last week.)

3. A: _____

   B: Yes, _____ (I ate lunch at the cafeteria.)

4. A: _____

   B: No, _____ (Bob didn't go to the library last night.)

5. A: _____

   B: Yes, _____ (I had a cup of coffee this morning.)

6. A: _____

   B: _____ (I went to a party last night.)

7. A: _____

   B: _____ (Ann studied English three years ago.)

8. A: _____

    B: _____ (I saw Jean at dinner last night.)

9. A: _____

    B: _____ (Sue and Dick didn't do their homework last night.)

10. A: _____

    B: _____ (I didn't dream in English last night.)

11. A: _____

    B: _____ (It isn't cold today.)

12. A: _____

    B: _____ (I come to class every day.)

13. A: _____

    B: _____ (John was absent yesterday.)

14. A: _____

    B: _____ (John stayed home yesterday.)

15. A: _____

    B: _____ (I don't watch television every day.)

16. A: _____

    B: _____ (George isn't in class today.)

    A: _____

    B: _____ (He was here yesterday.)

    A: _____

    B: _____ (He came to class the day before yesterday.)

    A: _____

    B: _____ (He usually comes to class every day.)

EXERCISE 17—ORAL (BOOKS CLOSED): Ask a classmate a question about his/her activities this morning.

> *Example:* walk to school
> *Student A:* Did you walk to school this morning?
> *Student B:* Yes, I did. OR: No, I didn't.

1. get up at seven
2. eat breakfast
3. study English
4. walk to class
5. talk to (. . .)
6. see (. . .)

7. smoke a cigarette
8. go shopping
9. have a cup of coffee
10. watch TV
11. listen to the radio
12. read a newspaper

EXERCISE 18—ORAL (BOOKS CLOSED): Ask questions about the present and the past.

(To the teacher: Use the entries in the preceding exercise.)

> *Example:* walk to school
> *Student A:* Do you walk to school every day?
> *Student B:* Yes, I do. OR: No, I don't.
> *Student A:* Did you walk to school this morning?
> *Student B:* Yes, I did. OR: No, I didn't.

EXERCISE 19—ORAL (BOOKS CLOSED): Review of irregular verbs.

Answer all of the questions "yes".

> *Example:* Did you come to class today?
> *Response:* Yes, I did. I came to class today.

1. Did you eat dinner last night?
2. Did (. . .) come to class today?
3. Did you get a letter yesterday?
4. Did (. . .) go shopping yesterday?
5. Did (. . .) do his/her homework last night?
6. Did you sleep well last night?
7. Did you have a cup of coffee this morning?

8. Did (. . .) go to a movie last night?

9. Did (. . .) sit in that chair yesterday?

10. Did you write a check yesterday?

11. (*Tell a student to stand up.*) Did (. . . .) stand up? (*Tell him/her to sit down.*) Did (. . .) sit down?

MORE IRREGULAR VERBS

bring – brought	read – read*
buy – bought	ride – rode
catch – caught	run – ran
drink – drank	teach – taught
drive – drove	think – thought

---

* The past form of *read* is pronounced the same way as the color *red*.

EXERCISE 20—ORAL (BOOKS CLOSED):

(To the teacher: The purpose of this exercise is to suggest a format for introducing irregular verbs orally. In addition to this chapter, Chapters 8, 9, and 11 contain short units that introduce irregular verbs. Oral exercises similar to this one may be found in the Teacher's Manual for all subsequent units on new irregular verbs.)

Example: *teach–taught*   I teach class every day. I taught class yesterday. What did I do yesterday?

Response: You taught class.

1. *bring–brought*   I bring my book to class every day. I brought my book to class yesterday. What did I do yesterday?

2. *buy–bought*   I buy books at the bookstore. I bought a book yesterday. What did I do yesterday?

3. *teach–taught*   I teach class every day. I taught class yesterday. What did I do yesterday?

4. *catch–caught*   I catch the bus every day. I caught the bus yesterday. What did I do yesterday?

5. *think–thought*   I often think about my family. I thought about my family yesterday. What did I do yesterday?

6. REVIEW:
    What did I bring to class yesterday? What did you bring to class yesterday?
    What did I buy yesterday? What did you buy yesterday?
    Did you teach class yesterday? Who did?

Did I walk to class yesterday or did I catch the bus?

What did I think about yesterday? What did you think about yesterday?

7. *run–ran*   Sometimes I'm late for class, so I run. Yesterday I was late, so I ran. What did I do yesterday?

8. *read–read*   I like to read books. I read every day. Yesterday I read a book. What did I do yesterday?

9. *drink–drank*   I usually drink a cup of coffee in the morning. I drank a cup of coffee this morning. What did I do this morning? Did you drink a cup of coffee this morning?

10. *drive–drove*   I usually drive my car to school. I drove my car to school this morning. What did I do this morning? Who has a car? Did you drive to school this morning?

11. *ride–rode*   Sometimes I ride the bus to school. I rode the bus yesterday morning. What did I do yesterday morning? Who rode the bus to school this morning?

12. REVIEW:

I was late for class yesterday morning, so what did I do?

What did I read yesterday? What did you read yesterday? Did you read a newspaper this morning?

What did I drink this morning? What did you drink this morning?

I have a car. Did I drive to school this morning? Did you?

Did you ride the bus to school this morning?

EXERCISE 21:   Complete the sentences. Use the words in parentheses.

1. A: I (*ride*) _____ the bus to school yesterday. How did you get to school?

   B: I (*drive*) _____ my car.

2. A: (*Ms. Carter, teach*) _____ class yesterday?

   B: No, she didn't. Mr. Adams (*teach*) _____ class.

3. A: Why are you sneezing and coughing? (*you, catch*)_____

   _____ a cold?

   B: Yes. I feel miserable.

4. A: Why are you out of breath?

   B: I (*run*) _____ to class because I was late.

5. A: Did you decide to change schools?

   B: I (*think*) _____ about it, but then I decided to stay here.

6. A: (*you, go*) _____ shopping yesterday?

   B: Yes. I (*buy*) _____ a new pair of shoes.

7. A: (*you, study*) _____ last night?

   B: No, I didn't. I was tired. I (*read*) _____ a

   magazine and then (*go*) _____ to bed early.

8. A: Do you like milk?

   B: No. I (*drink*) _____ milk when I (*be*)

   _____ a child, but I don't like milk now.

9. A: Did you leave your dictionary at home?

   B: No. I (*bring*) _____ it to class with me.

10. A: Did you enjoy your fishing trip?

    B: I had a wonderful time! I (*catch*) _____ a lot of
    fish.

EXERCISE 22:   Complete the sentences. Use the verbs in parentheses.

1. Ann and I (*go*) _____ to the bookstore yesterday. I

   (*buy*) _____ some stationery and a T-shirt.

2. I had to go downtown yesterday. I (*catch*) _____ the

   bus in front of my apartment and (*ride*) _____ to

   Grand Avenue. Then I (*get off*) _____ the bus and

   transferred to another one. It (*be*) _____ a long trip.

3. Sue (*eat*) _____ popcorn and (*drink*)

   _____ a cola at the movie theater last night. I (*eat,*

   not) _____ anything. I'm on a diet.

4. Mary (*ask*) _____ the teacher a question in class

   yesterday. The teacher (*think*) _____ about the
   question for a few minutes and then said, "I don't know."

5. I (*want*) _____ (*go*) _____

_____ to the basketball game last night, but I (*stay*)

_____ home because I had to study.

6. Last summer we (*drive*) _____ to Colorado for our

vacation. We (*visit*) _____ a national park, where we

(*camp*) _____ in our tent for a week. We (*go*)

_____ fishing one morning. I (*catch*)

_____ a very big fish, but my husband (*catch, not*)

_____ anything. We (*enjoy*) _____

_____ cooking and eating the fish for dinner. It (*be*)

_____ delicious. I like fresh fish.

7. Last night I (*read*) _____ an article in the newspaper.

It (*be*) _____ about the snowstorm in the Midwest.

8. Yesterday Yoko (*teach*) _____ us how to say "thank

you" in Japanese. Kim (*teach*) _____ us how to say
"I love you" in Korean.

9. I almost (*have*) _____ an accident yesterday. A dog

(*run*) _____ into the street in front of my car. I

(*slam*) _____ on my brakes and just (*miss*)

_____ the dog.

10. When Ben and I (*go*) _____ to the department store

yesterday, I (*buy*) _____ some new socks. Ben (*buy,

not*) _____ anything.

11. Marcia (*pass, not*) _____ the test yesterday. She

    (*fail*) _____ it.

12. Yesterday I (*play*) _____ ball with my little boy. He

    (*catch*) _____ the ball most of the time, but

    sometimes he (*drop*) _____ it.

EXERCISE 23—ORAL (BOOKS CLOSED):

Student A: Ask a classmate a question. Use the given verb. Use the past tense.

Student B: Answer the question. Give both a short answer and a long answer.

Example: drink
Student A: Did you drink a cup of coffee this morning?
Student B: Yes, I did. I drank a cup of coffee this morning. OR: No, I didn't. I didn't drink a cup of coffee this morning.

1. eat	7. drink	13. walk
2. buy	8. read	14. watch
3. get up	9. drive	15. listen to
4. have	10. sleep	16. see
5. go	11. go	17. think about
6. study	12. talk to	18. rain

EXERCISE 24—WRITTEN: Use the expressions in the list below to write sentences about yourself. When did you do these things in the past? Use the simple past tense and past time expressions (*yesterday, two days ago, last week, etc.*) in all of your sentences.

1. go downtown (*I went downtown yesterday/two days ago/last week, etc.*)

2. arrive in (*this city*)

3. write a letter to (*someone: mother, brother, friend, Bob, etc.*)

4. eat at a restaurant

5. go to bed early

6. go to bed late

7. get up early

8. be late for class

9. be in high school

10. be in elementary school

11. drink a cup of tea

12. talk to (*someone*) on the phone

13. go shopping

14. study English
15. read a newspaper
16. go on a picnic
17. go to a party
18. play (*soccer, a pinball machine, etc.*)

19. see (*someone or something*)
20. think about (*someone or something*)
21. buy (*something*)
22. do my homework
23. have a cold

7-7 THE SIMPLE PAST: USING *WHERE, WHEN, WHAT TIME,* **AND** *WHY*

QUESTION	SHORT ANSWER (+ LONG ANSWER)
(a) **Did you go** downtown?	**Yes, I did.** (I went downtown.) **No, I didn't.** (I didn't go downtown.)
(b) **Where did you go?**	**Downtown.** (I went downtown.)
(c) **Did Ann arrive** at six?	**Yes, she did.** (She arrived at six.) **No, she didn't.** (She didn't arrive at six.)
(d) **When / What time} did Ann arrive?**	**At six.** (She arrived at six.)
(e) **Did you run** because you were late?	**Yes, I did.** (I ran because I was late.) **No, I didn't.** (I ran because I needed exercise.)
(f) **Why did you run?**	**Because I was late.** (I ran because I was late.)

NOTE ON USING *WHEN* AND *WHAT TIME:*		
QUESTION	**SHORT ANSWER**	
(g) **What time** did Bob arrive?	**At six.** **Seven o'clock.** **Around 9:30.**	***What time*** usually asks specifically for time on a clock.
(h) **When** did Bob arrive?	**At six.** **Friday.** **June 15th.** **Last week.** **Three days ago.**	The answer to ***when*** can be any expression of time.

EXERCISE 25: Make questions. Use ***where, when, what time,*** or ***why.***

1. A: _____ Where did you go yesterday? _____

   B: To the zoo. (I went to the zoo yesterday.)

2. A: _____

    B: Last month. (Dick arrived in Canada last month.)

3. A: _____

    B: At 7:05. (My plane arrived at 7:05.)

4. A: _____

    B: Because I was tired. (I stayed home last night because I was tired.)

5. A: _____

    B: He had to study. (Tom stayed home last night because he had to study.)

6. A: _____

    B: At the library. (I studied at the library last night.)

7. A: _____

    B: Because it's dark in here. (I turned on the light because it's dark in here.)

8. A: _____

    B: To Alaska. (Sara went to Alaska for her vacation.)

9. A: _____

    B: Around midnight. (I finished my homework around midnight.)

10. A: _____

    B: Five weeks ago. (I came to the United States five weeks ago.)

11. A: _____

    B: Because Tom made a funny face. (I laughed because Tom made a funny face.)

12. A: _____

    B: At Emerhoff's Shoe Store. (I got my sandals at Emerhoff's Shoe Store.)

13. A: _____

    B: At home. (Nancy is at home.)

14. A: _____

    B: In the dormitory. (Ben lives in the dormitory.)

15. A: _____

    B: To the park. (I went to the park yesterday afternoon.)

16. A: _____

    B: Because he's sick. (Bobby is in bed because he's sick.)

17. A: _____

    B: Because he was sick. (Bobby stayed home because he was sick.)

18. A: _____
    B: 7:20. (The movie starts at 7:20.)

19. A: _____
    B: Because it's time for dinner. (I have to go home because it's time for dinner.)

20. A: _____
    B: Two days ago. (Sara got back from Chicago two days ago.)

21. A: _____
    B: Because she wanted to talk to Al. (Nancy called because she wanted to talk to Al.)

22. A: _____
    B: Around 5:30. (My wife usually gets home from class around 5:30.)

EXERCISE 26—ORAL (BOOKS CLOSED): Make questions. Use question words.

    Example: I got up at 7:30.
    Response: When/What time did you get up?

1. I went to the zoo.
2. I went to the zoo yesterday.
3. I went to the zoo yesterday because I wanted to see the animals.
4. (. . .) went to the park.
5. (. . .) went to the park yesterday.
6. (. . .) went to the park yesterday because the weather was nice.
7. I am in class.
8. I came to class (an hour) ago.
9. (. . .) is in class.
10. (. . .) came to class (an hour) ago.
11. (. . .) studied at the library last night.
12. (. . .) finished his/her homework around midnight.
13. (. . .) went to bed at 7:30 last night.
14. (. . .) went to bed early because he/she was tired.
15. (. . .) went to the park.
16. (. . .) went to the park yesterday.
17. (. . .) went to the park yesterday because he/she wanted to jog.
18. (. . .) is absent today because he/she is sick.
19. (. . .) is at home.
20. (. . .) stayed home because he/she is sick.

EXERCISE 27:   Make questions. Use *why.* Use ***didn't.***

1. A: ___Why didn't you come to class?___
   B: Because I was sick. (I didn't come to class because I was sick.)

2. A: _____
   B: Because I didn't have enough time. (I didn't finish my homework because I didn't have enough time.)

3. A: _____
   B: Because I forgot his phone number. (I didn't call George because I forgot his phone number.)

4. A: _____
   B: Because he didn't know the answer. (Tom didn't answer the question because he didn't know the answer.)

5. A: _____
   B: Because I had a headache. (I didn't do my homework because I had a headache.)

6. A: It's cold today. _____
   B: Because I lost it. (I didn't wear my hat today because I lost it.)

7. A: Why did you take the bus to school? _____
   B: Because it's cold. (I didn't walk to school because it's cold.)

8. A: I expected to see you at John's party. _____
   B: Because I had to study. (I didn't come because I had to study.)

MORE IRREGULAR VERBS

break – broke	ring – rang
fly – flew	send – sent
hear – heard	sing – sang
leave – left	speak – spoke
meet – met	take – took
pay – paid	

EXERCISE 28—ORAL (BOOKS CLOSED):   Practice using the irregular verbs in the above list.

Example: *break–broke*   Sometimes a person breaks an arm or a leg. I broke my arm five years ago. What happened five years ago?

Response: You broke your arm.

EXERCISE 29:   Complete the sentences. Use the words in parentheses.

1. A: What happened to your finger?

   B: I (*break*) _____ it.

2. A: Who did you talk to at the Dean's office?

   B: I (*speak*) _____ to the secretary.

3. A: When did Jessica leave for Europe?

   B: She (*leave*) _____ for Europe five days ago.

4. A: Did you write Ted a letter?

   B: No, but I (*send*) _____ him a postcard.

5. A: Do you know Meg Adams?

   B: Yes. I (*meet*) _____ her a couple of weeks ago.

6. A: Why did you call the police?

   B: Because I (*hear*) _____ a burglar!

7. A: Where did you go yesterday?

   B: I (*take*) _____ the children to the zoo.

8. A: What time did you get up this morning?
   B: 6:15.
   A: Why did you get up so early?

   B: The telephone (*ring*) _____.

9. A: Did you enjoy the party?

   B: Yes, I had a good time. We (*sing*) _____ songs and danced. It
       was fun.

10. A: Alice (*fly*) _____ to Hawaii last week.
    B: Is she taking a vacation there?
    A: No. She went there on business.

11. A: Bob (*pay*) _____ $150 for his car.
    B: $150???? Does it have an engine?

EXERCISE 30:   Complete the sentences. Use the words in parentheses.

(1)   Yesterday (*be*) _____ a terrible day. Everything (*go*)

(2)   _____ wrong.

(3)   First, I (*oversleep*) _____. My alarm clock (*ring, not*)

(4)   _____. I (*get*) _____ up when I (*hear*)

(5)   _____ some noise outside my window. It was 9:15. I (*get*)

(6)   _____ dressed quickly. I (*run*) _____ to class, but I

(7)   (*be*) _____ late. The teacher (*be*) _____ angry.

(8)   After my classes in the morning, I (*go*) _____ to the cafeteria.

(9)   I (*eat*) _____ a sandwich and (*drink*) _____ a glass of

(10)   milk for lunch. But I (*have*) _____ to pay for two sandwiches and

(11)   two glasses of milk because I (*drop*) _____ my first tray of food on

(12)   the floor. I (*go*) _____ back to the cafeteria line and (*get*)

(13)   _____ a second tray of food. I (*pay*) _____ for the

(14)   food again.

(15)   After lunch, I (*go*) _____ outside. I (*sit*) _____

(16)   under a tree near the classroom building. I (*see*) _____ a friend. I

(17)   (*call*) _____ to him. He (*join*) _____ me on the grass.

(18)   We (*talk*) _____ about our classes and (*relax*) _____.

(19)   Everything was fine. But then I (*stand*) _____ up. When I (*stand*)

(20) _____ up, I (*step*) _____ in a hole and (*break*)

(21) _____ my ankle.

(22)   My friend (*drive*) _____ me to the hospital. We (*go*)

(23) _____ to the emergency ward. The doctor (*take*)

(24) _____ X-rays of my ankle. Then he put a cast on it. I (*pay*)

(25) _____ my bill. Then we (*leave*) _____ the hospital.

(26) My friend (*take*) _____ me home and (*help*) _____

(27) me up the stairs to my apartment.

(28)   When we (*get*) _____ to the door of my apartment, I (*look*)

(29) _____ for my key. I (*look*) _____ in my purse and in

(30) my pockets. There was no key. I (*ring*) _____ the doorbell. I

(31) (*think*) _____ that my roommate might be at home, but she (*be,*

(32) *not*) _____ . So I (*sit*) _____ down on the floor

(33) outside my apartment and (*wait*) _____ for my roommate to get

(34) home.

(35)   Finally my roommate (*come*) _____ home and I (*get*)

(36) _____ into the apartment. I (*eat*) _____ dinner

(37) quickly and (*go*) _____ to bed. I (*sleep*) _____ for

(38) ten hours. I hope today is a better day than yesterday!

EXERCISE 31—WRITTEN: Write a composition.

> *Topic 1:*   Write about your activities yesterday, from the time you got up to the time you went to bed.
>
> *Topic 2:*   Write about one of the best days in your life. What happened?
>
> *Topic 3:*   Write about one of the worst days in your life. What happened?
>
> *Topic 4:*   Interview someone you know about his/her activities yesterday morning, yesterday afternoon, and last night. Then use this information to write a composition.

Use time expressions (*first, next, then, after that, at . . . o'clock, later,* etc.) to show the order of the activities.

chapter 8

Expressing Future Time

8-1 FUTURE TIME: USING *BE GOING TO*

(a) I **am going to go** downtown tomorrow. (b) Sue **is going to study** at the library tomorrow afternoon. (c) We **are going to come** to class tomorrow morning.	***Be going to*** expresses (talks about) the future. FORM: $\left. \begin{array}{c} \textbf{\textit{am}} \\ \textbf{\textit{is}} \\ \textbf{\textit{are}} \end{array} \right\}$ + ***going*** + *infinitive**
(d) **I'm not going to go** downtown tomorrow. (e) Ann **isn't going to study** tonight.	NEGATIVE: ***be*** + ***not*** + ***going to***
(f) **Are** you **going to come** to class tomorrow? (g) **Is** Jim **going to be** at the meeting tomorrow? (h) What time **are** you **going to go** to bed tonight? (i) Where **are** you **going to go** tomorrow?	QUESTION: ***be*** + *subject* + ***going to***
(j) I'm "gonna" go downtown tomorrow.	***Going to*** is often pronounced "gonna." "Gonna" is used in speaking, <u>not</u> in writing.

* Infinitive = ***to*** + *the simple form of a verb* (to come, to go, to see, to study, etc.)

EXERCISE 1—ORAL (BOOKS CLOSED): Use *I'm going to . . . tomorrow.*

Example: go downtown
Response: I'm going to go downtown tomorrow.

1. go shopping
2. buy a pair of boots
3. walk to school
4. go to a movie
5. study at the library
6. see a doctor
7. write a letter to my friend
8. go to bed early
9. get up at seven o'clock
10. call (. . .) on the phone
11. go to a party at (. . .)'s apartment
12. come to class
13. go dancing
14. play soccer
15. look for an apartment

EXERCISE 2—ORAL (BOOKS CLOSED):   Answer the questions.

Example: What are you going to do tomorrow?
Student A: I'm going to (go shopping).
Teacher: What is (. . .) going to do tomorrow?
Student B: He/She's going to go shopping.

What are you going to do:

1. tomorrow?
2. tomorrow morning?
3. tomorrow afternoon?
4. tomorrow night?
5. at 7:00 tomorrow morning?
6. at 9:00 tomorrow morning?
7. at noon tomorrow?
8. at 5:00 tomorrow afternoon?
9. at 6:30 tomorrow evening?
10. at 8:00 tomorrow night?

EXERCISE 3:   Complete the sentences. Use *be going to* + the following expressions (or your own words).

call the landlord
call the police
get something to eat
go to the beach
go to bed

go to the grocery store
go to an Italian
restaurant
lie down and rest for a
while
look it up in my
dictionary
major in psychology

see a dentist
stay in bed today
take a long walk in the
park
take it to the post office
take them to the
laundromat

1. I need to buy some tea. I _____ am going to go to the grocery store. _____

2. It's midnight now. I'm sleepy. I _____

3. Sue is hungry. She _____

4. My clothes are dirty. I _____

5. I have a toothache. My wisdom tooth hurts. I _____

6. I'm writing a composition. I don't know how to spell a word. I _____

_____

7. George has to mail a package. He _____

8. Lucy lives in an apartment. The plumbing doesn't work. She _____

_____

9. Sue and I want to go swimming. We _____

10. I have a headache. I _____

11. It's late at night. I hear a burglar! I _____

12. I want to be a psychologist. When I go to the university, I _____

_____

13. I feel terrible. I think I'm getting the flu. I _____

_____

14. John and Alice want to go out to eat. They _____

_____

15. It's a nice day today. Mary and I _____

EXERCISE 4—ORAL (BOOKS CLOSED): Answer the questions.

Teacher to A: You want to buy some tea. What are you going to do?

           A: I'm going to go to the grocery store.

Teacher to B: What is (. . .) going to do?

           B: He/She's going to go to the grocery store.

Teacher to B: Why?

           B: Because he/she wants to buy some tea.

1. You have a toothache. What are you going to do? What is (. . .) going to do? Why?

2. You have to mail a package. Where are you going to go? Where is (. . .) going to go? Why?

3. Your clothes are dirty.

4. It's midnight. You're sleepy.

5. It's late at night. You hear a burglar.

6. You need to buy some groceries.

7. You want to go swimming.

8. You want to go fishing.

9. You want to buy a new coat.

10. You're hungry.

11. You have a headache.

12. It's a nice day today.

13. You need to cash a check.

14. You want some (pizza) for dinner.

15. You're reading a book. You don't know the meaning of a word.

8-2 WORDS USED FOR PAST TIME AND FUTURE TIME

PAST	FUTURE	
yesterday	tomorrow	PAST: I **was** in class **yesterday morning.** FUTURE: I'**m going to be** in class **tomorrow morning.**
yesterday morning yesterday afternoon yesterday evening last night	tomorrow morning tomorrow afternoon tomorrow evening tomorrow night	
last week last month last year	next week next month next year	PAST: Mary **went** downtown **last week.** FUTURE: Mary **is going to go** downtown **next week.**
last spring last summer last fall last winter	next spring next summer next fall next winter	PAST: Bob **graduated** from high school **last spring.** FUTURE: Ann **is going to graduate** from high school **next spring.**
last Monday last Tuesday last Wednesday *etc.*	next Monday next Tuesday next Wednesday *etc.*	PAST: They **studied** at the library **last Monday.** FUTURE: They'**re going to study** at the library **next Monday.**
...minutes ago ...hours ago ...days ago ...weeks ago ...months ago ...years ago	in...minutes (*from now*) in...hours (*from now*) in...days (*from now*) in...weeks (*from now*) in...months (*from now*) in...years (*from now*)	PAST: I **finished** my homework **five minutes ago.** FUTURE: I'**m going to finish** my homework **in five minutes.**

EXERCISE 5: Complete the sentences. Use *yesterday, last, tomorrow,* or *next.*

1. I went swimming_____yesterday_____ morning.

2. Bob is going to go to the beach _____tomorrow_____ morning.

3. I'm going to take a trip _____ week.

4. Alice went to Miami _____ week for a short vacation.

5. We had a test in class _____ afternoon.

6. _____ afternoon we're going to go on a picnic.

7. My sister is going to arrive _____ Tuesday.

8. Sam bought a used car _____ Friday.

9. My brother is going to enter the university _____ fall.

10. _____ spring I took a trip to San Francisco.

11. We had a delicious meal at a restaurant _____ evening.

12. _____ evening I'm going to go to a baseball game.

13. Ann is going to fly to London _____ month.

14. Dick lived in Tokyo _____ year.

15. I'm going to study at the library _____ night.

16. _____ night I watched TV.

EXERCISE 6:   Complete the sentences. Use *yesterday, last, tomorrow,* or *next.*

1. I went to the zoo_____last_____ week.

2. Bob is going to go to the zoo _____ Saturday.

3. We're going to have company for dinner _____ night.

4. Mary Ann graduated from college _____ spring.

5. I'm going to take a vacation in Canada _____ summer.

6. _____ evening we're going to go to a concert.

7. _____ Friday I went to a party.

8. _____ morning the students took a test.

9. The students are going to have another test _____ Thursday.

10. Are you going to be home _____ afternoon around three?

11. My little sister arrived here _____ month.

12. _____ year Barbara is going to be a freshman in college.

EXERCISE 7:   Study the examples of expressions used with **ago** (past) and **in** (future):

PAST	FUTURE
a minute **ago**	**in** a minute
two minutes **ago** **three** minutes **ago** *etc.*	**in** **two** minutes **in** **two more** minutes **in** **three** minutes **in three more** minutes *etc.*
a few minutes **ago**	**in** **a few** minutes **in a few more** minutes
a couple of minutes **ago**	**in a couple of** minutes

Complete the sentences. Use the expressions in the examples above with the words in parentheses to complete the sentences.

1. (*days*)   We studied Chapter 7 ___a couple of days ago/three days ago/etc.___

2. (*days*)   We're going to study Chapter 9 ___in a couple of days/in three___
   ___days/in three more days/etc.___

3. (*hours*)   I ate breakfast _____

4. (*hours*)   I'm going to eat lunch/dinner _____

5. (*months*)   I arrived in this city _____

6. (*months*)   I'm going to leave this city _____

7. (*minutes*)   We finished Exercise 6 _____

8. (*minutes*)   We're going to finish this exercise _____

9. (*years*)   I was born _____

10. (*years*)   My sister/brother/cousin is going to graduate from high school/
    college _____

11. (*days*)   I went shopping _____

12. (*days*)   We're going to finish this chapter _____

EXERCISE 8:   Complete the sentences. Use your own words.

1. _____ a few days ago.

2. _____ in a few days (*from now*).

3. _____ in a few more minutes.

4. _____ three hours ago.

5. _____ in four more hours.

6. _____ a couple of days ago.

7. _____ in a couple of months (*from now*).

8. _____ a few minutes ago.

9. _____ 100 years ago.

10. _____ in a couple of minutes (*from now*).

EXERCISE 9—ORAL (BOOKS CLOSED):   Ask classmates questions. Use
be going to. Use a future time expression (*tomorrow morning, next week,
etc.*).

> *Example:*   go downtown
> *Student A:*   Are you going to go downtown tomorrow morning?
> *Student B:*   Yes, I am. OR: No, I'm not.
> *Student A:*   Is (. . .) going to go downtown tomorrow morning?
> *Student C:*   Yes, he/she is. OR: No, he/she isn't.

1. study at the library
2. go shopping
3. walk to school
4. have a sandwich for lunch
5. do your homework
6. get married
7. go to the zoo
8. visit (*a place in this city*)
9. cash a check
10. take the bus downtown
11. call (. . .) on the phone
12. go to (*name of restaurant*) for dinner
13. get up early
14. go to bed late
15. go on a picnic
16. be absent from class
17. be late for class
18. see (. . .)
19. buy a used car
20. quit smoking

EXERCISE 10—ORAL (BOOKS CLOSED):   Ask a classmate a question.
Use **when.** Use **be going to.**

> *Example:*   go downtown
> *Student A:*   When are you going to go downtown?
> *Student B:*   (*free response*)

1. get home tonight
2. go to the bank
3. eat dinner
4. go to bed tonight
5. get up tomorrow morning
6. call me on the phone

7. go to the grocery store
8. quit smoking
9. get married
10. go back to (*name of student's country*)
11. get a driver's license
12. go to the zoo

8-3   USING *TODAY, TONIGHT,* **AND** *THIS* + *MORNING, AFTERNOON, EVENING, WEEK, MONTH, YEAR*

PRESENT	(a) We **are studying** English **this morning**.	*today* *tonight* *this morning* *this afternoon* *this evening* *this week* *this month* *this year* can be used to express present, past, or future time
PAST	(b) Nancy **went** downtown **this morning**.	
FUTURE	(c) I**'m going to go** shopping **this morning**.	

EXERCISE 11:   Complete the sentences. Discuss the different tenses that are possible.

1. _____ today.

2. _____ this morning.

3. _____ this afternoon.

4. _____ this evening.

5. _____ tonight.

6. _____ this week.

7. _____ this month.

8. _____ this year.

EXERCISE 12—ORAL (BOOKS CLOSED):   Ask a classmate a question.

Example: tomorrow morning
Student A: Are you going to come to class tomorrow morning?
Student B: Yes, I am. OR: No, I'm not.

Example: yesterday morning
Student A: Did you eat breakfast yesterday morning?
Student B: Yes, I did. OR: No, I didn't.

1. last night	10. last week
2. tomorrow night	11. this week
3. tonight	12. yesterday morning
4. tomorrow afternoon	13. tomorrow morning
5. yesterday afternoon	14. this morning
6. this afternoon	15. today
7. last Friday	16. a couple of hours ago
8. next Friday	17. in a couple of hours (*from now*)
9. next week	

EXERCISE 13—ORAL: Ask a classmate a question. Use **What** + *a form of* **do** with the given time expressions.

PRESENT	(a) What **do** you **do** every day? (b) What **are** you **doing** right now?	**What** + *a form of* **do** is used to ask about activities.
PAST	(c) What **did** you **do** yesterday?	
FUTURE	(d) What **are** you **going to do** tomorrow?	

Example: yesterday
Student A: What did you do yesterday?
Student B: (*free response*)

1. last night	7. every morning
2. every day	8. right now
3. right now	9. last Saturday
4. tomorrow	10. next Saturday
5. yesterday afternoon	11. this morning
6. tomorrow morning	12. this afternoon

8-4 FUTURE TIME: USING *WILL*

STATEMENT:	(a) Dick **will go** to the library tomorrow. (b) Dick **is going to go** to the library tomorrow.	(a) and (b) have basically the same meaning.

CONTRACTIONS:	(c)	I will come. =	**I'll** come	
		You will come. =	**You'll** come.	
		He will come. =	**He'll** come.	
		She will come. =	**She'll** come.	
		It will come. =	**It'll** come.	
		We will come. =	**We'll** come.	
		They will come. =	**They'll** come.	
NEGATIVE:	(d) Bob **will not be** here tomorrow.			Negative contraction:
	(e) Bob **won't be** here tomorrow.			**will** + **not** = **won't**

EXERCISE 14:   Rewrite the sentences. Use **will** to express future time.

1. I'm going to arrive around six tomorrow.

   I'll arrive around six tomorrow.

2. Fred isn't going to come to our party.

3. He's going to be out of town next week.

4. Sue is going to be in class tomorrow.

5. She has a cold, but she isn't going to stay home.

6. Jack and Mary are going to meet us at the movie theater.

7. They are going to be there at 7:15.

8. It's an important letter. I'm going to send it by special delivery.

9. We're going to stay at a hotel in Honolulu.

10. Hurry up, or we're going to be late for the concert.

11. Be careful! You're going to hurt yourself!

12. I'm not going to be at home this evening.

_____

13. According to the newspaper, it isn't going to rain tomorrow.

_____

8-5   ASKING QUESTIONS WITH *WILL*

QUESTION					ANSWER	
(QUESTION WORD) + *WILL* + SUBJECT + MAIN VERB						Note:
(a)		**Will**	**Dick**	**come**	tomorrow?	**Yes, he will.** **No, he won't.**	*will* is not con-
(b)		**Will**	**you**	**be**	at home tonight?	**Yes, I will.** **No, I won't.**	tracted with a pronoun
(c)	When	**will**	**Ann**	**arrive?**		**Next Saturday.**	in a short
(d)	What time	**will**	**the plane**	**arrive?**		**3:30 p.m.**	answer.
(e)	Where	**will**	**you**	**be**	tonight?	**At home.**	

EXERCISE 15:   Make questions.

1. A: ____Will you be at home tomorrow night?_____

B: Yes, ____I will._____ (I'll be at home tomorrow night.)

2. A: ____Will Ann be in class tomorrow?_____

B: No, ____she won't.____ (Ann won't be in class tomorrow.)

3. A: _____

B: Yes, _____ (The plane will be on time.)

4. A: _____

B: Yes, _____ (Dinner will be ready in a few minutes.)

5. A: _____

B: In a few minutes. (Dinner will be ready in a few minutes.)

6. A: _____

B: Next year. (I'll graduate next year.)

7. A: _____
    B: In October. (The weather will turn cold in October.)

8. A: _____
    B: At the junior college. (Mary will go to school at the junior college next year.)

9. A: _____
    B: No, _____ (Jane and Mark won't be at the party.)

10. A: _____
    B: Yes, _____ (Dick will arrive in Chicago next week.)

11. A: _____
    B: No, _____ (I won't be home early tonight.)

12. A: _____
    B: In Chicago. (My plane will stop in Chicago *en route* to New York.)

13. A: _____
    B: In a few minutes. (Dr. Smith will be back in a few minutes.)

14. A: _____
    B: At 6:30. (The limousine will leave for the airport at 6:30.)

15. A: _____
    B: Yes, _____ (I'll be ready to leave at seven o'clock.)

8-6 USING *MAYBE:* USING *MAY* AND *MIGHT*

(a) —Will Dick be in class tomorrow? —I don't know. **Maybe.**	*maybe = possibly*
(b) **Maybe Dick will be** in class tomorrow, and **maybe he won't.**	*Maybe* (one word) comes in front of a subject and verb.
s v (c) Dick **may be** in class tomorrow.	*may be* (two words) = the verb of the sentence.
(d) It **may rain tomorrow.**	*May + verb (simple form)* expresses possibility in the future or at present.
(e) John **may be** at home **now.**	
(f) It **might rain tomorrow.**	*Might* has the same meaning as *may.*
(g) John **might be** at home **now.**	

EXERCISE 16:   Use *maybe* or *may/might.*

1. A: Is David going to come to the party?

   B: I don't know. _____Maybe._____

2. A: What are you going to do tomorrow?

   B: I don't know. I ____may/might____ go swimming.

3. A: What are you going to do tomorrow?

   B: I don't have any plans. _____ I'll go swimming.

4. A: Where is Donald?

   B: I don't know. He _____ be at his office.

5. A: Where is Donald?

   B: I don't know. _____ he's at his office.

6. A: Are Kathy and Steve going to get married?

   B: _____. Who knows?

7. A: Are you going to move to Portland or Seattle?

   B: I don't know. I _____ move to San Francisco.

8. A: Do you hear that noise?
   B: Yes!
   A: What is it?

   B: It _____ be a burglar!

9. A: Where are you planning to go on your vacation?

   B: _____ we'll go to Mexico. We haven't decided yet. We

   _____ go to Florida.

10. A: Is Margaret married?

    B: Hmmm. I'm not sure. _____ she is, and _____
    she isn't.

11. A: Do you think it will rain tomorrow?

    B: I have no idea. _____ it will, and _____ it won't.

12. A: It _____ be cold tomorrow.
    B: That's okay. Let's go to the beach anyway.

13. A: Are you going to study English next semester?

    B: _____ Are you?

14. A: Will the plane be on time?

    B: I think so, but it _____ be a few minutes late.

15. A: I'd like to have a pet.

    B: Oh? What kind of pet would you like to get?

    A: Oh, I don't know. I haven't decided yet. _____ I'll get a canary.

    Or _____ I'll get a snake. I'm not sure. I _____

    get a frog. Or I _____ get a tiger.

    B: What's wrong with a cat or dog?

EXERCISE 17—ORAL (BOOKS CLOSED): Answer the question by using
"I don't know" + *maybe* or *may/might.*

    Example: What are you going to do tonight?
    Response: I don't know. Maybe I'll watch TV.
                OR: I may watch TV.
                OR: I might watch TV.

1. What are you going to do tonight?
2. What are you going to do tomorrow?
3. What are you going to do after class today?
4. What are you going to do this weekend?
5. What are you going to do this evening?
6. Who is going to go shopping tomorrow? What are you going to buy?
7. Who is going to go out to eat tonight? Where are you going to go?
8. Who is going to get married? When?
9. Who is going to watch TV tonight? What are you going to watch?
10. Who is absent today? Where is he/she?
11. Is it going to rain tomorrow?
12. Who is planning to go on a vacation? Where are you going to go?
13. Who wants to have a pet? What kind of pet are you going to get?

EXERCISE 18—WRITTEN: Complete the sentences. Write about your activities <u>tomorrow</u>. Use *be going to* and *may/might.*

1. I'm going to get up at . . . tomorrow
   morning.
2. Then. . . .
3. After that. . . .
4. Around . . . o'clock. . . .
5. Later. . . .

6. At . . . o'clock. . . . .
7. Then. . . .
8. After that. . . .
9. Next. . . .
10. Then at . . . o'clock. . . .

EXERCISE 19—WRITTEN: Complete the sentences. Write about your activities <u>yesterday.</u>

1. I got up at . . . yesterday morning.
2. I . . . and . . . .
3. Then I . . . .
4. I didn't . . . because. . . .
5. Later. . . .
6. Around . . . o'clock. . . .
7. Then. . . .

8. After that. . . .
9. At . . . o'clock. . . .
10. I didn't . . . because. . . .
11. At . . . I . . . .
12. . . . after that.
13. Then at. . . .

MORE IRREGULAR VERBS

begin – began	steal – stole
find – found	sell – sold
lose – lost	tell – told
hang – hung	tear – tore
say – said	wear – wore
	wake up – woke up

EXERCISE 20—ORAL (BOOKS CLOSED): Practice using the irregular verbs in the above list.

> *Example:* *begin–began* Our class begins at 9:00 every day. Class began at 9:00 this morning. When did class begin this morning?
> *Response:* It began at 9:00.

EXERCISE 21: Complete the sentences. Use the words in parentheses.

1. A: Did you go to the park yesterday?

   B: No. We stayed home because it (*begin*) _____ to rain.
2. A: Susie is in trouble.

   B: Why?

   A: She (*tell*) _____ a lie. Her mom and dad are upset.
3. A: May I please have your homework?

   B: I don't have it. I (*lose*) _____ it.

   A: You (*lose*) _____ it!

4. A: Where's my coat?

B: I (*hang*) _____ it up in the closet.

5. A: Why were you late for class?

B: I (*wake*) _____ up late. My alarm clock didn't go off.

SHELLS

6. A: Where did you get that pretty shell?

B: I (*find*) _____ it on the beach.

7. A: Do you still have your bicycle?

B: No. I (*sell*) _____ it.

8. A: I'm tired.

B: Excuse me? What did you say?

A: I (*say*) _____, "I'm tired."

9. A: Why did you take the bus to school this morning? Why didn't you drive?

B: Because somebody (*steal*) _____ my car.

10. A: Did you wear your blue jeans to the job interview?

B: Of course not! I (*wear*) _____ a suit.

11. A: What happened to your sleeve?

B: I (*tear*) _____ it on a nail.

A: That's too bad.

EXERCISE 22: Complete the sentences. Use the words in parentheses. Use any appropriate tense.

1. A: (*you, be*) _____ at home tomorrow morning around ten?

B: No. I (*be*) _____ out.

2. A: I (*lose*) _____ my sunglasses yesterday.

   B: Where?

   A: I (*think*) _____ that I (*leave*) _____

   _____ them on a table at the restaurant.

3. A: How are you getting along?

   B: Fine. I'm making a lot of friends and my English (*improve*) _____

   _____.

```
┌─────────────────────────┐
│ APTS., UNFURN.          │
│                         │
│ 2 BR. $225/mo. Lake St. │
│ Near bus. All utils. incl. │
│ No pets. 361-3663. eves. │
└─────────────────────────┘
```

4. A: May I see the classified section of the newspaper?

   B: Sure. Here it is.

   A: Thanks. I (*want, look*) _____ at the want ads. I (*need,*

   find) _____ a new apartment.

5. A: Sometimes children tell little lies. You talked to Annie. (*she, tell*)_____

   _____ the truth or (*she, tell*)_____

   _____ a lie?

   B: She (*tell*) _____ the truth. She's honest.

6. A: (*you, write*) _____ a letter to George yesterday?

   B: Yes, I _____. I (*send*) _____ him
   a letter yesterday.

7. A: Where (*you, go*) _____ yesterday?

   B: I (*go*) _____ to my cousin's house. I (*see*) _____

   _____ Jean there and (*talk*) _____

   _____ to her for a while. And I (*meet*)_____

   _____ my cousin's neighbors, Mr. and Mrs. Dalton.
   They're nice people. I like them.

8. A: What are you going to do tonight? (*you, study*)_____?

   B: No. I don't think so. I'm tired. I think I (*watch*) _____

   TV for a while or maybe I (*listen*) _____ to some

music. Or I might read a novel. But I (*want, not, study*) _____

_____ tonight.

9. A: (*you, do*) _____ your homework last night?

   B: No. I (*be*) _____ too tired. I (*go*)_____

   _____ to bed early and (*sleep*) _____

   _____ for nine hours.

10. A: Good morning.

    B: Excuse me?

    A: I (*say*) _____, "Good morning."

    B: Oh! Good morning! I'm sorry. I (*understand, not*) _____

    _____ you at first.

11. A: What did you do yesterday?

    B: Well, I (*wake up*) _____ around nine and (*go*)

    _____ shopping. While I was downtown, someone

    (*steal*) _____ my purse. I (*take*) _____

    _____ a taxi home. When I (*get*)_____

    _____ out of the taxi, I (*tear*) _____

    _____ my blouse. I (*borrow*) _____

    _____ some money from my roommate to pay the taxi

    driver.

    A: Did anything good happen to you yesterday?

    B: Hmmm. Let me think. Oh yes. I (*lose*) _____ my

    grammar book, but I (*find*) _____ it later.

MORE IRREGULAR VERBS

cost – cost	forget – forgot
cut – cut	give – gave
hit – hit	make – made
put – put	understand – understood
shut – shut	lend – lent
	spend – spent

EXERCISE 23—ORAL (BOOKS CLOSED): Practice using the irregular verbs in the list on page 167.

> *Example:* cost–cost   I bought a hat yesterday. I paid twenty dollars for it. It cost twenty dollars. What did I buy yesterday? How much did it cost?
>
> *Response:* You bought a hat. It cost twenty dollars.

EXERCISE 24: Complete the sentences. Use the words in parentheses.

1. A: How much (*a telephone call, cost*) _____

   _____ if you use a pay phone?

   B: It (*cost*) _____ twenty-five cents.

2. A: That's a nice hat. Was it expensive?

   B: Not at all. It (*cost*) _____ three bucks.

3. A: Where's your dictionary?

   B: I (*give*) _____ it to Robert.

4. A: I had a car accident yesterday morning.
   B: What happened?

   A: I (*hit*) _____ a telephone pole.

5. A: May I have your homework please?

   B: I'm sorry, but I don't have it. I (*forget*) _____ it.

   A: You (*forget*) _____ it!

6. A: Did you eat breakfast?

   B: Yeah. I (*make*) _____ some scrambled eggs and toast for myself.

7. Bob (*put*) _____ on his clothes every morning.

8. Bob (*put*) _____ on his clothes this morning after he got up.

9. A: Did you enjoy going into the city to see a show?

   B: Yes, but I (*spend*) _____ a lot of money. I can't afford to do that very often.

10. A: May I see your dictionary?

   B: I don't have it. I (*lend*) _____ it to George.

11. A: Why are you wearing a bag over your head?

   B: I went to a barber this morning. He (*cut*) _____ my hair too short.

   A: Let me see.

   B: Okay.

   A: Oh, no! You're bald! I don't believe it!

EXERCISE 25—ORAL:* Give the past form. Make sentences using the past form.

1. come	11. get	21. pay
2. eat	12. forget	22. cost
3. stand	13. steal	23. spend
4. understand	14. meet	24. sell
5. drink	15. speak	25. buy
6. break	16. take	26. take
7. hear	17. wear	27. make
8. lose	18. write	28. do
9. find	19. fly	29. say
10. begin	20. leave	30. catch

EXERCISE 26: Complete the sentences. Use the words in parentheses.

1. A: I (*cut*)_____ am going to cut _____ class tomorrow.

   B: Why?

---

* *To the teacher:* You may wish to make a game out of this exercise by dividing the class into two teams and asking each player in turn to say and spell the past form. Give the teams points for each correct answer.

A: Why not?

B: That's not a very good reason.

2. A: How did you get here?

B: I (*take*) _____ a plane. I (*fly*)

_____ here from Bangkok.

3. A: How do you usually get to class?

B: I (*walk, usually*) _____, but sometimes I (*take*)

_____ the bus.

4. A: Where's my book! Someone (*steal*) _____ it!

B: Take it easy. Your book (*be*) _____ right here.

A: Oh.

5. A: Where (*you, meet*) _____ your wife?

B: I (*meet*) _____ her at a party ten years ago.

6. A: Did you see that?

B: What?

A: The man in the red shirt (*hit*) _____ the man in the blue shirt.

B: Really?

7. A: Were you late for the movie?

B: No. The movie (*begin*) _____ at 7:30, but we (*get*)

_____ to the theater at 7:26.

8. A: What time (*the movie, begin*) _____ last night?

B: 7:30.

A: (*you, be*) _____ late?

B: No. We (*make*) _____ it in time.

9. A: Do you hear that noise?

B: What noise?

A: (*you, listen*) _____?

B: Yes, but I (*hear, not*) _____ anything.

10. A: Where's your homework?

B: I (*lose*) _____ it.

A: Oh?

B: I (*forget*) _____ it.

A: Oh?

B: Someone (*steal*) _____ it.

A: Oh?

B: Well, actually I (*have, not*) _____ enough time to finish it.

A: I see.

11. A: (*you, stay*) _____ here during vacation next week?

B: No. I (*take*) _____ a trip to Miami. I (*visit*)

_____ my aunt and uncle.

A: How long (*you, be*) _____ away?

B: About five days.

12. A: Why (*you, wear*) _____ a cast on your foot?

B: I (*break*) _____ my ankle.

A: How?

B: I (*step*) _____ in a hole while I was running in the park.

13. A: (*you, want, go*) _____ to the zoo tomorrow?

B: I'd like to go, but I can't because I have to study.

A: That's too bad.

B: (*you, go*) _____ to the zoo?

A: Yes. The weather is perfect, and I (*want, get*) _____

outside and (*enjoy*) _____ it.

14. A: (*you, see*) _____ Randy yesterday?

B: No, but I (*speak*) _____ to him on the phone. He (*call*)

_____ me yesterday evening.

A: Is he okay?

B: Yes. He still has a cold, but he's feeling much better.

A: That's good.

15. A: Is Carol here?

B: No, she _____ . She (*leave*) _____ a few minutes ago.

A: (*she, be*) _____ back soon?

B: I think so.

A: Where (*she, go*) _____?

B: She (*go*) _____ to the drugstore.

8-7   USING *SHOULD*

(a) My clothes are dirty. I **should wash** them. (b) Tom is sleepy. He **should go** to bed. (c) You're sick. You **should go** to a doctor.	***Should*** means: *This is a good idea. This is good advice.*

(d)   I should go.
      You should go.
      She should go.
      He should go.
      It should go
      We should go.
      They should go.
	Should is followed by the simple form of a verb.

(e) You **should eat** fruit. It's good for your health. (f) You **shouldn't eat (should not eat)** candy. It's not good for you. It's bad for your teeth.	 NEGATIVE: ***should not*** CONTRACTION: ***should + not = shouldn't***

EXERCISE 27:   Complete the sentences. Use ***You should.*** Use the expressions in the list or your own words.

buy a new pair of shoes
call the landlady
go on a diet
go to the bank
go to the immigration office
go to the post office
go to bed and take a nap
see a dentist
study harder
take it to an automobile service center

1. A: I want to mail a package.

    B: You should go to the post office.

2. A: I'm sleepy.

    B: _____

3. A: I need to cash a check.

    B: _____

4. A: My shoes have holes in the bottom.

 B: _____

5. A: I have a toothache.

 B: _____

6. A: I'm flunking all of my courses at school.

 B: _____

7. A: I'm gaining weight. My old clothes are too small for me.

 B: _____

8. A: The plumbing in my apartment doesn't work.

 B: _____

9. A: I need to renew my visa.

 B: _____

10. A: Something is wrong with my car. It sounds funny.*

 B: _____

EXERCISE 28:   Complete the sentences. Use **should** or **shouldn't.**

1. Students _____should_____ come to class every day.

2. Students _____shouldn't_____ cut class.

3. We _____ waste our money on things we don't need.

4. Life is short. We _____ waste it.

5. It's raining. You _____ take your umbrella when you leave.

6. Jimmy, you _____ pull the cat's tail!

7. People _____ be cruel to animals.

8. Your plane leaves at 8:00. You _____ get to the airport by 7:00.

—————————
* funny = strange

9. We _____ cross a street at an intersection. We _____ jaywalk.

10. You _____ smoke in a crowded room because the smoke bothers other people.

11. When you go to New York City, you _____ see a play on Broadway.

12. You _____ walk alone on city streets after midnight. It's dangerous.

13. When you go to San Francisco, you _____ ride on the cable cars.

14. When you go to a football game, you _____ throw things on the field.

15. Sue is a lazy student. She nevers does her homework. She's flunking her English

course. She _____ study harder.

EXERCISE 29—WRITTEN: Write about your hometown. Use a separate piece of paper.

I'm a tourist. I'm going to visit your hometown. Is your hometown a good place for a tourist to visit? Why? What should I do when I'm there? Where should I go? What should I see? What shouldn't I do? Are there places I shouldn't visit? Will I enjoy my visit?

Write a composition in which you tell me (a tourist) about your hometown.

8-8 USING *MUST*

(a) People need food. People **have to eat** food.	(a) and (b) have the same meaning.
(b) People need food. People **must eat** food.	*must eat = have to eat**
(c) I must work. You must work. She must work. He must work. It must work. We must work. They must work.	Notice in (c): *must + main verb (simple form)*

* See 6–2 for a discussion of *have to.*

Study the following examples. Notice the difference between *should* and *must.*

MUST	*SHOULD*
SOMETHING IS VERY IMPORTANT. SOMETHING IS NECESSARY. YOU DO NOT HAVE A CHOICE.	SOMETHING IS A GOOD IDEA, BUT YOU HAVE A CHOICE.
(a) I **must go** to the bank today. I don't have any money. I need some money because I'm going to take my girlfriend to a movie tonight.	(b) I **should go** to the bank today, but maybe I'll wait and go tomorrow.
(c) I **must stop** smoking. Cigarettes are killing me.	(d) I **should stop** smoking, but I like to smoke. Maybe I'll stop smoking next year.
(e) You **must take** an English course. You cannot graduate without it.	(f) You **should take** an English course. It will help you.
(g) Johnny, this is your mother speaking. You **must eat** your vegetables. You can't leave the table until you eat your vegetables.	(h) Johnny, you **should eat** your vegetables. They're good for you. You'll grow up to be strong and healthy.
(i) I **must study** tonight. I'm going to take a very important test tomorrow.	(j) I **should study** tonight. I have some homework to do, but I'm tired. I'll study tomorrow night. I'm going to go to bed.

EXERCISE 30:   Complete the sentences. Use *must.* Use the expressions in the list.

> close the door behind you
> go to medical school
> ✔ have a driver's license
> have a library card
> have a passport
> pay an income tax
> speak English outside of class every day, listen to the radio, watch television, read newspapers, make new friends, and talk to myself in English
> stop
> study harder
> take one pill every six hours

1. According to the law,* a driver _____ must have a driver's license. _____

---

* *according to the law = the law says*

2. If a traffic light is red, a car _____

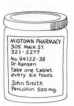

3. My doctor gave me a prescription. According to the directions on the bottle, I ___

_____

4. If you want to check a book out of the library, you _____

_____

5. Nancy has a job in Chicago. She earns $20,000 a year. According to the law, she

_____

6. I failed the last two tests in my biology class. According to my professor, I _____

_____

7. I want to travel abroad. According to the law, I _____

_____

8. If you want to become a doctor, you _____

9. Jimmy! It's cold outside. When you come inside, you _____

_____

10. I want to improve my English. According to my teacher, I _____

_____

_____

8-9   USING *LET'S*

(a) Bob: What should we do tonight? Ann: **Let's go to a movie.** Bob: Okay.	*Let's (do something) = I have a suggestion for you and me.*
(b) Sue: I'm tired. Don: I'm tired, too. **Let's take a break.** Sue: That's a good idea!	*let's = let us* In (a): **Let's go to a movie.** *= I think we should go to a movie. Do you want to go a movie?*

EXERCISE 31:   Complete the dialogs. Use *let's*. Use the expressions in the list or your own words.

eat	*go to a seafood restaurant*
get a cup of coffee	*go to the zoo*
go dancing	*leave at six-thirty*
go to Florida	*walk*
go to a movie	

1. A: What time should we leave for the airport?

   B: _____ Let's leave at six-thirty. _____

   A: Okay.

2. A: Where should we go for our vacation?

   B: _____

   A: That's a good idea.

3. A: Where do you want to go for dinner tonight?

   B: _____

4. A: The weather is beautiful today. _____

   B: Okay. Great!

5. A: I'm bored. _____

   B: I can't. I have to study.

6. A: Should we take the bus downtown or walk downtown?

   B: It's a nice day. _____

   A: Okay.

7. A: Dinner's ready! The food's on the table!

   B: Great! _____ I'm starving!

8. A: Where should we go Saturday night?

   B: _____

   A: Good idea!

9. A: We have an hour between classes. _____

   B: Okay. That sounds like a good idea.

chapter 9

Expressing Ability

9-1 USING CAN

(a) I have some money. I **can buy** a book.	**Can** expresses *ability* and *possibility*.
(b) We have time and money. We **can go** to a movie.	
(c) Tom is strong. He **can lift** the heavy box.	

(d)   **I can speak** English.
  You can speak English.
  He can speak English.
She can speak English.
   It can happen.
 We can speak English.
They can speak English.
	Notice in (d):
	
	can + main verb (simple form) *

(e) NEGATIVE: Alice **can not** come.
              Alice **cannot** come.
              Alice **can't**   come.
	NEGATIVE:
	  can + not = can not or *cannot*
	CONTRACTION:
	  can + not = can't

* Common problems with **can:**
(1) Do not use **to** after **can.** (Do not use an infinitive.)
    WRONG: *I can to come.*
    RIGHT: *I can come.*
(2) Do not use **-s** on the main verb.
    WRONG: *She can comes.*
    RIGHT: *She can come.*

EXERCISE 1—ORAL: Make sentences from the given words. Use **can** or **can't.**

Example: A bird/sing
Response: A bird can sing.

Example: A horse/sing
Response: A horse can't sing.

1. A bird/fly
2. A pig/fly
3. A dog/drive a car
4. A newborn baby/walk
5. A cat/climb trees
6. A fish/breathe air
7. A fish/swim

8. A deaf person/hear
9. A blind person/see
10. A doctor/prescribe medicine
11. A banker/lend money
12. A boat/float on water
13. A rock/float on water

EXERCISE 2—ORAL: Make sentences from the given words. Use **I can** or **I can't.**

Example: speak Chinese
Response: I can speak Chinese. OR: I can't speak Chinese.

1. whistle
2. ride a bicycle
3. touch my ear with my elbow
4. play the piano*
5. play the guitar
6. lift a piano
7. drive a stick-shift car
8. fix a flat tire

9. swim
10. float on water
11. ski
12. do arithmetic
13. make a paper airplane
14. sew a button on a shirt
15. eat with chopsticks
16. wiggle my ears

9-2 USING *CAN:* QUESTIONS

(QUESTION WORD) + *CAN* + SUBJECT + MAIN VERB				ANSWER
(a)	Can	you	speak	Arabic?	Yes, I can. No, I can't.
(b)	Can	Marge	come	to the party?	Yes, she can. No, she can't.

* In expressions with ***play, the*** is usually used with musical instruments: *play the piano, play the guitar, play the violin,* etc.

(QUESTION WORD) + *CAN* + SUBJECT + MAIN VERB					ANSWER
(c)	Where	can	I	buy	a hammer?	At a hardware store.
(d)	When	can	you	help	me?	Tomorrow afternoon.

EXERCISE 3:   Make yes/no questions. Give short answers.

1. A: _____ Can Jean speak English? _____

    B: _____ Yes, she can. _____ (Jean can speak English.)

2. A: _____ Can you speak French? _____

    B: _____ No, I can't. _____ (I can't speak French.)

3. A: _____

    B: _____ (Bob can't play the piano.)

4. A: _____

    B: _____ (I can whistle.)

5. A: _____

    B: _____ (I can go shopping with you this afternoon.)

6. A: _____

    B: _____ (Martha can't ride a bicycle.)

7. A: _____

    B: _____ (I can drive a stick-shift car.)

8. A: _____

    B: _____ (Children can't see an X-rated movie.)

9. A: _____

    B: _____ (The students can finish this exercise quickly.)

10. A: _____

    B: _____ (The doctor can see you tomorrow.)

11. A: _____

    B: _____ (We can't have pets in the dormitory.)

12. A: _____

    B: _____ (I can stand on my head.)

EXERCISE 4—ORAL (BOOKS CLOSED): Ask a classmate a question. Use *Can you . . . ?*

    Example: speak Arabic
    Student A: Can you speak Arabic?
    Student B: Yes, I can. OR: No, I can't.

1. ride a bicycle
2. ride a motorcycle
3. ride a horse
4. play the piano
5. play the guitar
6. play the violin
7. cook (*nationality*) food
8. sing
9. whistle
10. float on water
11. spell Mississippi
12. see the back of (. . .)'s head
13. count to five in (*language*)
14. stand on your head
15. touch your knee with your nose
16. touch your ear with your elbow
17. touch the ceiling of this room
18. drive a stick-shift car
19. fix a flat tire
20. ski

EXERCISE 5—ORAL: Ask a classmate a question. Use *Where can I . . . ?*

    Example: buy a notebook
    Student A: Where can I buy a notebook?
    Student B: (*free response*)

1. buy a camera
2. buy a dozen eggs
3. buy a window fan
4. buy a diamond ring
5. buy a hammer
6. buy an airplane ticket
7. catch a bus
8. mail a package

9. get a good dinner
10. go swimming
11. see a zebra
12. find the foreign student advisor

13. find an encyclopedia
14. get a limousine to the airport
15. get a sandwich

9-3 USING *KNOW HOW TO*

(a) I can swim. (b) I **know how to swim.**	(a) and (b) have basically the same meaning. ***Know how to*** expresses ability.
(c) Can you cook? (d) **Do** you **know how to cook?**	(c) and (d) have basically the same meaning.

EXERCISE 6—ORAL: Ask a classmate a question. Use ***know how to*** in your question.

> *Example:* swim
> *Student A:* Do you know how to swim?
> *Student B:* Yes, I do. OR: No, I don't.

1. cook
2. dance
3. play the piano
4. play the guitar
5. fix a flat tire
6. drive a stick-shift car
7. eat with chopsticks
8. sew

9. get to the post office from here
10. get to the airport from here
11. get to (*name of a store*) from here
12. use a hammer
13. use a screwdriver
14. count to five in (*name of language*)
15. add, subtract, multiply, and divide
16. find the square root of 9

EXERCISE 7—ORAL/WRITTEN:

Walk around and talk to your classmates. Ask them questions. Find people who have the abilities listed below. Ask them questions about their abilities. Write a report of the information you get from your classmates.

1. play a musical instrument
2. play a sport
3. speak three or four languages
4. cook
5. sing

6. sew
7. fix a car
8. draw
9. swim
10. wiggle your ears

9-4   USING *COULD:* **PAST OF** *CAN*

(a) I am in Hawaii. I can go to the beach every day.	*could* = the past form of *can*
(b) I was in Hawaii **last month. I could go** to the beach every day when I was there.	
(c) I can't go to the movie today. I have to study.	
(d) I {**couldn't go** to the movie **last night.** I had to study. \quad **could not go**	*could* + *not* = *couldn't*

EXERCISE 8:   Complete the sentences by using *couldn't.* Use the expressions in the list or your own words.

call you	*go to the movie*
come to class	*listen to music*
do my homework	*smoke his pipe*
get into my car	*use the pay phone*
go swimming	*watch TV*

1. I _____couldn't do my homework_____ last night because I was too tired.

2. I _____ yesterday because I lost your telephone number.

3. I _____ last night because my TV set is broken.

4. Tom _____ because he didn't have any matches.

5. The teacher _____ yesterday because he was sick.

6. I _____ last night because my record player doesn't work.

7. I _____ because I didn't have any change in my pocket.

8. We _____ yesterday because the water was too cold.

9. I _____ yesterday because I locked all the doors and left the keys inside.

10. I _____ last night because I had to study.

EXERCISE 9—ORAL (BOOKS CLOSED):   Answer the questions. Use *No, I couldn't . . . because. . . .*

> *Example:*   Did you finish your homework last night?
> *Response:*   No, I couldn't finish my homework because (I was tired, I had a headache, etc.)

1. go shopping yesterday
2. study last night
3. go swimming yesterday
4. watch TV last night

5. go to (. . .)'s party last night
6. come to class yesterday
7. go downtown yesterday afternoon
8. wash your clothes yesterday

9-5   USING *TOO* AND *VERY*

(a) The box is **very heavy**, but I **can lift** it.	*Very* and *too* come in front of adjectives.
(b) The box is **too heavy. I can't lift** it.	*Very* and *too* do not have the same meaning. In (a): *very heavy* = It is possible but difficult for me to lift the box. In (b): *too heavy* = It is impossible for me to lift the box.
(c) The weather is too cold. *Negative result:* We can't go to the beach. (d) The coffee is too hot. *Negative result:* I can't drink it.	In the speaker's mind, the use of *too* implies a negative result.

EXERCISE 10:   Complete the sentences. Use the expressions in the list or your own words.

buy it
do his homework
drink it
go swimming

lift it
reach the cookie jar
sleep
take a break

TOO + ADJECTIVE	NEGATIVE RESULT

1. The coffee is too hot. I can't _____

2. The diamond ring is too expensive. I can't _____

3. The weather is too cold. We can't _____

4. Bob is too tired. He can't_____

5. I am too busy. I can't _____

6. It's too noisy in the dorm at night. I can't _____

7. A piano is too heavy. I can't_____

8. Peggy is too short. She can't _____

EXERCISE 11: Complete the sentences. Use **too.** Use an adjective in the list or your own words.

cold	*small*
expensive	*tall*
fat	*tired*
heavy	*young*
noisy	

1. You can't lift a car. A car is _____

2. Jimmy can't go to the X-rated movie. He's _____

3. I can't study in the dorm at night. It's _____

4. I don't want to go to the zoo. The weather is _____

5. Ann doesn't want to play tennis this afternoon. She's _____

6. I can't buy a new car. A new car is_____

7. The basketball player can't stand up straight in the subway. He's_____

8. John can't wear his old shirt. It's _____. John is

_____.

EXERCISE 12:   Complete the sentences. Use *too* or *very*.

1. The coffee is _____very_____ hot, but I can drink it.

2. The coffee is _____too_____ hot. I can't drink it.

3. I have $5.00. The book costs $10.00. I can't buy the book. It's

_____ expensive.

4. The book costs $75.00. The book is _____ expensive, but I can buy
it if I want to. I have $75.00.

5. I can't put my dictionary in my pocket. My dictionary is _____ big.

6. An elephant is _____ big. A mouse is _____ small.

7. We went to the Rocky Mountains for our vacation. The mountains are

_____ beautiful.

8. I can't eat this food. It's _____ salty.

9. Nancy doesn't like her room in the dorm. She thinks it is _____
small.

10. I lost your dictionary. I'm _____ sorry. I'll buy you a new one.

11. A: Do you like your math course?

    B: Yes. It's _____ difficult, but I enjoy it.

12. A: Do you like your math course?

    B: No. It's _____ difficult. I don't like it because I can't
    understand the math.

13. A: It's seven-thirty. Do you want to go to the movie?

    B: We can't. It's _____ late. The movie started at seven.

14. A: Did you enjoy your dinner last night?

    B: Yes. The food was _____ good!

15. A: Are you going to buy that dress?

B: No. It doesn't fit. It's _____ big.

16. A: Do you think Carol is smart?

B: Yes, I do. I think she's _____ intelligent.

17. A: My daughter wants to get married.

B: What? But she can't! She's _____ young.

18. A: Can you read that sign across the street?

B: No, I can't. It's _____ far away.

EXERCISE 13:   Complete the sentences. Use *too many* or *too much.* Use *too many* with plural count nouns. Use *too much* with noncount nouns.

1. I can't go to the movie tonight. I have ___too much___ homework to do.

2. Mr. and Mrs. Smith have six cars. They have ___too many___ cars.

3. Don is nervous and jumpy. He drinks _____ coffee.

4. Fred is a commuter. He drives to and from work every day. Yesterday afternoon he tried to get home early, but he couldn't because there was

   _____ traffic. There were _____ cars on the highway during rush hour.

5. There are _____ students in my chemistry class. I can't remember all of their names.

6. You use _____ salt on your food. A lot of salt isn't good for you.

7. It's not possible for a person to have _____ friends.

8. The restaurant was crowded, so we left. There were _____ people at the restaurant.

9. This food is too hot! I can't eat it. There's _____ pepper in it.

10. Mike is gaining weight because he eats _____ food.

11. I can't buy this watch. It costs _____ money.

12. Ann doesn't study because she's always busy. She has

   _____ boyfriends.

13. I have to study for eight hours every night. My teachers assign

_____ homework.

14. I invited three friends to my house for lunch. I made twelve sandwiches for them,

but they ate only six. I made _____ sandwiches. I made

_____ food for my guests.

9-6 USING *TOO* + ADJECTIVE + INFINITIVE

(a) Susie can't go to school because she is too young.	(a) and (b) have the same meaning.
(b) Susie is **too young to go** to school.	

TOO + ADJECTIVE + INFINITIVE			
(c) Susie is **too**	**young**	**to go**	to school.
(d) Peggy is **too**	**short**	**to reach**	the cookie jar.
(e) Bob is **too**	**tired**	**to do**	his homework.

EXERCISE 14: Write sentences that have the same meaning as the given sentences by using an infinitive after *too* + *adjective.*

1. Jimmy can't go to the movie because he's too young.

   Jimmy is too young to go to the movie.

2. Charlotte doesn't want to go to the party because she is too tired.

   _____

3. The basketball player can't stand up straight in the subway because he's too tall.

   _____

4. Robert can't touch the ceiling because he's too short.

   _____

5. I don't want to do my homework because I'm too sleepy.

   _____

6. I couldn't finish my work because I was too sleepy.

   _____

7. Mary doesn't want to go the park with us this afternoon because she is too busy.

   _____

8. Ed didn't want to go to the zoo yesterday afternoon because he was too busy.
   _____

9. Jack can't get married. He's too young.
   _____

10. I can't eat another sandwich. I'm too full.
    _____

9-7 USING TOO + ADJECTIVE + *FOR (SOMEONE)* + INFINITIVE

(a) Bob can't lift the box because it is too heavy.	(a) and (b) have the same meaning.
(b) The box is **too heavy for Bob to lift.**	

TOO + ADJECTIVE + ***FOR*** *(SOMEONE)* + INFINITIVE				
(c) The box is	**too**	**heavy**	**for Bob**	**to lift.**
(d) The dorm is	**too**	**noisy**	**for me**	**to study.**
(e) The ring is	**too**	**expensive**	**for Alice**	**to buy.**

EXERCISE 15: Write sentences that have the same meaning as the given sentences by using *too* + *adjective* + *for* (someone) + *infinitive*.

1. Robert can't touch the ceiling because it's too high.

   The ceiling is too high for Robert to touch. _____

2. I can't do the homework because it's too difficult.
   _____

3. Ed can't drink this coffee because it's too hot.
   _____

4. Ann can't carry that suitcase because it's too heavy.
   _____

5. I can't buy this book because it's too expensive.
   _____

6. We can't go swimming because it's too cold.
   _____

7. We can't go to the movie because it's too late.
   _____

8. Mrs. Rivers can't swallow the pill. It's too big.

EXERCISE 16—ORAL (BOOKS CLOSED): Answer *no* and explain *why.*

*(To the teacher: The intended emphasis in this exercise is on infinitive usage but encourage and discuss responses with **because** too.)*

> *Example:* The coffee is too hot. Can you drink it?
> *Response:* No. The coffee is too hot (for me) to drink.

1. This desk is heavy. Can you lift it?
2. (. . .)'s shoe is small. Can you wear it?
3. (. . .)'s shoe is big. Can you wear it?
4. Can you touch the ceiling?
5. I have an orange in my hand. Can you swallow it whole?
6. Who is tired? Do you want to play tennis?
7. Is the weather perfect today?
8. Who lives in the dorm? Is it quiet? Can you study?
9. Who wants to buy a Rolls-Royce? How much does a Rolls-Royce cost? Can you buy one?
10. The weather is cold. Do you want to go on a picnic?
11. The weather is hot. Do you want to go jogging in the park?
12. Who is a parent? Son or daughter? How old? Can he/she/walk/read/go to college/get a job/get married?

9-8 USING ADJECTIVE + *ENOUGH*

(a) Peggy can't go to school. She is too young.	(a) and (b) give the same meaning.
(b) Peggy can't go to school. She is not **old enough.**	Notice: **enough** follows an adjective.

	ADJECTIVE + **ENOUGH**
(c) I can't hear the radio. It's not **loud enough.** (d) Bobby can read. He's **old enough.** (e) We can go swimming. The weather is **warm enough.**	old enough loud enough warm enough

Enough is pronounced "enuf."

EXERCISE 17: Complete the sentences. Use *too* or *enough.* Use the words in parentheses.

1. (*young, old*) Susie can't go to school. She's _____

    __too young_____ . She's not _____

    __old enough_____ .

2. (*loud, soft*) I can't hear the music. It's_____

    _____ . It's not _____

    _____ .

3. (*big, small*) Jack is gaining weight. He can't wear his old coat. It's

    _____ . It's not _____

    _____ .

4. (*short, tall*) Cindy can't reach the book on the top shelf. She's

    _____ . She's not _____

    _____ .

5. (*cold, hot*) I don't want to finish my coffee because it's _____

    _____ . It's not _____

    _____ .

6. (*weak, strong*) Don can't lift the heavy box. He's not _____

    _____ . He's_____

    _____ .

7. (*sweet, sour*) I don't want to finish eating this orange. It's _____

    _____ . It's not _____

    _____ .

8. (*old, fresh*) Don't buy that fruit. It's _____ .

    It's not _____ .

9. (*young, old*)   Jimmy is an infant. He can't talk yet. He's not _____

_____. He's_____

_____.

10. (*wide, narrow,*   Anne and Sue can't carry the love seat through the door.
    large, small)

The door is _____. The door

isn't _____. The love seat is

_____. The love seat isn't

_____.

11. (*strong, weak*)   This coffee looks like dirty water. It's_____

_____. It's not _____

_____.

12. (*big, small*)   I can put my dictionary in my shirt pocket. My pocket is

_____. It's not _____

_____.

13. (*comfortable,*   I don't want to sit in that chair. It's _____
    uncomfortable)

_____. It's not_____

_____.

14. (*warm, cold*)   We can go to the beach today. The weather is _____

_____. It's not _____

_____.

9-9 USING *ENOUGH* + NOUN AND *MORE* + NOUN

(a) I can't buy this book. I need **more money**.	*more* = additional *enough* = sufficient

(b) I can't buy this book. I don't have **enough money**.	Notice: *more* comes in front of a noun.
	      MORE + NOUN
	  more money
	  more time

(c) I can't finish my work. I need some **more time**.	

(d) I can't finish my work. I don't have **enough time**.	Notice: *enough* comes in front of a noun.*
	      ENOUGH + NOUN
	  enough money
	  enough time

* *Enough* may also follow a noun: *I don't have money enough.* In everyday English, *enough* usually comes in front of a noun.

EXERCISE 18: Complete the sentences. Use your own words.

1. I can't _____ because I don't have enough money.

2. I can't _____ because I don't have enough time.

3. I couldn't _____ because I didn't have enough money.

4. I couldn't _____ because I didn't have enough time.

5. I don't want to _____ because I don't have enough time.

6. I would like to _____, but I can't because I don't have enough money.

EXERCISE 19: Complete the sentences. Use *more* or *enough.* Use the words in the list; use the plural form if necessary

✔ *bread*	*gas*	*sugar*	*vocabulary*
desk	*light*	*tea*	
✔ *egg*	*minute*	*time*	

1. I'm hungry. I want to make a sandwich, but I can't. There isn't

   ____enough bread____.

2. According to the cake recipe I need three eggs, but I have only one. I need two

___more eggs_____.

3. Bob isn't finished with his test. He needs ten _____.

4. I can't go skiing Saturday. I'm too busy. I don't have _____

_____.

5. My tea isn't sweet enough. I need some _____.

6. We need five _____. There are fifteen students in the
class, but there are only ten desks.

7. I can't understand the front page of the newspaper because I don't know

_____.

8. It's too dark in here. I can't read my book. There isn't_____

_____.

9. A: Do we have _____?
   B: No. We have to stop at a gas station.

10. A: Would you like _____?
    B: Yes, thank you. I'd like one more cup.

9-10   USING *ENOUGH* + INFINITIVE

(a) Peggy can go to school because she is old enough.	(a) and (b) give the same meaning.
ADJECTIVE + ***ENOUGH*** + INFINITIVE (b) Peggy is **old** **enough** **to go** to school.	
(c) I can't buy this book because I don't have enough money.	(c) and (d) give the same meaning.
ENOUGH + NOUN + INFINITIVE (d) I don't have **enough** **money** **to buy** this book.	

EXERCISE 20:   Write sentences that have the same meaning as the given sentences by using an infinitive.

1. Bob can reach the top shelf because he's tall enough.

___Bob is tall enough to reach the top shelf._____

2. Sue can't reach the ceiling because she isn't tall enough.

_____

3. Johnny can't get married because he isn't old enough.

_____

4. I can't finish my work because I don't have enough time.

_____

5. Dick can buy a new car because he has enough money.

_____

6. I can eat a horse. I'm hungry enough.*

_____

7. Sally bought enough food. She can feed an army.

_____

8. Did you have enough time? Did you finish your homework last night?

_____

9. Can you buy a ticket to the show? Do you have enough money?

_____

10. I can't understand this article in the newspaper because I don't know enough
    vocabulary.

_____

EXERCISE 21:   Complete the sentences. Use your own words.

1. I'm old enough to _____

2. I'm strong enough to _____

3. I'm not strong enough to _____

4. I'm not hungry enough to _____

5. I have enough money to _____

6. I don't have enough money to _____

7. I have enough time to _____

---

*_I'm hungry enough to eat a horse_ is an English idiom. The speaker is saying, "I'm very hungry." The speaker does not really want to eat a horse.
    Other examples of idioms:
I put my foot in my mouth. = I said something stupid. I said something to the wrong person at the wrong time.
Watch your step. = Be careful.
It's raining cats and dogs. = It's raining hard.
    Every language has idioms. They are common expressions that have special meanings.

8. I don't have enough time to _____

9. I know enough English to _____

10. I don't know enough English to _____

EXERCISE 22—ORAL (BOOKS CLOSED): Answer *no* and explain *why.* Use *too* or *enough.*

> *Example:*   Is the weather perfect today?
> *Response:*   No, it's too cold./No, it's not warm enough.

1. I have a daughter. She is two years old. Can she go to school?
2. Can you touch the ceiling without jumping?
3. Can you lift a piano?
4. Can you wear (. . .)'s shoe? Does it fit?
5. I'm making a noise (*a very soft noise*). Can you hear it?
6. Bobby is ten years old. He's in love. He wants to get married. Is that a good idea?
7. Can you put my briefcase/purse/etc. in your shirt pocket?
8. Can you understand everything on the front page of a newspaper?
9. Can an elephant walk through that door?
10. Do you like the weather (*in this city*) in the winter/summer?
11. Did you finish your homework last night?
12. Do you want to go on a picnic Saturday?
13. Would you like to eat your lunch on the floor of this room?
14. Can you buy an airplane?

9-11   USING *BE ABLE TO*

PRESENT:	(a) I **am able to touch** my toes. (b) I **can touch** my toes.	(a) and (b) have basically the same meaning.
FUTURE:	(c) I **will be able to go** shopping tomorrow. (d) I **can go** shopping tomorrow.	(c) and (d) have basically the same meaning.
PAST:	(e) I **wasn't able to finish** my homework last night. (f) I **couldn't finish** my homework last night.	(e) and (f) have basically the same meaning.

EXERCISE 23:   Rewrite the sentences. Use *be able to.*

1. I can be here tomorrow at ten o'clock.

> _____ I'll (I will) be able to be here tomorrow at ten o'clock. _____

2. Mark is bilingual. He can speak two languages.

    _____ Mark is bilingual. He's (He is) able to speak two languages. _____

3. It was a hard test. Two students couldn't finish it.

    _____ It was a hard test. Two students weren't able to finish it. _____

4. Animals can't speak.

    _____

5. Can animals speak?

    _____

6. Can you touch your toes?

    _____

7. Sue can get her own apartment next year.

    _____

8. My best friend couldn't come to my party last night.

    _____

9. Could you do the homework?

    _____

10. It's snowing. We can go skiing tomorrow.

    _____

11. I couldn't sleep last night. My apartment was too hot.

    _____

12. My roommate can speak four languages. He's multilingual.

    _____

13. I'm sorry that I couldn't call you last night.

    _____

14. Can we take vacations on the moon in the 21st century?

    _____

15. I'm sorry, but I can't come to your party next week.

    _____

EXERCISE 24:   Complete the sentences.

1. I wasn't able to _____ last night because _____

    _____

2. We'll be able to _____ in the 21st century.

3. I'm sorry, but I won't be able to _____

4. Birds are able to _____

5. My friend is multilingual. She's able to _____

6. I'm bilingual. I'm able to _____

7. The students weren't able to _____ in class yesterday

   because _____

8. Will you be able to _____ tomorrow?

9. _____ wasn't able to _____ because

   _____

10. _____ isn't able to _____ because

    _____

11. _____ won't be able to _____ because

    _____

12. I wasn't able to _____ at the zoo because _____

    _____

9-12 USING *TWO, TOO,* AND *TO*

	Two, too, and **to** have the same pronunciation.
TWO (a) I have **two** children.	In (a): **two** = a number.
TOO (b) Timmy is **too** young. He can't read.	In (b): **too young = not old enough.**
(c) Ann saw the movie. I saw the movie **too.***	In (c): **too = also.**
TO (d) I talked **to** Jim.	In (d): **to** = a preposition.
(e) I want **to** watch television.	In (e): **to** = part of an infinitive.

*Often a comma is used in front of **too** (meaning *also*), especially in formal writing: *I saw the movie, too.*

EXERCISE 25: Complete the sentences. Use **two, too,** or **to.**

1. I had _____ cups of coffee yesterday.

2. I'd like a cup of coffee. Bob would like a cup _____.

3. I can't drink my coffee. It's _____ hot. The coffee is

   _____ hot for me _____ drink.

4. I want _____ drink a cup of coffee.

5. I talked _____ Jim. Jane wants _____ talk

   _____ Jim _____.

6. I walked _____ school today. Bob walked _____

   school today _____.

7. I'm going _____ take the bus _____ school
   tomorrow.

8. Shh. I want _____ listen _____ the news broadcast.

9. I can't study. The music is _____ loud.

10. Could I borrow _____ dollars from you?

11. The weather is _____ cold for us _____ go

    _____ the beach.

12. I have _____ apples. Bob wants _____ have

    _____ apples _____.

MORE IRREGULAR VERBS

fall – fell	blow – blew
feel – felt	draw – drew
hurt – hurt	grow – grew
keep – kept	know – knew
swim – swam	throw – threw
win – won	

EXERCISE 26—ORAL (BOOKS CLOSED): Practice using the irregular verbs in the above list.

Example: *fall–fell*   Rain falls. Leaves fall. Sometimes people fall. Yesterday I fell down. I hurt my knee. How did I hurt my knee yesterday?

Response: You fell (down).

EXERCISE 27:   Complete the sentences. Use the past form of the verbs in the list.

blow	*grow*	*swim*
draw	*hurt*	*throw*
fall	*keep*	*win*
feel	*know*	

1. A: Did you enjoy your tennis game with Jackie?

   B: Yes, but I lost. Jackie _____.

2. A: How did you break your leg?

   B: I _____ down on the ice on the sidewalk.

3. A: Ouch!

   B: What's the matter?

   A: I _____ my finger.

   B: How?

   A: I pinched it in the door.

4. A: Did you give the box of candy to your girlfriend?

   B: No, I didn't. I _____ it and ate it myself.

5. A: That's a nice picture.

   B: I agree. Anna _____ it. She's a good artist.

6. A: Did you have a garden when you lived at home?

   B: Yes. I _____ vegetables and flowers.

7. A: I burned my finger.

   B: Did you put ice on it?

   A: No. I _____ on it.

8. A: Did you finish the test?

   B: No. I didn't have enough time. I _____ all of the answers, but I ran out of time.

9. A: Did you have fun at the beach?

   B: Lots of fun. We sunbathed and _____ in the ocean.

10. A: What's the matter? You sound like you have a frog in your throat.

   B: I think I'm catching a cold. I _____ okay yesterday, but I don't feel very good today.

11. A: How did you break the window, Tommy?

   B: Well, I _____ a ball to Annie, but I missed Annie and hit the window instead.

EXERCISE 28:   Complete the sentences. Use the past form of the verbs in the list.

begin	*fly*	*make*	*take*
break	*grow*	*meet*	*tell*
catch	*know*	*sing*	*throw*
cost	*leave*	*spend*	*wear*
fall	*lose*	*steal*	*win*

1. When I went to the airport yesterday, I _____ a taxi.

2. I _____ my winter jacket yesterday because the weather was cold.

3. Tom bought a new tie. It _____ ten dollars.

4. Laurie doesn't feel good. She _____ a cold a couple of days ago.

5. Leo could read the story easily. The words in the story weren't new for him. He _____ the vocabulary in the story.

6. I know Ronald Sawyer. I _____ him at a party a couple of weeks ago.

7. My hometown is Ames, Iowa. I _____ up there.

8. I dropped my book. It _____ to the floor.

9. Dick couldn't get into his apartment because he _____ his keys.

10. We _____ fifty dollars at the restaurant last night. The food was good, but expensive.

11. The baseball player _____ the ball to the catcher.

12. I wrote a check yesterday. I _____ a mistake on the check, so I tore it up and wrote another one.

13. Someone _____ my bicycle, so I called the police.

14. Maggie didn't tell a lie. She _____ the truth.

15. Rick _____ his arm when he fell on the ice.

16. We were late for the movie. It _____ at 7:00, but we didn't get there until 7:15.

17. We _____ songs at the party last night and had a good time.

18. I _____ to Chicago last week. The plane was only five minutes late.

19. My plane _____ at 6:03 and arrived at 8:45.

20. We played a soccer game yesterday. The other team _____. We lost.

chapter **10**

Nouns and Pronouns

10-1 NOUNS: SUBJECTS AND OBJECTS

(a) <u>S</u> <u>V</u> Birds fly. (*noun*) (*verb*) (b) <u>S</u> <u>V</u> <u>O</u> Mary needs a pen. (*noun*) (*verb*) (*noun*)	**S** = Subject **V** = Verb **O** = Object A noun is used as the subject of a sentence. A noun is used as the object of a verb.*
(c) <u>S</u> <u>V</u> <u>PREP</u> <u>O of PREP</u> Birds fly in the sky. (*noun*) (d) <u>S</u> <u>V</u> <u>O</u> <u>PREP</u> <u>O of PREP</u> John is holding a pen in his hand. (*noun*)	**PREP** = Preposition** **O of PREP** = Object of the preposition A noun is used as the object of a preposition.

*Some verbs are followed by an object. These verbs are called transitive verbs (*v.t.* in a dictionary).
Some verbs are not followed by an object. These verbs are called intransitive verbs (*v.i.* in a dictionary).

**Examples of some common prepositions: *about, across, at, between, by, for, from, in, of, on, to, with.*

EXERCISE 1: Find each noun. Is the noun used as:

(a) the subject of the sentence?
(b) the object of the verb?
(c) the object of a preposition?

1. Marie studied chemistry.
2. The sun is shining.
3. Children like candy.
4. The teacher erased the board with her hand.
5. Jack is wearing a blue shirt.
6. Judy usually drinks tea in the afternoon.
7. Two students didn't do their homework.
8. Dick is reading a book about butterflies.
9. Mary and Bob helped Sue with her homework.
10. Sue thanked her friends for their help.
11. The students have rooms in the dormitory.
12. The ship sailed across the ocean.
13. Jean and Fred bought some furniture for their new house.
14. Is Barbara living in an apartment?
15. Does water contain hydrogen and oxygen?

10-2 SUBJECT PRONOUNS AND OBJECT PRONOUNS

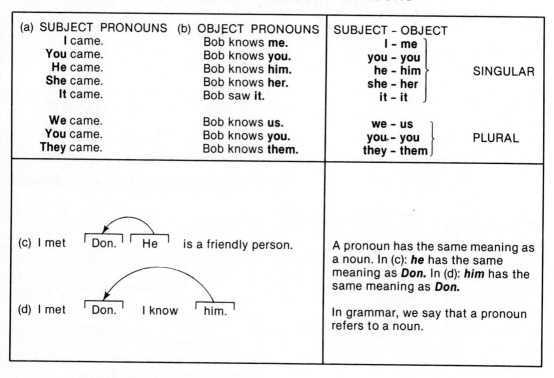

(a) SUBJECT PRONOUNS	(b) OBJECT PRONOUNS	SUBJECT – OBJECT	
I came.	Bob knows **me**.	**I – me**	
You came.	Bob knows **you**.	**you – you**	
He came.	Bob knows **him**.	**he – him**	SINGULAR
She came.	Bob knows **her**.	**she – her**	
It came.	Bob saw **it**.	**it – it**	
We came.	Bob knows **us**.	**we – us**	
You came.	Bob knows **you**.	**you – you**	PLURAL
They came.	Bob knows **them**.	**they – them**	

(c) I met Don. He is a friendly person.

(d) I met Don. I know him.

A pronoun has the same meaning as a noun. In (c): **he** has the same meaning as **Don.** In (d): **him** has the same meaning as **Don.**

In grammar, we say that a pronoun refers to a noun.

EXERCISE 2:   Complete the sentences. Use pronouns (**I/me, he/him,** etc.).

1. Mary has a book. _____She_____ bought____it_____ last week.

2. I met the new students, but Bob didn't meet _____.

3. I wrote a letter, but I didn't send _____ because I didn't have a stamp.

4. Marie studied chemistry. _____ studied _____ in high school.

5. Tom is in Canada. _____ is studying at a university.

6. Bill was at the party last night. I saw _____ there.

7. Ann was also at the party last night. I talked to _____ for a long time. _____ had an interesting conversation together.

8. We need some help. Please help _____.

9. I read two books last week. I liked _____. _____ were interesting.

10. Barb and Paul went shopping yesterday. I saw _____ downtown. _____ bought some new clothes.

11. Ann and I have a dinner invitation. Mr. and Mrs. Brown invited _____ to come to dinner at their house.

12. Judy bought a new car. _____ is a Toyota.

13. My husband and I have a new car. _____ got _____ last month.

14. I saw Paul yesterday at the cafeteria. I talked to _____ for a while. _____ is taking four courses this semester.

15. Are Liz and you going to come to the party tomorrow night? I hope so. _____ will have a good time.

EXERCISE 3:   Complete the sentences. Use pronouns. Use short answers to questions.

1. A: Do you know Bob and Mary?

   B: Yes, _____I do_____. I met____them_____ a couple of weeks ago.

2. A: Did you see Linda at the party last night?

   B: No, _____. Was _____ there? I didn't see

   _____.

3. A: Is the chemical formula for water H_3O?

   B: No, _____. _____ is H_2O.

4. A: Would Judy and you like to come to the movie with us?

   B: Yes, _____. Judy and _____ would enjoy going

   to the movie with _____.

5. A: Do Mr. and Mrs. Kelly live in the city?

   B: No, _____. _____ live in the suburbs. I visited

   _____ last month. _____ live about ten miles
   from downtown.

6. A: Do you know how to spell "Mississippi?"

   B: Sure _____. I can spell _____.

7. A: Was Paul at the party Saturday night?

   B: Yes, _____. I danced with _____ a couple of

   times. _____ is a good dancer. _____ had a good
   time together.

8. A: Liz and I are going to go downtown this afternoon. Do you want to come
   with _____?

   B: I don't think so, but thanks anyway. Don and _____ are going

   to go to the library. _____ need to study for our test.

9. A: Hi, Ann. Did you talk to Barbara?

   B: Yes, _____. She called _____ last night.

   A: I talked to _____ last night, too. _____ called me
   around nine.

   B: She has a lot of problems. I feel sorry for _____.

10. A: Did George and Mike come over to your house last night?

    B: No, _____. I'm angry at _____. I waited for

    _____ for three hours. They promised to come over, but

    _____ didn't.

10-3   INDIRECT OBJECTS

(a) I wrote $\overbrace{\text{a letter}}^{\text{D.O.}}$ $\overbrace{\text{to Jim.}}^{\text{I.O.}}$	Some verbs are followed by two objects: a direct object (D.O.) and an indirect object (I.O.).	
	(a) and (b) have the same meaning.	
(b) I wrote $\overbrace{\text{Jim}}^{\text{I.O.}}$ $\overbrace{\text{a letter.}}^{\text{D.O.}}$	Notice in (b): Do not use *to* when the indirect object is first and the direct object is second.	

VERBS FOLLOWED BY INDIRECT OBJECTS:

give	Please give	your pen	**to me.**	send	I sent	a postcard	**to Alice.**
	Please give	**me**	your pen.		I sent	**Alice**	a postcard.
hand	Please hand	that book	**to me.**	write	I wrote	a letter	**to Don.**
	Please hand	**me**	that book.		I wrote	**Don**	a letter.
pass	Please pass	the salt	**to me.**	tell	Ann told	a story	**to us.**
	Please pass	**me**	the salt.		Ann told	**us**	a story.
lend	I lent	my car	**to Tom.**	show	He showed	a picture	**to us.**
	I lent	**Tom**	my car.		He showed	**us**	a picture.

EXERCISE 4—ORAL: Change the position of the indirect object in the following sentences. Be sure to omit **to.**

Example: I gave a book to John.
Response: I gave John a book.

1. I gave my pen to Ann.
2. I wrote a letter to John.
3. I sent a package to Sue.
4. I told a story to Mary.
5. I showed a picture to Liz.
6. Ann gave some money to me.
7. Bob wrote a letter to me.
8. Please pass the butter to me.
9. Please lend a dime to me.
10. Please write a letter to me.
11. Please hand that book to me.
12. Please tell a story to us.
13. I gave a birthday present to Bob.
14. My uncle wrote a letter to me.
15. Please pass the salt and pepper to me.
16. Would you please hand that hammer to me?
17. Did you send a package to your parents?
18. Carol told a bedtime story to her son.
19. Could you lend a dollar to me?
20. Bob showed a photograph of his wife to me.
21. Jean gave some money to her roommate yesterday.
22. Mr. Winston gave some good advice to his children.
23. Please hand that piece of chalk to me.
24. Mrs. Johnson is going to write a letter to the President of the United States.

EXERCISE 5—ORAL (BOOKS CLOSED):   Change the position of the indirect object.

> *Example:*   I gave my book to (. . .).
> *Response:*   I gave (. . .) my book.

1. I gave my pen to (. . .).
2. I passed my dictionary to (. . .).
3. I handed my notebook to (. . .).
4. I wrote a letter to (. . .).
5. I sent a package to (. . .).
6. I told a funny story to (. . .).
7. I showed a photograph to (. . .).

8. I sent a check to the telephone company.
9. I lent fifty cents to (. . .).
10. Please hand that pen to (. . .).
11. Please pass this pencil to (. . .).
12. Please give this book to (. . .).
13. Please tell a joke to the class.
14. Please lend a million dollars to me.

EXERCISE 6:   Rewrite each sentence. Change the position of the indirect object. Be sure to add *to.*

1. I wrote my sister a letter yesterday.   I wrote a letter to my sister yesterday.
   _____

2. I sent my parents a telegram two days ago. _____
   _____

3. Mrs. Kelly gave her children some candy after dinner. _____
   _____

4. Sue is going to lend me her car tomorrow. _____
   _____

5. Sam told the class a joke yesterday._____
   _____

6. I'm going to write the newspaper a letter._____
   _____

7. Did you hand John the scissors? _____
   _____

8. Could you please pass me the ketchup? _____
   _____

9. Mr. Schwartz showed Liz a picture of his baby daughter. _____

_____

10. Yesterday the teacher gave the students some good advice. _____

_____

EXERCISE 7—ORAL (BOOKS CLOSED): Perform the action. Answer the question.

Example: Give your book to (. . .). What did you do?
Response: I gave my book to (. . .). OR: I gave (. . .) my book.

1. Pass your dictionary to (. . .).
2. Hand me your pen/pencil.
3. Lend (. . .) a quarter.
4. Tell me your name.

5. Pass my pen to (. . .).
6. Give (. . .) a penny.
7. Show (. . .) a picture.
8. Write (. . .) a note and pass it to him/her.

10-4 INDIRECT OBJECTS: USING *FOR*

<table>
<tr>
<td>(a) Bob opened ⌐the door⌐ ⌐for Mary.⌐
              D.O   I.O

(b) Sue answered ⌐a question⌐ ⌐for me.⌐
                D.O.   I.O.</td>
<td>With some verbs, *for* is used with the indirect object. With these verbs, the indirect object follows the direct object. *For* is not omitted. The position of the indirect object is not changed.</td>
</tr>
<tr>
<td>VERBS FOLLOWED BY INDIRECT OBJECTS WITH *FOR:*

answer   He answered a question **for me.**

cash   The teller cashed a check **for me.**

fix   Can you fix my car **for me?**

open   Mr. Smith opened the door **for his wife.**

pronounce The teacher pronounced the word **for the students.**

translate I translated a letter **for my brother.**</td>
<td>Notice in the examples: All of the sentences give the idea that someone is helping another person.</td>
</tr>
</table>

EXERCISE 8:   Complete the sentences by adding *for* or *to*.

1. The teacher answered a question _____ me.

2. I opened the door _____ my mother.

3. My roommate translated a newspaper story _____ me.

4. Fred gave some candy _____ his girlfriend.

5. The teller cashed a check _____ me.

6. The mechanic fixed my car _____ me.

7. Mrs. Baker handed the baby _____ her husband.

8. The teacher pronounced "bat" and "but" _____ the students.

9. Our landlord fixed the air conditioner _____ us.

10. Could you please answer a question _____ me?

EXERCISE 9:   Study the examples.

(a) A: **Could you please** open the door for me? 　　B: **Certainly. I'd be happy to.**	**Could you please...?** is used to ask a polite question. **Certainly. I'd be happy to** is a common response to a polite question.
(b) A: **Could you please** open the door for me? 　　B: **Sure.**	In (b): **Sure** is an informal response. People often use informal English when they are talking to people they know well: friends, family members, classmates, etc.

Make dialogs from the given words.

STUDENT A: Use *could you please... + for me.*

STUDENT B: Answer the question.

1. (*open the window*)　　　A:　 Could you please open the window for me?

　　　　　　　　　　　　　　　　　　_____

　　　　　　　　　　　　　　B:　 Certainly, I'd be happy to./Sure.

　　　　　　　　　　　　　　　　　　_____

2. (*answer a question*)   A: _____

_____

B: _____

_____

3. (*translate this word*)   A: _____

_____

B: _____

_____

4. (*pronounce this word*)   A: _____

_____

B: _____

_____

5. (*cash a check*)   A: _____

_____

B: _____

_____

6. (*fix it*)   A: The plumbing in my apartment doesn't work.

_____

B: _____

_____

7. (*open this jar of pickles*) A: My hands are wet._____

_____

B: _____

_____

EXERCISE 10—ORAL (BOOKS CLOSED):   Ask and answer questions.

STUDENT A: Ask a question using *Could you please . . . ?* Use *me, to me,* or *for me* in your question.

STUDENT B: Answer the question.

> *Example:*   pass the salt
> *Student A:*   Could you please pass me the salt/pass the salt to me?
> *Student B:*   Certainly. I'd be happy to./Sure.

1. pass the butter
2. pass the sugar
3. hand the ketchup
4. pass the salt and pepper
5. lend your dictionary
6. lend a dime

7. answer a question
8. pronounce this word
9. open the door
10. lend some money
11. translate this paragraph
12. hand that book

10-5   USING INDIRECT OBJECTS WITH *EXPLAIN*

(a) The teacher **explained** the grammar **to us**. (b) The teacher **explained** the grammar **for us**.	Either *to* or *for* is used with indirect objects after *explain*. With *explain,* the indirect object always follows the direct object. (INCORRECT: *The teacher explained us the grammar.*)

EXERCISE 11:   Complete the sentences. Use the words in parentheses.

1. (*the problem, me*)   Elizabeth explained____ the problem to me/for me._____

_____

2. (*the students, the   The professor explained _____
   chemistry formula*)

_____

3. (*the lesson, the class*)   The teacher explained _____

_____

4. (*the patient, the   The doctor explained_____
   problem*)

_____

5. (*me, this sentence*)   Could you please explain _____

_____

6. (*his ideas, us*)   Fred explained _____

_____

7. (*the doctor, his problem*)   Mr. Schwartz explained_____

_____

EXERCISE 12:   Rewrite. Add the word(s) in parentheses. If necessary, add **to** or **for.**

1. (*Bob*)   I wrote a letter.

     I wrote Bob a letter.   OR: I wrote a letter to Bob.* _____

2. (*my cousin*)   I sent a postcard.

_____

3. (*me*)   The teacher answered a question.

_____

4. (*his girlfriend*)   Jim opened the car door.

_____

5. (*the bride and groom*)   Ann Miller gave a nice wedding present.

_____

6. (*the class*)   The teacher pronounced the new vocabulary words.

_____

---

* *I wrote a letter for Bob* is possible, but it has a special meaning: It gives the idea that I helped Bob. (*For example:* Bob broke his hand. He can't write. He wanted to write a letter. I helped him by writing the letter.)

7. (*us*)   The teacher explained the meaning of the word.

_____

8. (*my roommate*)   I translated the title of a book.

_____

9. (*me*)   Please translate the title of this book.

_____

10. (*me*)   My friend answered the phone because my hands were full.

_____

11. (*the University of Texas*)   I sent an application.

_____

12. (*the students*)   The teacher explained the assignment.

_____

13. (*his wife*)   Ron fixed the sewing machine.

_____

14. (*us*)   Don told a funny joke at the party.

_____

15. (*me*)   Jane explained her problem.

_____

16. (*me*)   My father wrote a letter.

_____

17. (*the teacher*)   Bill showed a picture of his family.

_____

EXERCISE 13—WRITTEN: Write complete sentences by adding direct objects and indirect objects. (Use your own paper.)

1. I wrote _____ _____ yesterday.

2. I sent _____ _____ last week.

3. Please pass _____ _____.

4. The taxi driver opened _____ _____.

5. Bob gave _____ _____.

6. Could you please pronounce _____ _____?

7. Could you please lend _____ _____?

8. Ann translated _____ _____.

9. Could you please answer _____ _____?

10. My friend explained _____ _____.

10-6 MAKING POLITE REQUESTS

(a) **Would you please open** the door? (b) **Could you please open** the door? (c) **Please open** the door.	(a), (b), and (c) have the same meaning: I want you to open the door. I am asking you politely to open the door.
(d) **May I please borrow** your pen? (e) **Can I please borrow** your pen? (f) **Could I please borrow** your pen?	(d), (e) and (f) have the same meaning: I want to borrow your pen. I am asking politely to borrow your pen.

EXERCISE 14—ORAL (BOOKS CLOSED): Ask and answer polite questions.

STUDENT A: Ask a classmate a polite question. Use
Would you please . . . ? or
Could you please . . . ? or
Please . . .

STUDENT B: Answer the question. Possible answers:
Certainly. I'd be happy to.
Of course. I'd happy to.
Sure. (informal)
Okay. (informal)

1. You want your classmate to open the door.
   A: *Would you please open the door?*
   B: *Certainly. I'd be happy to.*
   A: *Thank you.*
2. You want a classmate to close the door.
3. You want a classmate to turn on the light.
4. You want a classmate to turn off the light.
5. You want a classmate to pass you the salt and pepper.
6. You want a classmate to hand you that book.
7. You want a classmate to translate a word for you.
8. You want a classmate to tell you the time.

9. You want a classmate to open the window.

10. You want a classmate to hold your books for a minute.

EXERCISE 15—ORAL (BOOKS CLOSED):   Ask and answer polite questions.

STUDENT A: Ask a classmate a polite question. Use
             May I please...? or
             Can I please...? or
             Could I please...?

STUDENT B: Answer the question. Possible answers:
             Certainly.
             Of course.
             Sure. (informal)

1. Your classmate has a pen. You want to borrow it.

   A: *May I please borrow your pen?*

   B: *Certainly. Here it is.*

   A: *Thank you.*

2. Your classmate has a dictionary. You want to borrow it.

3. Your classmate has a pen. You want to use it for a minute.

4. Your classmate has an eraser. You want to use it for a minute.

5. Your classmate has a pencil sharpener. You want to borrow it.

6. Your classmate has a book. You want to see it.

7. Your classmate has a dictionary. You want to see it.

8. You are at your classmate's home. You want to use the phone.

9. You are at your classmate's home. You want a glass of water.

10. You are at a restaurant. Your classmate is a waiter/waitress. You want to have a cup of coffee.

11. Your classmate is a waiter/waitress. You want to have a hamburger with everything.*

12. Your classmate is a waiter/waitress. You want to have the check.

---

*a hamburger with everything = a hamburger with ketchup, mustard, onions, and pickles.

10-7 INDEFINITE PRONOUNS: USING *SOMETHING, SOMEONE, ANYTHING, ANYONE*

STATEMENT:	(a) Mary **bought something** at the store. (b) Jim **talked to someone** after class.	In a statement, use *something* or *someone*.
NEGATIVE:	(c) Mary **didn't buy anything** at the store. (d) Jim **didn't talk to anyone** after class.	In a negative sentence, use *anything* or *anyone*.
QUESTION:	(e) **Did** Mary **buy something** at the store? **Did** Mary **buy anything** at the store? (f) **Did** Jim **talk to someone** after class? **Did** Jim **talk to anyone** after class?	In a question, use either *something/someone* or *anything/anyone*.

EXERCISE 16: Complete the sentences. Use *something, someone, anything* or *anyone.**

1. I have _____ in my pocket.

2. Do you have _____ in your pocket?

3. Bob doesn't have _____ in his pocket.

4. I bought _____ when I went shopping yesterday.

5. Alice didn't buy _____ when she went shopping.

6. Did you buy _____ when you went shopping?

7. My roommate is speaking to _____ on the phone.

8. Ann didn't tell _____ her secret.

9. I talked to _____ at the phone company about my bill.

10. Did you talk to _____ about your problem?

11. Jane gave me _____ for my birthday.

12. Paul didn't give me _____ for my birthday.

13. Did Paul give you _____ for your birthday?

14. My brother is sitting at his desk. He's writing a letter to _____.

---

* *Someone* and *somebody* have the same meaning. *Anyone* and *anybody* have the same meaning. You may also wish to include practice with *somebody* and *anybody* in this exercise.

15. The hall is empty. I don't see _____.

16. A: Listen. Do you hear a noise?

    B: No, I don't. I don't hear _____.

17. A: Did you talk to Jim on the phone last night?

    B: No. I didn't talk to _____.

18. A: Where's your bicycle?

    B: _____ stole it.

19. A: Does _____ have a couple of dimes? I need to use the pay phone.

    B: Here.

    A: Thanks. I'll pay you back later.

20. A: What did you do last weekend?

    B: I didn't do _____. I stayed home.

10-8 INDEFINITE PRONOUNS: USING *NOTHING* AND *NO ONE*

(a) I **didn't say anything.**	(a) and (b) have the same meaning.
(b) I **said nothing.**	*Anything* is used when the verb is negative. *Nothing* is used when the verb is affirmative.
(c) Bob **didn't see anyone** at the park.	(c) and (d) have the same meaning.
(d) Bob **saw no one** at the park.	*Anyone* is used when the verb is negative. *No one* is used when the verb is affirmative.

EXERCISE 17: Complete the sentences by using **anything, nothing, anyone,** or **no one.** *

1. Jim doesn't know _____ about butterflies.

2. Jim knows _____ about butterflies.

3. Jean didn't tell _____ about her problem.

4. Jean told _____ about her problem.

5. There's _____ in my pocket. It's empty.

---

* Just as *anyone* and *anybody* have the same meaning, *no one* and *nobody* have the same meaning. Include practice with *nobody* in the exercise if you wish.

6. There isn't _____ in my pocket.

7. Liz went to a shoe store, but she didn't buy _____.

8. Liz bought _____ at the shoe store.

9. I got _____ in the mail today. My mailbox was empty.

10. George sat quietly in the corner. He didn't speak to _____.

11. The office is closed from 12:00 to 1:00. _____ is there during the lunch hour.

12. I know _____ about nuclear physics.

13. _____ was at home last night. Both my roommate and I were out.

14. Joan has a new apartment. She doesn't know _____ in her apartment building yet.

10-9 QUESTIONS WITH *WHAT*

(QUESTION WORD)	+ HELPING VERB	+ SUBJECT	+ MAIN VERB		ANSWER
(a)	**Did**	Carol	**buy**	a car?	**Yes, she did.** (She bought a car.)
(b)	**What**	**did**	Carol	**buy?**	**A car.** (She bought a car.)
(c)		**Is**	Fred	**holding**	a book?	**Yes, he is.** (He's holding a book.)
(d)	**What**	**is**	Fred	**holding?**	**A book.** (He's holding a book.)
(e)		**Can**	you	**see**	that bird?	**Yes, I can.** (I can see that bird.)
(f)	**What**	**can**	you	**see?**	**That bird.** (I can see that bird.)

(g) Carol bought ⌐a car.⌐ O	In (g): *a car* is the object of the verb.
(h) ⌐What⌐ did Carol buy? O	In (h): *what* is the object of the verb.
	What is used in a question when you want to find out about a thing. (*Who* is used when you want to find out about a person. See 10–10.)

EXERCISE 18: Make questions.

1. A: ____Did you buy a new tape recorder?_____

    B: Yes, I did. (I bought a new tape recorder.)

2. A: _What did you buy?_ _____

   B: A new tape recorder. (I bought a new tape recorder.)

3. A: _____

   B: Yes, she is. (Mary is carrying a suitcase.)

4. A: _____

   B: A suitcase. (Mary is carrying a suitcase.)

5. A: _____

   B: Yes, I can. (I can see that airplane.)

6. A: _____

   B: That airplane. (I can see that airplane.)

7. A: _____

   B: Jeans. (I'm going to wear jeans to the party tonight.)

8. A: _____

   B: Yes, I am. (I'm going to wear jeans to the party tonight.)

9. A: _____

   B: A hamburger. (Bob ate a hamburger for lunch.)

10. A: _____

   B: Yes, he did. (Bob ate a hamburger for lunch.)

EXERCISE 19:   Make questions.

1. A: _What did John talk about?*_ _____

   B: His country. (John talked about his country.)

2. A: _Did John talk about his country?_ _____

   B: Yes, he did. (John talked about his country.)

3. A: _____

   B: A bird. (I'm looking at a bird.)

_____

* In this question, *what* is the object of the preposition *about.* In formal English a preposition may come at the beginning of a question:

   About what did John talk?

In usual, everyday English a preposition rarely comes at the beginning of a question.

4. A: _____

   B: Yes, I am. (I'm looking at that bird.)

5. A: _____

   B: Yes, I am. (I'm interested in science.)

6. A: _____

   B: Science. (I'm interested in science.)

7. A: _____

   B: Nothing in particular. (I'm thinking about nothing in particular.)

8. A: _____

   B: English grammar. (I dreamed about English grammar last night.)

9. A: _____

   B: No, I'm not. (I'm not afraid of snakes.) Are you?

10. A: _____

   B: The map on the wall. (The teacher is pointing at the map on the wall.)

EXERCISE 20—ORAL (BOOKS CLOSED): Ask a classmate a question. Use *what.* Use any tense.

> *Example:*   eat
> *Student A:*   What did you eat for breakfast this morning?/What are you going to eat for dinner tonight?/etc.
> *Student B:*   (free response)

1. eat	6. be interested in
2. wear	7. be afraid of
3. look at	8. dream about
4. study	9. have
5. think about	10. need to buy

10-10 QUESTIONS WITH *WHO*

QUESTION	ANSWER	
(a) **What** did they see?	**A boat.** (They saw **a boat.**)	***What*** is used to ask questions about *things*.
(b) **Who** did they see?	**Jim.** (They saw **Jim.**)	***Who*** is used to ask questions about *people*.
(c) **Who** did they see? (d) **Whom** did they see? (*formal*)	**Jim.** (They saw **Jim.**) **Jim.** (They saw **Jim.**)	(c) and (d) have the same meaning. **Whom** is used in formal English as the object of a verb or a preposition. In (c): **who,** not **whom,** is usually used in everyday English. In (d): **whom** is used in very formal English. **Whom** is rarely used in everyday spoken English.

O
(e) **Who(m)** did they see?
 	
    S
(f) **Who** came?
	O
	Jim. (They saw **Jim.**)
	
	    S
	Mary. (Mary came.)
		In (e): **who(m)** is the object of the verb. Usual question word order (*question word + helping verb + subject + main verb*) is used.
		
		In (f): **who** is the subject of the question. Usual question word order is *not* used.

(g) **Who lives** there? (h) **Who can help** us? (i) **Who saw** the accident? (j) **Who saw** Jim?	**Mr. Lee. (Mr. Lee lives** there.) **Nancy. (Nancy can help** us.) **Ann. (Ann saw** the accident.) **Ann. (Ann saw** Jim.)	When **who** is the subject of a question, do *not* use **does, do,** or **did.** Do *not* change the verb in any way: the verb form in the question is the same as the verb form in the answer.

EXERCISE 21: Make questions.

1. A: _____

   B: Mary. (I saw Mary at the party.)

2. A: _____

   B: Mary. (Mary came to the party.)

3. A: _____

   B: John. (John lives in that house.)

4. A: _____

   B: John. (I called John.)

5. A: _____

   B: My aunt and uncle. (I visited my aunt and uncle.)

6. A: _____
   B: My cousin. (My cousin visited me.)

7. A: _____
   B: Bob. (Bob helped Ann.)

8. A: _____
   B: Ann. (Bob helped Ann.)

9. A: _____
   B: Yes, he did. (Bob helped Ann.)

10. A: _____
    B: No, I'm not. (I'm not confused.)

EXERCISE 22:   Make questions.

1. A: _____
   B: Dick. (I saw Dick.)

2. A: _____ *
   B: Dick. (I talked to Dick.)

3. A: _____
   B: Nancy. (I visited Nancy.)

4. A: _____
   B: Mary. (I'm thinking about Mary.)

5. A: _____
   B: Sue. (I'm going to talk to Sue.)

6. A: _____
   B: Alice Jennings. (I met Alice Jennings at the party.)

7. A: _____
   B: Marcia. (Marcia called.)

8. A: _____
   B: Donald. (Donald answered the question.)

9. A: _____
   B: Carol. (Carol taught the English class.)

---

*In formal English a preposition may come at the beginning of a question:
  To whom** (not **who**) **did you talk?
In usual, everyday English a preposition rarely comes at the beginning of a question.

10. A: _____

     B: David. (David helped me.)

11. A: _____

     B: Barbara. (Barbara wrote me a letter.)

12. A: _____

     B: My brother. (My brother carried my suitcase.)

EXERCISE 23: Make questions. Use any appropriate question word: *where, when, what time, why, who, what.*

1. A: _____

     B: To the zoo. (Ann went to the zoo.)

2. A: _____

     B: Yesterday. (Ann went to the zoo yesterday.)

3. A: _____

     B: Ann. (Ann went to the zoo yesterday.)

4. A: _____

     B: Bob. (I saw Bob.)

5. A: _____

     B: At the zoo. (I saw Bob at the zoo.)

6. A: _____

     B: Yesterday. (I saw Bob at the zoo yesterday.)

7. A: _____

     B: Because the weather was nice. (I went to the zoo yesterday because the weather was nice.)

8. A: _____

     B: In an apartment. (I'm living in an apartment.)

9. A: _____

     B: Dick. (Dick is sitting next to me.)

10. A: _____

     B: All of my friends. (I'm going to invite all of my friends to my party.)

11. A: _____

     B: Dr. Jones. (I talked to Dr. Jones.)

12. A: _____

    B: Dr. Jones. (Dr. Jones called.)

13. A: _____

    B: Yesterday afternoon. (Dr. Jones called yesterday afternoon.)

14. A: _____

    B: Tomorrow. (I can help you tomorrow.)

15. A: _____

    B: At 6:05. (My plane will arrive at 6:05.)

16. A: _____

    B: My keys. (I lost my keys.)

17. A: _____

    B: Grammar. (The teacher is talking about grammar.)

18. A: _____

    B: A frog. (Annie has a frog in her pocket.)

EXERCISE 24—ORAL: Study the examples.

(a) **What does** "pretty" **mean?**	(a) and (b) have the same meaning.
(b) **What is the meaning of** "pretty"?	*INCORRECT: What means "pretty"?*

Ask a classmate for the meaning of the following words:

1. muggy	6. listen	11. discover	16. forest
2. awful	7. supermarket	12. simple	17. possess
3. quiet	8. crowd	13. empty	18. invite
4. century	9. lend	14. enjoy	19. modern
5. finish	10. murder	15. ill	20. pretty difficult

10-11   ASKING QUESTIONS ABOUT QUANTITY: *HOW MANY* AND *HOW MUCH*

	QUESTION				ANSWER	
COUNT NOUN		**COUNT HOW MANY + NOUN***				
students	(a)	**How many**	**students**	are there in your class?	Sixteen.	***How many*** is used with count nouns.
children	(b)	**How many**	**children**	do you have?	Three.	
cups	(c)	**How many**	**cups** of coffee	do you drink every day?	Four.	
NONCOUNT NOUN		**NONCOUNT HOW MUCH + NOUN***				
money	(d)	**How much**	**money**	do you have in your pocket?	Two dollars.	***How much*** is used with noncount nouns.
rice	(e)	**How much**	**rice**	did you buy?	Five pounds.	
coffee	(f)	**How much**	**coffee**	do you drink every day?	Four cups.	

*Often a noun is omitted after ***how many*** and ***how much*** when the speaker's intended meaning is clear:
There are fifteen students in my class. How many are there in your class?
How much does that book cost?

EXERCISE 25:   Make questions. Use ***how much*** or ***how many.***

1. A: _____ How much money do you have? _____
   B: Six dollars. (I have six dollars.)

2. A: _____
   B: Three dollars. (I gave Tom three dollars.)

3. A: _____
   B: Three. (I have three sisters.)

4. A: _____
   B: Five. (I have five brothers and sisters.)

5. A: _____
   B: A dollar. (This pen costs a dollar.)

6. A: _____

    B: Two dollars. (My pen cost two dollars.)

7. A: _____

    B: Thirteen. (There are thirteen people in this room.)

8. A: _____

    B: Fifty. (There are fifty states in the United States.)

9. A: _____

    B: Forty dollars. (We spent forty dollars at the restaurant last night.)

10. A: _____

    B: Two. (The Wilsons have two children.)

11. A: _____

    B: Three. (I drank three cups of coffee this morning.)

12. A: _____

    B: Three cups. (I drank three cups of coffee this morning.)*

13. A: _____

    B: Eight. (A spider has eight legs.)

14. A: _____

    B: Eight glasses. (I drink eight glasses of water every day.)

15. A: _____

    B: 33,333. (There are 33,333 books in the library.)

EXERCISE 26:   Make questions. Use your own words.

1. A: _____

    B: Yesterday.

2. A: _____

    B: My brother.

3. A: _____

    B: A new pair of sandals.

4. A: _____

    B: At 7:30.

---

*There are two possible questions in #12: *How much coffee did you drink this morning?* OR: *How many cups of coffee did you drink this morning?*

5. A: _____
   B: At Rossini's Restaurant.

6. A: _____
   B: Tomorrow afternoon.

7. A: _____
   B: In an apartment.

8. A: _____
   B: My roommate.

9. A: _____
   B: Because I wanted to.

10. A: _____
    B: Ann.

11. A: _____
    B: A bird.

12. A: _____
    B: The zoo.

13. A: _____
    B: Five.

14. A: _____
    B: Two sisters and three brothers.

15. A: _____
    B: Ten dollars.

EXERCISE 27—ORAL (BOOKS CLOSED): Make questions that would produce the following answers.

> *Example:*   At 7 o'clock.
> *Response:*   When did you get up this morning?/What time does the movie start?/etc.

1. In an apartment.
2. Yesterday.
3. Six dollars.
4. (. . .).
5. At seven-thirty.
6. A shirt.
7. A hamburger.
8. Five.
9. Because I wanted to.
10. One sister and two brothers.

11. Twenty.
12. Grammar.
13. (. . .).
14. Nothing.
15. Last night.
16. Yes.
17. No.
18. In the dormitory.
19. Ten dollars.
20. (. . .).

21. At nine o'clock.
22. A new pair of shoes.
23. Eighteen.
24. Because I was tired.
25. Tomorrow.
26. Nothing.
27. (. . .).
28. On (*name of street in this city*).
29. In (*name of this state or province*).
30. Certainly. I'd be happy to.

chapter **11**

Making Comparisons—
Part I

11-1 POSSESSIVE PRONOUNS: *MINE, YOURS, HIS, HERS, OURS, THEIRS*

	POSSESSIVE ADJECTIVE	POSSESSIVE PRONOUN	
(a) This book belongs to me. It is **my** book. It is **mine.**			A possessive adjective is used in front of a noun.
(b) That book belongs to you. It is **your** book. It is **yours.**	**my** **your** **her** **his** **our** **their**	**mine** **yours** **hers** **his** **ours** **theirs**	A possessive pronoun is used alone, without a noun.

EXERCISE 1: Complete the sentences. Use object pronouns, possessive adjectives, and possessive pronouns.

1. **I** own this book.
   This book belongs to

   _____me_____.

   This is _____my_____ book.

   This is _____mine_____.

2. **She** owns this pen.
   This pen belongs to

   _____.

   This is _____ pen.

   This is _____.

3. **They** own these books.
   These books belong to

   _____.

   These are _____
   books.

   These are _____.

4. **You** own that book.
   That books belongs to

   _____.

   That is _____ book.

   That is _____.

5. **He** owns that pen.
   That pen belongs to

   _____.

   That is _____ pen.

   That is _____.

6. **We** own those books.
   Those books belong to

   _____.

   Those are _____
   books.

   Those are _____.

EXERCISE 2:   Complete the sentences. Use the correct possessive form of the words in parentheses.

1. (*I*)   This bookbag is _____mine_____.

2. (*Sue*)   That bookbag is _____Sue's_____.

3. (*I*)   _____My_____ bookbag is red.

4. (*she*)   _____Hers_____ is green.

5. (*we*)   These books are _____.

6. (*they*)   Those books are _____.

7. (*we*)   _____ books are on the table.

8. (*they*)   _____ are on the desk.

9. (*Tom*)   This raincoat is _____.

10. (*Mary*)   That raincoat is _____.

11. (*he*)   _____ is light brown.

12. (*she*)   _____ is light blue.

13. (*I*)   This notebook is _____.

14. (*you*)   That one is _____.

15. (*I*)   _____ has _____ name on it.

16. (*you*)   _____ has _____ name on it.

17. (*Dick*) _____ apartment is on Pine Street.

18. (*we*) _____ is on Main Street.

19. (*he*) _____ apartment has three rooms.

20. (*we*) _____ has four rooms.

21. (*I*) This is _____ pen.

22. (*you*) That one is _____.

23. (*I*) _____ is in _____ pocket.

24. (*you*) _____ is on _____ desk.

25. (*we*) _____ car is a Chevrolet.

26. (*they*) _____ is a Volkswagen.

27. (*we*) _____ gets 17 miles to the gallon.

28. (*they*) _____ car gets 30 miles to the gallon.

29. (*Ann*) These books are _____.

30. (*Paul*) Those are _____.

31. (*she*) _____ are on _____ desk.

32. (*he*) _____ are on _____ desk.

11-2 COMPARISONS: USING *THE SAME (AS), SIMILAR (TO),* AND *DIFFERENT (FROM)*

THE SAME (AS)	SIMILAR (TO)	DIFFERENT (FROM)
A and B are **the same.** A is **the same as** B.	C and D are **similar.** C is **similar to** D.	E and F are **different.** E is **different from** F.

EXERCISE 3: Complete the sentences. Use *the same (as), similar (to),* and *different (from)* in your completions.

1. A _____ is the same as _____ F.

2. D and E _____ are similar OR: are different _____ .*

3. C _____ D.

4. B _____ D.

5. B and D _____ .

6. C and D _____ .

7. A and F _____ .

8. F and G _____ .

9. F _____ G.

10. G _____ A and F, but

_____ C.

EXERCISE 4:   Answer the questions.

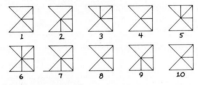

1. Which of the figures are the same?
2. Is there at least one figure that is different from all the rest?
3. How many triangles are there in figure 1? (*answer: Seven.*)
4. How many triangles are there in figure 2?
5. How many triangles are there in figure 6?

11-3   COMPARISONS: USING *LIKE* AND *ALIKE*

You have a ballpoint pen with blue ink. *I have a ballpoint pen with blue ink.*	
(a) Your pen **is like** my pen.	***like*** = *similar to*
(b) Your pen and my pen **are alike.** Our pens **are alike.**	***alike*** = *similar*
	Like and ***alike*** have the same meaning, but the sentence patterns are different: *This + **be** + **like** + that.* *This and that + **be** + **alike.***

---

* *Similar* gives the idea that two things are the same in some ways (e.g., both D and E have four edges) but different in other ways (e.g., D is a rectangle and E is a square).

EXERCISE 5:   Make sentences from the given information. Use *like* and
alike.

1. (*You and I have similar books.*)

    _____Your book is like my book/mine.____Our books are alike.____

2. (*Bob and I have similar coats.*)

    _____

3. (*Ted and Sue have similar cars.*)

    _____

4. (*The Smiths and we have similar houses.*)

    _____

5. (*A town and a city are similar in some ways.*)

    _____

6. (*Tom and Alice have similar jobs.*)

    _____

7. (*A foot and a hand are similar in some ways.*)

    _____

8. (*A motorcycle and a bicycle are similar in some ways.*)

    _____

9. (*You and I have similar hats.*)

    _____

10. (*A dormitory is similar to an apartment building in many ways.*)

    _____

EXERCISE 6—ORAL: Make sentences with **like.** Compare the things in
Column A with the things in Column B. Discuss the ways in which the two
things you are comparing are similar.

Example: A pencil is like a pen in some ways.

COLUMN A

   an alley
   a bus
   a bush
   a cup
   a hill

COLUMN B

   a glass
   a human hand
   a lemon
   a chair
   a mountain

COLUMN A	COLUMN B
honey	an ocean
a monkey's hand	✓ a pen
an orange	a street
✓ a pencil	sugar
a sea	a suit coat
a sofa	a taxi
a sports jacket	a tree

11-4   THE COMPARATIVE: USING *-ER* AND *MORE*

<table>
<tr>
<td colspan="3">
Mary is 25 years old.
John is 20 years old.

(a) Mary is older than John.
</td>
<td rowspan="2">
When we use adjectives (e.g., old, ex—pensive) to compare two people or two things, the adjectives have special forms. We either add -er to an adjective or use more in front of an adjective. The use of -er or more is called the comparative form.
Notice in the examples: than follows the comparative form: older than, more expensive than.
</td>
</tr>
<tr>
<td colspan="3">
This watch costs $100.
That watch costs $50.

(b) This watch is more expensive than that watch.
</td>
</tr>
<tr>
<td></td>
<td>ADJECTIVE</td>
<td>COMPARATIVE FORM</td>
<td></td>
</tr>
<tr>
<td rowspan="3">ADJECTIVES WITH ONE SYLLABLE</td>
<td>old</td>
<td>older</td>
<td rowspan="3">Add -er to one-syllable adjectives.

Spelling note: If an adjective ends in one vowel and one consonant, double the consonant: fat-fatter, thin-thinner, hot-hotter.</td>
</tr>
<tr>
<td>cheap</td>
<td>cheaper</td>
</tr>
<tr>
<td>big</td>
<td>bigger</td>
</tr>
<tr>
<td rowspan="2">ADJECTIVES THAT END IN -Y</td>
<td>pretty</td>
<td>prettier</td>
<td rowspan="2">If an adjective ends in -y, change the -y to i and add -er.</td>
</tr>
<tr>
<td>funny</td>
<td>funnier</td>
</tr>
<tr>
<td rowspan="3">ADJECTIVES WITH TWO OR MORE SYLLABLES</td>
<td>famous</td>
<td>more famous</td>
<td rowspan="3">Use more in front of adjectives that have two or more syllables (except adjectives that end in -y).</td>
</tr>
<tr>
<td>expensive</td>
<td>more expensive</td>
</tr>
<tr>
<td>interesting</td>
<td>more interesting</td>
</tr>
<tr>
<td rowspan="3">IRREGULAR COMPARATIVE FORMS</td>
<td>good</td>
<td>better</td>
<td rowspan="3">The comparative forms of good, bad, and far are irregular.</td>
</tr>
<tr>
<td>bad</td>
<td>worse</td>
</tr>
<tr>
<td>far</td>
<td>farther/further</td>
</tr>
</table>

EXERCISE 7:   Write the comparative forms for the following adjectives.

1. old ____older (than)____   9. sweet_____

2. small _____   10. expensive_____

3. big _____   11. hot _____

4. important _____   12. cheap _____

5. easy _____   13. good_____

6. difficult _____   14. bad_____

7. long _____   15. far _____

8. heavy _____   16. lazy_____

EXERCISE 8:   Complete the sentences. Use the comparative form of the words in parentheses.

1. (*comfortable*)   This chair is ____more comfortable than____ that chair.

2. (*large*)   Your apartment is _____ mine.

3. (*warm*)   It's _____ today _____ it was yesterday.

4. (*dark*)   Tom's mustache is _____ Don's.

5. (*important*)   Love is _____ than money.

6. (*lazy*)   I'm _____ my roommate.

7. (*tall*)   My brother is _____ than I am.*

8. (*heavy*)   Iron is _____ wood.

_____

*Formal written English: *My brother is taller than I (am).*
Informal spoken English: *My brother is taller than me.*

Note: In formal English a subject pronoun follows **than.** However, in informal spoken English people frequently use an object pronoun after **than.**

9. (*difficult*) My physics course is _____

_____ my math course.

10. (*good*) Her English is _____ her husband's.

11. (*long*) The Nile River is _____ the Mississippi.

12. (*intelligent*) A dog is _____ a chicken.

13. (*good*) My wife's cooking is _____

_____ mine.

14. (*bad*) My cooking is _____ my wife's.

15. (*short*) My little finger is _____ my middle finger.

16. (*pretty*) This dress is _____ that one.

17. (*far*) Your apartment is _____

from school _____ mine.

18. (*strong*) A horse is _____ a person.

19. (*curly*) Tom's hair is _____ mine.

20. (*beautiful*) A rose is _____ a weed.

EXERCISE 9: Same as the preceding exercise.

1. (*good*) The weather today is _____ it was yesterday.

2. (*bad*) The weather yesterday was _____

_____ it is today.

3. (*funny*) This story is _____ that story.

4. (*interesting*) This book is _____ that book.

5. (*smart*)   Bob is _____ his brother.

6. (*famous*)   A movie star is _____ I am.

7. (*wide*)   A highway is _____ an
                  alley.

8. (*deep*)   The Pacific Ocean is _____
                  the Mediterranean Sea.

9. (*confusing*) This story is _____ that
                  story.

10. (*fat*)   A pig is _____ a chicken.

11. (*thin*)   A giraffe's neck is _____
                  an elephant's neck.

12. (*far*)   My house is _____ from

                  downtown _____ your
                  house is.

13. (*good*)   Reading a good book is _____

                  _____ watching television.

14. (*easy*)   My English class is _____
                  my history class.

15. (*nervous*)   The groom was _____ at

                  the wedding _____ the
                  bride.

EXERCISE 10—ORAL: Compare the following. Use the adjective in parentheses. Use **more** or **-er.** (*Example: A mouse is smaller than an elephant.*)

1. a mouse
   an elephant
   (*small*)

2. my old shoes
   my new shoes
   (*comfortable*)

3. your hair
   my hair
   (*dark*)

4. my arm
   your arm
   (*long*)

5. biology
   chemistry
   (*interesting*)

6. I
   my brother
   (*thin*)

7. my hair
   her hair
   (*curly*)

8. her hair
   his hair
   (*straight*)

9. this book
   that one
   (*good*)

10. the weather here
    the weather in my
    hometown
    (*bad*)

11. this chapter
    Chapter 10
    (*easy*)

12. Japanese grammar
    English grammar
    (*difficult*)

EXERCISE 11—ORAL (BOOKS CLOSED):

A. Compare this book to that book. (The books are imaginary.)

> *Example:* big
> *Response:* This book is bigger than that book/that one.

1. large	5. expensive	9. difficult
2. interesting	6. easy	10. cheap
3. small	7. good	11. funny
4. heavy	8. bad	12. important

B. Compare John to Dick. (The two people are imaginary.)

1. tall	5. young	9. friendly*
2. strong	6. happy	10. thin
3. lazy	7. kind	11. famous
4. intelligent	8. interesting	12. busy

EXERCISE 12: Complete the sentences. Use the comparative form of the words in the list (or your own words).

big	*easy*	*important*
bright	*expensive*	*intelligent*
cheap	*fast*	*large*
cold	*high*	*small*
comfortable	*hot*	*sweet*

1. An elephant is ___bigger than/larger than___ a mouse.

2. A lemon is sour. An orange is _____ a lemon.

3. Texas is a large state, but Alaska is _____ Texas.

4. A diamond costs a lot of money. A diamond is _____

   _____ a ruby.

5. Hamburger is expensive, but it's _____ steak.

---

*The comparative of **friendly** has two possible forms: *friendlier than* or *more friendly than*.

6. An airplane moves quickly. An airplane is _____

_____ an automobile.

7. A lake is _____ an ocean.

8. A person can think logically. A person is _____

_____ an animal.

9. Hills are low. Mountains are _____ hills.

10. The sun gives off a lot of light. The sun is_____

_____ the moon.

11. Sometimes my feet hurt when I wear high heels. Bedroom slippers are

_____ shoes with high heels.

12. Arithmetic isn't difficult. Arithmetic is _____

_____ algebra.

13. Good health is _____ money.

14. The weather today is _____ it was yesterday.

EXERCISE 13—ORAL (BOOKS CLOSED):   Compare the following.

Example: an elephant to a mouse
Response: An elephant is bigger than a mouse/more intelligent than a mouse,
              etc.

1. an orange to a lemon
2. a lake to an ocean
3. good health to money
4. hamburger to steak
5. an airplane to an automobile
6. Alaska to Texas
7. a person to an animal
8. the sun to the moon
9. a mountain to a hill
10. arithmetic to algebra
11. a diamond to a ruby
12. bedroom slippers to high heels
13. a child to an adult
14. a horse to a person
15. the Nile River to the Mississippi River
16. your little finger to your ring finger
17. love to money
18. your hair to (. . .)'s hair
19. food in your country to food in the U.S./Canada
20. the weather today to the weather yesterday

EXERCISE 14—ORAL (BOOKS CLOSED): Make comparisons by using *-er/more* with these adjectives.

Example: large
Response: Canada is larger than Mexico./My feet are larger than yours./etc.

1. tall	6. long	11. small	16. sweet
2. important	7. easy	12. intelligent	17. high
3. cold	8. comfortable	13. big	18. interesting
4. curly	9. old	14. heavy	19. good
5. expensive	10. strong	15. cheap	20. bad

11-5 USING *AS...AS;* USING *LESS*

John is 21 years old. *Mary is 21 years old.* (a) John **is as old as** Mary.	Notice the pattern: **as** + adjective + **as** In (a): Their ages are the same.
This watch costs $100.00. *That watch costs $100.00.* (b) This watch **is as expensive as** that watch.	In (b): The price of the watches is the same.
Fred is 20 years old. *Jean is 21 years old.* (c) Fred **isn't as old as** Jean. (d) Fred **is younger than** Jean.	(c) and (d) have the same meaning.
This book costs $3.00. *That books costs $5.00.* (e) This book **isn't as expensive as** that book. (f) This book **is cheaper than** that book.	(e) and (f) have the same meaning.
(g) This book **isn't as expensive as** that book. (h) This book **is less expensive than** that book.	(g) and (h) have the same meaning. ***Less*** is the opposite of ***more***. ***Less*** is used with adjectives that have two or more syllables (except adjectives that end in **-y**). ***Less*** is usually not used with one-syllable adjectives or adjectives that end in **-y**. INCORRECT: *Fred is less old than Jean.* CORRECT: *Fred isn't as old as Jean.* *Fred is younger than Jean.*

EXERCISE 15:   Complete the following sentences by using *as...as* and the adjective in parentheses.

1. (*tall*)   Mary is ____as tall as____ her brother.

2. (*sweet*)   A lemon isn't _____ an orange.

3. (*big*)   A donkey isn't _____ a horse.

4. (*friendly*)   People in this city are _____ the people in my hometown.

5. (*dark*)   Paul's hair isn't _____ his brother's.

6. (*cold*)   The weather isn't _____ today _____ it was yesterday.

7. (*pretty*)   This dress is _____ that one.

8. (*expensive*)   A pencil isn't _____ a pen.

EXERCISE 16:   Make sentences with the same meaning by using *less,* if *possible.*

1. This book isn't as expensive as that book. ____This book is less expensive than____ ____that book.____

2. Bob isn't as old as Jim. ____(no change)____ _____

3. Arithmetic isn't as difficult as algebra. _____

4. Arithmetic isn't as hard as algebra. _____

5. This chair isn't as comfortable as that chair. _____

6. This box isn't as heavy as that box. _____

7. A hill isn't as high as a mountain. _____

8. Swimming isn't as dangerous as boxing. _____

_____

9. I'm not as tall as my brother. _____

_____

10. This letter isn't as important as that letter. _____

_____

EXERCISE 17: Make sentences with the same meaning by using **as . . . as** with the adjective in parentheses.

1. Bob is younger than Sally. (*old*)

   Bob isn't as old as Sally. _____

2. This book is less expensive than that one. (*expensive*)

   This book isn't as expensive as that one. _____

3. I'm shorter than my sister. (*tall*)

   _____

4. This exercise is more difficult than the last one. (*easy*)

   _____

5. My new shoes are less comfortable than my old shoes. (*comfortable*)

   _____

6. My little finger is shorter than my index finger. (*long*)

   _____

7. Hamburger is less expensive than steak. (*expensive*)

   _____

8. This book is worse than that book. (*good*)

   _____

9. My apartment is smaller than yours. (*big*)

   _____

10. In my opinion, chemistry is less interesting than psychology. (*interesting*)

    _____

EXERCISE 18:   Make sentences with the same meaning by using *as . . . as.*

1. This room is smaller than that room.

   <u>   This room isn't as big as that room.   </u>

2. An animal is less intelligent than a human being.

   _____

3. Soda pop is less expensive than beer.

   _____

4. The Mississippi River is shorter than the Nile River.

   _____

5. Tom's pronunciation is worse than Sue's.

   _____

6. Algebra is more difficult than arithmetic.

   _____

7. Money is less important than good health.

   _____

8. American coffee is weaker than Turkish coffee.

   _____

9. A limousine is smaller than a bus.

   _____

10. A wooden chair is less comfortable than a sofa.

   _____

EXERCISE 19:   Complete the following with your own words.

1. I'm taller _____

2. I'm not as old _____

3. A chicken isn't as big _____

4. Food in the United States/Canada isn't as good _____

5. An ocean is deeper _____

6. An apple is less expensive _____

7. It's warmer today _____

8. My hair isn't as curly _____

9. A hill isn't as high _____

10. A dog is less intelligent _____

11. My hair is darker _____

12. My apartment is less comfortable _____

13. The moon isn't as bright _____

14. Money is more important _____

15. English grammar isn't as difficult _____

11-6 USING *BUT*

(a) John is rich, **but** Mary is poor.	*But* gives the idea that "This is the opposite of that."
(b) John is rich, **but** Mary isn't.	

Note: A comma usually precedes *but.*

EXERCISE 20: Complete the following sentences by using adjectives.

1. An orange is sweet, but a lemon is ____sour_____.

2. The weather is hot today, but it was _____ yesterday.

3. These dishes are clean, but those dishes are _____.

4. This suitcase is heavy, but that suitcase is _____.

5. My hair is light, but my brother's hair is _____.

6. These shoes are uncomfortable, but those shoes are _____.

7. Linda is tall, but her sister is _____.

8. This street is narrow, but that street is_____.

9. This exercise is easy, but that exercise is _____.

10. My old apartment is big, but my new apartment is _____.

11. This food is good, but that food is _____.

12. A chicken is stupid, but a human being is _____.

13. Dick is fat, but his brother is _____.

14. This answer is right, but that answer is _____.

15. This towel is dry, but that towel is _____.

16. This cup is full, but that cup is _____.

17. This street is noisy, but that street is _____.

18. This picture is ugly, but that picture is _____.

19. This sentence is confusing, but that sentence is _____.

20. This car is safe, but that car is _____.

21. A kitten is weak, but a horse is_____.

22. This watch is expensive, but that watch is _____.

23. Tom is hard-working, but his brother is _____.

24. A pillow is soft, but a rock is _____.

25. My apartment is messy, but Bob's apartment is always_____.

EXERCISE 21: Study the examples. Complete the sentences.

1. Mary is at home, but her husband ___isn't_____.

2. Bob isn't at home, but his wife ___is_____.

3. Beds are comfortable, but park benches ___aren't_____.

4. I wasn't at home last night, but my roommate ___was_____.

5. Bob was in class yesterday, but Ann and Linda ___weren't_____.

6. Jack wants to go to the zoo, but Barbara ___doesn't_____.

7. I don't want to go to the movie, but my friends ___do_____.

8. Tom went to the party, but Steve ___didn't_____.

9. Jerry can speak French, but I ___can't_____.

10. Mary will be at the meeting, but Helen ___won't_____.

11. I was at home yesterday, but my roommate_____.

12. This shirt is clean, but that one _____.

13. These shoes aren't comfortable, but those shoes _____.

14. I like strong coffee, but Karen_____.

15. Mike doesn't write clearly, but Ted _____.

16. I ate breakfast this morning, but my roommate _____.

17. Carol has a car, but Jerry _____.

18. Jerry doesn't have a car, but Carol_____.

19. Ron was at the party, but his wife _____.

20. Ron went to the party, but his wife _____.

21. Ellen can speak Spanish, but her husband _____.

22. Ted can't speak Spanish, but his wife _____.

23. I won't be at home tonight, but Sue _____.

24. Dan will be in class tomorrow, but Eddie _____.

25. Mary won't be here tomorrow, but Alice _____.

EXERCISE 22—ORAL (BOOKS CLOSED): Complete the sentences. Use *but....*

> *Example:*   (Ali) went to a party last night. . . .
> *Response:*   (Ali) went to a party last night, but (Carlos) didn't.
>
> *Example:*   (Anna) likes strong coffee. . . .
> *Response:*   (Anna) likes strong coffee, but (I) don't.

1. (. . .) is in class today. . . .

2. (. . .) can speak (*language*). . . .

3. (. . .) was at home last night. . . .

4. (. . .) lives in the dorm. . . .

5. (. . .) went to a movie last night. . . .

6. (. . .) likes hamburgers. . . .

7. (. . .) will be here tomorrow. . . .

8. (. . .) wears glasses. . . .

9. (. . .) isn't in class today. . . .

10. (. . .) can't speak (*language*). . . .

11. (. . .) wasn't in class yesterday. . . .

12. (. . .) doesn't live in an apartment. . . .

13. (. . .) didn't study last night. . . .

14. (. . .) won't be here tomorrow. . . .

15. (. . .) doesn't have a car. . . .

16. (. . .) didn't go to a movie last night. . . .

17. (. . .) has a mustache. . . .

18. (. . .) doesn't smoke. . . .

19. (. . .) is from (*country*). . . .

20. (. . .) was in class yesterday. . . .

21. (. . .) can't play (*instrument*). . . .

22. (. . .) didn't watch TV last night. . . .

23. (. . .) stayed home last night. . . .

24. (. . .) will be at home tonight. . . .

25. (. . .) has curly hair. . . .

26. (. . .) isn't hungry right now. . . .

27. (. . .) likes hot food. . . .

28. (. . .) went to a Chinese restaurant last night. . . .

29. (. . .) doesn't live in an apartment. . . .

30. (. . .) is married. . . .

31. (. . .) can wiggle his/her ears. . . .

32. (. . .) has a car. . . .

33. (. . .) carries a bookbag to class. . . .

34. (. . .) doesn't have a (*language*) dictionary. . . .

35. (. . .) went to the library last night. . . .

EXERCISE 23: Picture A and Picture B are not the same. There are many differences between A and B. Can you find all of the differences?

| A | B |

Example: There's a wooden chair in Picture A, but there isn't a chair in B.

EXERCISE 24—WRITTEN:

1. Write about this city. Compare it to your hometown.
2. Write about your present residence. Compare it to a past residence. For example, compare your new apartment to your old apartment.

CHECKLIST OF WORDS AND STRUCTURES USED IN COMPARISONS:

the same (as)	*–er/more*
similar (to)	*less*
like	*as . . . as*
alike	*but*
different (from)	

MORE IRREGULAR VERBS

become – became	feed – fed
bend – bent	fight – fought
bite – bit	hide – hid
build – built	hold – held
choose – chose	shake – shook

EXERCISE 25—ORAL (BOOKS CLOSED): Practice using the irregular verbs in the above list.

Example: *shake-shook* People often shake hands when they meet. I'm shaking hands with (. . .). (. . .) and I shook hands. What did we do?

Response: You shook hands.

EXERCISE 26:   Complete the sentences. Use the words in parentheses.

1. I (*hide*) _____ my husband's birthday present in the closet
   yesterday.

2. A: Ow!

   B: What's the matter?

   A: I (*bite*) _____ my tongue.

3. When I asked Dennis a question, he (*shake*) _____ his head no.

4. Diane is a computer programmer. Yesterday she (*feed*) _____
   information into the computer.

5. A: I've lost touch with some of our childhood friends. What happened to Greg
      Jones?

   B: He (*become*) _____ a doctor.

   A: What happened to Sandy Peterson?

   B: She (*become*) _____ a lawyer.

6. I offered the child a red lollipop or a green lollipop. He (*choose*)

   _____ the red one.

7. Doug is a new father. He felt very happy when he (*hold*) _____ his
   baby for the first time.

8. Nancy and Tom saved money. They didn't buy a bookcase for their new

   apartment. They (*build*) _____ one.

9. We saw a strong man at the circus. He (*bend*) _____ an iron bar.

10. A: Why did the children fight?

    B: They (*fight*) _____ because both of them wanted the same toy.

EXERCISE 27—ORAL (BOOKS CLOSED):   In order to practice irregular
verbs, answer **yes**.

   Example: Did you write a letter yesterday?
   Response: Yes, I did. I wrote a letter yesterday.

1. Did you fly to (*this city*)?
2. Did you drink a cup of tea this morning?
3. Did you come to class yesterday?
4. Did you go downtown yesterday?
5. Did you eat breakfast this morning?
6. Did you lend some money to (. . .)?
   (. . .), did you spend the money?
7. Did you lose your pen yesterday? Did you find it?
8. Did you give your dictionary to (. . .)?
   (. . .), did you keep it?
9. Did you throw your book to (. . .)?
   (. . .), did you catch it?
10. Did someone steal your wallet? Did you get it back?
11. Did you wake up at seven this morning?
12. Did you get up at seven this morning?
13. Did the wind blow yesterday?
14. Did you shut the door?
15. Did class begin at . . .?
16. Did you say hello to (. . .)?
17. Did you tell (. . .) to sit down?
    (. . .), did you sit down?
18. Did you hear my last question?
19. Did you teach your daughter/son to count to ten?
20. Did you bring your books to class today?
21. Did you forget your books?
22. Did you see (. . .) yesterday? Did you speak to him/her?
23. Did you meet (. . .)'s wife/husband yesterday?
24. Did you leave your sunglasses at the restaurant?
25. Did you read the newspaper this morning?
26. Did you go shopping yesterday? Did you buy something?
27. Did you drive your car to school today?
28. Did you ride a horse to school today?
29. Did a barber cut your hair?
30. Did you run to class this morning?
31. Did your pen cost 89¢?
32. Did you understand my question?
33. Did you come to class yesterday?
34. Did you make a mistake?
35. Did you take the bus to school today?
36. Did you write a letter yesterday? Did you send it?
37. Did the telephone ring?
38. Did you break your arm?
39. Did you shake your head?
40. Did you draw a picture?
41. Did you bend your elbow?
42. Did you win a million dollars?
43. Did you feel good yesterday?
44. Did you feed the birds at the park?
45. Did you bite your finger?
46. Did you hurt your finger?
47. Did you hold (. . .)'s hand?
48. Did you build a bookcase?
49. Did you stand at the bus stop?
50. Did you sing in the shower this morning?
51. Did you grow up in (*country*)?
52. Did you become an adult?
53. Did (*name of a sports team*) win yesterday?
54. Did you fall down yesterday?
55. Did you think about me yesterday?
56. Did you fight yesterday?

57. Which pen do you want? Did you choose this one?

58. Did you hide your money under your mattress?

59. Did your car hit a telephone pole yesterday?

60. Did you put your books under your desk?

chapter *12*

Making Comparisons — Part II

12-1 THE SUPERLATIVE: USING *-EST* AND *MOST*

(a) COMPARATIVE: My thumb is **shorter than** my index finger.	The comparative *(-er/more)* compares two things or people.
(b) SUPERLATIVE: My hand has five fingers. My thumb is **the shortest** (finger) of all.	The superlative *(-est/most)* compares three or more things or people.

	ADJECTIVE	COMPARATIVE	SUPERLATIVE
ADJECTIVES WITH ONE SYLLABLE	old	older (than)	the oldest (of all)
	big	bigger (than)	the biggest (of all)
ADJECTIVES THAT END IN *-Y*	pretty	prettier (than)	the prettiest (of all)
	easy	easier (than)	the easiest (of all)
ADJECTIVES WITH TWO OR MORE SYLLABLES	expensive	more expensive (than)	the most expensive (of all)
	important	more important (than)	the most important (of all)
IRREGULAR FORMS	good	better (than)	the best (of all)
	bad	worse (than)	the worst (of all)
	far	farther/further (than)	the farthest/furthest (of all)

EXERCISE 1:   Write the comparative and superlative forms of the following adjectives.

	COMPARATIVE	SUPERLATIVE
1. long	_longer (than)_	_the longest (of all)_
2. small	_____	_____
3. heavy	_____	_____
4. comfortable	_____	_____
5. hard	_____	_____
6. difficult	_____	_____
7. easy	_____	_____
8. good	_____	_____
9. bad	_____	_____
10. far	_____	_____

EXERCISE 2:   Complete the sentences. Use the adjectives in parentheses.

1. (*long*)   The Nile is ____the longest____ river in the world.

2. (*large*)   The USSR is _____ country in the world in area.

3. (*large*)   The People's Republic of China is _____ _____ country in the world in population.

4. (*high*)   Mt. McKinley in Alaska is _____ mountain in North America.

5. (*tall*)   The Sears Tower in Chicago is _____ _____ building in the world.

6. (*big*)   Lake Superior is _____ lake in North America.

7. (*short*)   February is _____ month of the year.

8. (*far*)   Pluto is _____ planet from the sun.

9. (*beautiful*)   In my opinion, Seattle is _____ city in the United States.

10. (*bad*)   In my opinion, Harry's Steak House _____

_____ restaurant in the city.

11. (*good*)   In my opinion, the Doghouse Bar and Grill has

_____ hamburgers in the city.

12. (*comfortable*)   Bob is sitting in _____ chair in the room.

13. (*fast*)   _____ way to travel is by airplane.

14. (*good*)   When you feel depressed, laughter is _____

_____ medicine.

15. (*large*)   Asia is _____ continent in the world.

16. (*small*)   Australia is _____ continent in the world.

17. (*expensive*)   Sally ordered _____ food on the menu for dinner last night.

18. (*easy*)   Taking a taxi is _____ way to get to the airport.

19. (*important*)   I think good health is _____ thing in life.

20. (*famous*)   The Gateway Arch is _____ landmark in St. Louis, Missouri.

21. (*large*)   _____ city in Canada is Toronto.

EXERCISE 3:   Make at least four statements of comparison about each group of pictures.

A. COMPARE THE WEIGHT OF THE THREE PIGS

PORKY   OINKY   PIGGY

1. Porky is _____ thinner than _____ Oinky.

2. Piggy is _____ fatter than _____ Oinky.

3. Piggy is _____ the fattest _____ of all.

4. Porky is _____ the thinnest _____ of all.

B. COMPARE THE AGES OF THE CHILDREN

TOMMY
(3 YEARS OLD)   HELEN
(6 YEARS OLD)   ANN
(8 YEARS OLD)

5. Ann is _____ Helen.

6. Ann is _____ Tommy.

7. Ann is _____ of all.

8. Tommy is _____ of all.

C. COMPARE THE HEIGHT OF THE THREE WOMEN

LINDA   KAREN   ALICE

9. _____ is the tallest.

10. _____ is the shortest.

11. _____ is taller than _____

    but shorter than _____

12. _____ isn't as tall as _____.

D. COMPARE THE STRENGTH OF THE THREE MEN

MIKE   JOE   DON

13. _____

14. _____

15. _____

16. _____

E. COMPARE THE PRICES OF THE THREE BOOKS

17. _____

18. _____

19. _____

20. _____

F. COMPARE THE DIFFICULTY OF THE THREE PROBLEMS

$$2+2=$$
PROBLEM A

$$650 \div 7 =$$
PROBLEM B

SOLVE FOR X

$$\frac{2(2x+3)}{6(2x-3)} + \frac{3(x+2)}{5(2x-3)} = 2$$

PROBLEM C

21. _____

22. _____

23. _____

24. _____

G. COMPARE THE TEST PAPERS

25. _____

26. _____   _____

27. _____

28. _____

EXERCISE 4:   Complete the sentences. Use the correct form (comparative or superlative) of the adjectives in parentheses.

1. (*long*)   The Yangtze River is __longer than__ the Mississippi.

2. (*long*)   The Nile is __the longest__ river in the world.

3. (*large*)   The Caribbean Sea is _____ the Mediterranean Sea.

4. (*large*)   The Caribbean Sea is _____ sea in the world.

5. (*high*)   Mt. Everest is _____ mountain in the world.

6. (*high*)   Mt. Everest is _____ Mt. McKinley.

7. (*big*)   Africa is _____ North America.

8. (*small*)   Europe is _____ South America.

9. (*large*)   Asia is _____ continent in the world.

10. (*big*)   Canada is _____ the United States in area.

11. (*large*)   Indonesia is _____ Japan
in population.

12. (*good*)   Fruit is _____ for your

health _____ candy.

13. (*good*)   The student cafeteria has_____
roast beef sandwiches in the city.

14. (*comfortable*)   I have a pair of boots, a pair of sandals, and a pair of running

shoes. The sandals are_____

the boots, but the running shoes are _____

_____ of all.

15. (*easy*)   This exercise is _____

that one. This is one of _____
exercises in the book.

EXERCISE 5:   Study the examples.

(a) The Amazon is **one of the longest rivers** in the world.	The superlative often follows **one of.** Notice the pattern: **one of** + *superlative* + *plural noun*
(b) A Rolls-Royce is **one of the most expensive cars** in the world.	
(c) Alice is **one of the most intelligent people** in our class.	

Make sentences about the following. Use *one of* + *superlative* + *plural noun.*

1. a long river in the world

_____The Mississippi is one of the longest rivers in the world._____

2. a nice park in (*this city*)

_____Forest Park is one of the nicest parks in St. Louis._____

3. a tall person in our class

_____Talal is one of the tallest people* in our class._____

4. a big city in the world

_____

_____

* People is usually used instead of *persons* in the plural.

5. a beautiful city in the world

_____

6. a nice person in our class

_____

7. a high mountain in the world

_____

8. a good restaurant in (*this city*)

_____

9. a famous landmark in Canada/the United States

_____

EXERCISE 6—WRITTEN: Write sentences using **one of** + *superlative* + *plural noun.* (Use your own paper.)

1. a big city in Canada
2. a large state in the U.S.
3. a beautiful country in the world
4. a friendly person in our class
5. a good place to visit in the world
6. a famous person in the world
7. an important thing in life
8. a bad restaurant in (*this city*)
9. a famous landmark in (*name of a country*)
10. a tall building in (*this city*)
11. a dangerous sport in the world
12. a serious problem in the world

EXERCISE 7: Take this quiz. If you don't know an answer, guess. After you take the quiz, look at information on pages 262–263 to determine the correct answers.*

PART A

1. What is the longest river in the world?
   (a) the Yangtze
   (b) the Amazon
   (c) the Nile
   (d) the Mississippi

_____

* *To the teacher:* When everyone has finished the quiz, divide the class into small groups. Ask each group to determine and discuss the correct answers by using the information on pages 262–263.

2. Is the Amazon River longer than the Mississippi River?
   (a) yes
   (b) no

3. Is the Yangtze River longer than the Mississippi River?
   (a) yes
   (b) no

4. Is the Yangtze River as long as the Nile River?
   (a) yes
   (b) no

5. Which of the two rivers are almost the same length?
   (a) the Nile and the Amazon
   (b) the Amazon and the Yangtze
   (c) the Nile and the Mississippi
   (d) the Mississippi and the Amazon

PART B

6. What is the largest sea in the world?
   (a) the Mediterranean Sea
   (b) the South China Sea
   (c) the Caribbean Sea

7. Is the South China Sea the smallest of the three seas listed above?
   (a) yes
   (b) no

PART C

8. What is the highest mountain in the world?
   (a) Mt. Everest
   (b) Mt. McKinley
   (c) Mt. Fuji

9. What is the tallest building in the world?
   (a) the Empire State Building (New York City)
   (b) the Sears Tower (Chicago)
   (c) the World Trade Center (New York City)

PART D

10. Below is a list of the continents in the world. List them in order according to size, from the largest to the smallest.

Africa   Europe
✔ Antarctica   North America
Asia   South America
Australia

(1) _____ (*the largest*)

(2) _____

(3) _____

(4) _____

(5) ____Antarctica_____

(6) _____

(7) _____ (*the smallest*)

PART E

11. Which of the following countries is the largest in area in the world?
    (a) Canada
    (b) the People's Republic of China
    (c) the United States
    (d) the USSR (the Union of Soviet Socialist Republics)

12. Which of the following four countries is the largest in area?
    (a) Brazil
    (b) Canada
    (c) the People's Republic of China
    (d) the United States

13. Which of the following countries is the largest in population in the world?
    (a) India
    (b) the People's Republic of China
    (c) the United States
    (d) the USSR

14. Which of the following two countries is larger in population?
    (a) India
    (b) the USSR

15. Which of the following two countries is larger in population?
    (a) Brazil
    (b) Japan

16. Which of the following two countries is smaller in population?
    (a) Brazil
    (b) Indonesia

Use the following information to determine the correct answers for the quiz in Exercise 7.* (Note: Each list is in alphabetical order.)

PART A

RIVER	LENGTH
the Amazon River	3,915 miles
the Mississippi River	2,348 miles
the Nile River	4,145 miles
the Yangtze River	3,900 miles

PART B

SEA	SIZE
the Caribbean Sea	970,000 square miles
the Mediterranean Sea	969,000 square miles
the South China Sea	895,000 square miles

PART C

MOUNTAIN	HEIGHT
Mt. Everest	29,028 feet
Mt. Fuji	12,389 feet
Mt. McKinley	20,320 feet

BUILDING	HEIGHT
the Empire State Building	1,136 feet
the Sears Tower	1,451 feet
the World Trade Center	1,350 feet

PART D

CONTINENT	SIZE
Africa	11,707,000 square miles
Antarctica	5,500,000 square miles
Asia	17,129,000 square miles
Australia	2,942,000 square miles

---

*Source of figures: *The Hammond Almanac, 1982 Edition.*

Europe . . . . .4,057,000 square miles
North America . . . . .9,363,000 square miles
South America . . . . .6,886,000 square miles

PART E

COUNTRY	AREA	POPULATION
Brazil	3,286,470 sq. mi.	119 million
Canada.	3,851,809 sq. mi.	24 million
India.	1,269,339 sq. mi.	651 million
Indonesia	788,430 sq. mi.	148 million
Japan	145,730 sq. mi.	116 million
the People's Republic of China	3,691,000 sq. mi.	945 million
the United States of America	3,615,123 sq. mi.	221 million
the USSR	8,649,490 sq. mi.	263 million

12-2 ADJECTIVES AND ADVERBS

	ADJECTIVE	ADVERB	
(a) Ann is a ⌐*adjective* careful ⌐ driver. (b) Ann drives ⌐*adverb* carefully. ⌐	careful slow quick easy	carefully slowly quickly easily	An adjective describes a noun. In (a): *careful* describes *driver*. An adverb describes the action of a verb. In (b): *carefully* describes *drives*. Most adverbs are formed by adding *-ly* to an adjective.
(c) John is a ⌐adjective fast ⌐ driver. (d) John drives ⌐*adverb* fast. ⌐	fast hard early late	fast hard early late	The adjective form and the adverb form are the same for *fast, hard, early, late.*
(e) Linda is a ⌐*adjective* good ⌐ writer. (f) Linda writes ⌐*adverb* well. ⌐	good	well	*Well* is the adverb form of *good.**

* *Well* can also be used as an adjective to mean "not sick". *Paul was sick last week, but now he's well.*

EXERCISE 8:   Complete the sentences by using the adjective or adverb in parentheses.

1. (*quiet, quietly*)   My hometown is small and _____quiet_____.

   I like living in a _____quiet_____ town.

2. (*quiet, quietly*)   Mr. Wilson whispered. He spoke _____

   _____quietly_____.

3. (*clear, clearly*)   Anna pronounces every word _____

   _____.

4. (*clear, clearly*)   We like to go boating in _____ weather.

5. (*careless, carelessly*)   Ed makes a lot of mistakes when he writes. He's a

   _____ writer.

6. (*careless, carelessly*)   Ed writes _____.

7. (*easy, easily*)   The teacher asked an _____ question.

8. (*easy, easily*)   I answered the teacher's question _____

   _____.

9. (*good, well*)   Jake can't see _____ without his glasses. He has poor eyesight.

10. (*good, well*)   David is kind, generous, and thoughtful. He is a

    _____ person.

EXERCISE 9:   Complete the sentences by using the correct form (adjective or adverb) of the word in parentheses.

1. (*careful*)   Do you drive _____carefully_____?

2. (*correct*)   Mary Ellen gave the _____ answer to the question.

3. (*correct*)   She answered the question _____.

4. (*fast*)   George is a _____ reader.

5. (*quick*)   George reads _____.

6. (*fast*)   George reads _____.

7. (*neat*)   Barbara has _____ handwriting. It is easy to read what she writes.

8. (*neat*)   Barbara writes _____.

9. (*hard*)   I study _____.

10. (*hard*)   The students took a _____ test.

11. (*honest*)   Jerry answered the question _____.

12. (*slow*)   Karen and Helen walked through the park

_____.

13. (*careless*) I made some _____ mistakes in my last composition.

14. (*quick*)   We were in a hurry, so we ate lunch _____.

15. (*early*)   Last night we had dinner _____ because we had to leave for the theater at 6:00.

16. (*early*)   We had an _____ dinner last night.

17. (*good*)   You speak English very _____.

18. (*good*)   Your English is very _____.

19. (*loud*)   I speak _____ when I talk to my grandfather because he has trouble hearing.

20. (*slow, clear*) Kim speaks English _____ and

_____.

EXERCISE 10:   The same as the preceding exercise.

1. (*good*)   Did you sleep _____well_____ last night?

2. (*fast*)   Karen is a _____ learner.

3. (*quick*)   She learns everything _____.

4. (*fast*)   Steve walks too _____. I can't keep up with him.

5. (*soft*)   Please speak _____. The children are asleep.

6. (*easy*)   This is an _____ exercise.

7. (*hard*)   It rained _____ yesterday.

8. (*clear*)   Our teacher explains everything _____.

9. (*late*)   Tim came to class _____ yesterday.

10. (*safe*)   The plane arrived at the airport _____.

11. (*hard*)   Helen is a _____ worker.

12. (*hard*)   She works _____.

13. (*late*)   I paid my telephone bill _____.

14. (*easy*)   Ron lifted the heavy box _____. He's very strong.

15. (*quiet*)   Joan entered the classroom _____ because she was late for class.

16. (*fast*)   Mike talks too _____. I can't understand him.

17. (*honest*)   Carol is an _____ person. I trust her completely.

18. (*good*)   I didn't understand the teacher's explanation very

     _____.

19. (*good*)   We had a _____ time at the party last night.

20. (*good*)   Linda speaks _____, but she doesn't write

     _____.

21. (*fluent*)   Alice speaks French _____.

12-3   MAKING COMPARISONS WITH ADVERBS

	COMPARATIVE	SUPERLATIVE	
(a) Kim speaks **more fluently than** Ali (does). (b) Anna speaks **the most fluently of all.**	more fluently more slowly more quickly	the most fluently the most slowly the most quickly	Use **more** and **most** with adverbs that end in **-ly.** *
(c) Tom worked **harder than** Bob (did). (d) Sue worked **the hardest of all.**	harder faster earlier later	the hardest the fastest the earliest the latest	Use **-er** and **-est** with irregular adverbs (**hard, fast, early, late**).
(e) Mary writes **better than** I do. (f) Dick writes **the best of all.**	better	the best	

* Exception: *early-earlier-earliest.*

EXERCISE 11:   Complete the sentences by using the correct form (comparative or superlative) of the adverbs in parentheses.

1. (*late*)   Karen got home _____later than_____ Alice (did.)

2. (*quickly*)   I finished my work _____ Tom (did).

3. (*beautifully*) Sue sings _____ Mary (does).

4. (*beautifully*) Ann sings _____ of all.

5. (*hard*)   My sister works _____ I (do).

6. (*hard*)   My brother works _____ of all.

7. (*carefully*)   My husband drives _____ I (do).

8. (*early*)   We arrived at the party _____ the Smiths (did).

9. (*early*)   The Wilsons arrived at the party _____

        _____ of all.

10. (*well*)   You can write _____ I (can).

11. (*well*)   Dick can write _____ of all.

12. (*clearly*)   Karen pronounces her words _____ Mary (does).

13. (*fast*)   I work _____ Jim (does).

14. (*fast*)   Tom finished his work _____ of all.

15. (*loudly*)   Ali speaks _____ Yoko (does).

16. (*fluently*)   Sue speaks Spanish _____ I (do).

17. (*fluently*)   Ted speaks Spanish _____ of all.

18. (*slowly*)   A turtle moves _____ a rabbit (does).

EXERCISE 12:   Use the correct form (adjective or adverb, comparative or superlative) of the words in parentheses.

1. (*careful*)   Karen drives _____more carefully than_____ her brother does.

2. (*beautiful*)   A tiger is _____ a pig.

3. (*neat*)   Tom's apartment is _____ mine.

4. (*neat*)   Dick's apartment is _____ of all.

5. (*neat*)   You write _____ I do.

6. (*neat*)   Ann writes _____ of all.

7. (*heavy*)   This suitcase is _____ that one.

8. (*clear*)   This author explains her ideas _____ that one.

9. (*good*)   I like rock music _____ classical music.

10. (*good*)   My husband can sing _____ I can.

11. (*good*)   My daughter can sing _____ of all.

12. (*hard*)   Sue studies _____ Fred.

13. (*hard*)   Jean studies _____ of all.

14. (*dangerous*)   A motorcycle is _____ a bicycle.

15. (*salty*)   Bacon is _____ beef.

16. (*late*)   Bob usually goes to bed _____ his roommate.

17. (*clear*)   Anna pronounces her words _____ of all the students in the class.

18. (*sharp*)   A razor blade is usually _____ a kitchen knife.

19. (*artistic*)   My son is _____ my daughter.

20. (*slow*)   I eat _____ my husband does.

12-4   USING *AS...AS* WITH ADVERBS

(a) Bob doesn't study **as hard as** his brother (does). (b) I didn't finish my work **as quickly as** Sue (did). (c) Yoko speaks English **as well as** Tony (does).	Notice the pattern in the examples: *as* + *adverb* + *as*

(d) I'm working **as fast as I can.** (e) I'm working **as fast as possible.** (f) Bob came **as quickly as he could.** (g) Bob came **as quickly as possible.**	Notice the patterns in the examples: **as** + *adverb* + **as** is frequently followed by *subject* + **can/could** or by **possible.**

EXERCISE 13: Complete the sentences. Compare John to your class-mates or yourself.

1. John is lazy. He doesn't work as hard___ as Yoko (does)./as I (do).___

2. John is a reckless driver. He doesn't drive as carefully _____

3. I can't read John's handwriting. He doesn't write as neatly _____

4. John goes to bed late. He doesn't go to bed as early _____

5. John was the last person to finish the test. He didn't finish it as quickly _____

   _____

6. John speaks softly. He doesn't speak as loudly _____

7. John is never in a hurry. He takes his time. He doesn't walk as fast _____

   _____

8. John is an insomniac. He doesn't sleep as well _____

9. John was the last person to finish the test. He didn't finish it as quickly _____

   _____

10. John rarely studies. He doesn't study as hard _____

EXERCISE 14:—ORAL: Change the sentences by using **as . . . as** + **possible** or **can/could.**

Examples: Please come early.
Please come as early as possible./Please come as early as you can.

Bob walked fast.
Bob walked as fast as possible./Bob walked as fast as he could.

1. Please come quickly.
2. Ann came quickly.
3. Please write neatly.
4. I opened the door quietly.
5. Please come soon.
6. Dick came soon.
7. Pronounce each word clearly.
8. Do you study hard?
9. I write to my parents often.
10. When Bobby saw a mean dog, he ran home fast.
11. I'm working fast.
12. Please give me your homework soon.
13. I'll get home early.
14. Steve answered the question well.
15. I'll call you soon.
16. I go swimming often.
17. Please finish the test soon.
18. I'll pay my telephone bill soon.

EXERCISE 15—WRITTEN:

Compare things and people you see in the classroom right now. Look at this thing and that thing and then compare them. Look at this person and that person and then compare them.

Write as quickly as you can.

EXERCISE 16—WRITTEN:

1. Write about your family. Compare the members of your family. Include yourself in the comparisons. (Who is younger than you? Who is the youngest of all? Etc.)
2. Write about your childhood friends when you were ten years old. Compare them. Include yourself in the comparisons. (Who could run faster than you? Who could run the fastest of all? Etc.)

12-5 USING LINKING VERBS

LINKING VERB		LINKING VERB + ADJECTIVE		
taste	(a) Candy	**tastes**	**sweet.**	Some verbs are followed by adjectives. These verbs are called *linking verbs*.
smell	(b) Flowers	**smell**	**good.**	
feel	(c) I	**feel**	**good.**	
look	(d) That chair	**looks**	**comfortable.**	
sound	(e) That book	**sounds**	**interesting.**	

EXERCISE 17—ORAL: Do any of the following adjectives describe how you feel today?

1. good
2. fine
3. terrible
4. terrific
5. lazy

6. sleepy
7. tired
8. old
9. nervous
10. sick

EXERCISE 18—ORAL: Name things that . . .

1. taste good
2. taste terrible
3. taste delicious
4. taste sweet

5. taste sour
6. smell good
7. smell bad
8. smell wonderful

EXERCISE 19—ORAL:

1. Name something in this room that . . .
   looks clean
   looks dirty
   looks new
   looks old
   looks expensive
   looks comfortable
   looks nice

2. Name an animal that . . .
   looks strong
   looks intelligent
   looks dangerous

3. Name a sport that . . .
   looks easy
   looks hard

EXERCISE 20—ORAL:

1. You're not angry, but can you look angry?
2. Can you look sad?
3. Can you look happy?
4. Can you look tired?

5. Can you look nervous?
6. Can you look busy?
7. Can you look comfortable?

EXERCISE 21:   Complete the sentences. Use the words in the list or your own words.

easy   *good/terrific/wonderful*   *interesting*   *tired*
hard   *terrible/awful*

1. Mary told me about a new book. I want to read it. It sounds _____.

2. Al told me about a movie he saw. A mad killer murders 27 people with a knife.

   It sounds _____!

3. Karen learned how to make paper flowers. She told me how to do it. It sounds

   _____.

4. There's a new play at the community theater. I read a review of it in the

   newspaper. It sounds _____. I'd like to see it.

5. Professor Wilson is going to lecture on the problems of overpopulation

   tomorrow evening. I think I'll go. It sounds _____.

6. Chris explained how to fix a flat tire. It sounds _____. I think I can
   do it.

7. Ann didn't finish her dinner because it didn't taste _____.

8. What's for dinner? Something smells _____. Ummm! What is it?

9. Karen didn't get any sleep last night because she studied all night for a test.

   Today she looks _____.

10. A: What's the matter? Do you feel okay?

    B: No. I feel _____. I think I'm getting a cold.

11. A: Do you want to go to the movie tonight? *The Mad Knife Killer* is playing at
        the theater on 5th Street.

    B: My sister saw that movie last night. She told me all about it. It sounds

        _____.

12. A: Do you like my new dress, darling?

    B: You look _____, honey.

13. A: Pyew!* Something smells _____! Do you smell it too?

    B: I sure do. It's the garbage in the alley.

14. A: Do you want to go the lecture tonight?

    B: Yes. I'd like to. It sounds _____.

---

* "Pyew" is sometimes said "P.U." Both "pyew" and "p.u." mean that something smells very bad.

appendix *1*

Numbers

1	one	1st	first
2	two	2nd	second
3	three	3rd	third
4	four	4th	fourth
5	five	5th	fifth
6	six	6th	sixth
7	seven	7th	seventh
8	eight	8th	eighth
9	nine	9th	ninth
10	ten	10th	tenth
11	eleven	11th	eleventh
12	twelve	12th	twelfth
13	thirteen	13th	thirteenth
14	fourteen	14th	fourteenth
15	fifteen	15th	fifteenth
16	sixteen	16th	sixteenth
17	seventeen	17th	seventeenth
18	eighteen	18th	eighteenth
19	nineteen	19th	nineteenth
20	twenty	20th	twentieth
21	twenty-one	21st	twenty-first

22	twenty-two		22nd	twenty-second
23	twenty-three		23rd	twenty-third
30	thirty		30th	thirtieth
40	forty		40th	fortieth
50	fifty		50th	fiftieth
60	sixty		60th	sixtieth
70	seventy		70th	seventieth
80	eighty		80th	eightieth
90	ninety		90th	ninetieth
100	one hundred		100th	one hundredth
200	two hundred		200th	two hundredth

1000	one thousand
10,000	ten thousand
100,000	one hundred thousand
1,000,000	one million

appendix 2

DAYS

Monday	(Mon.)
Tuesday	(Tues.)
Wednesday	(Wed.)
Thursday	(Thurs.)
Friday	(Fri.)
Saturday	(Sat.)
Sunday	(Sun.)

MONTHS

January	(Jan.)
February	(Feb.)
March	(Mar.)
April	(Apr.)
May	(May)
June	(June)
July	(July)
August	(Aug.)
September	(Sept.)
October	(Oct.)
November	(Nov.)
December	(Dec.)

Using numbers to write the date:

month/day/year
10/31/41 = October 31, 1941
4/15/82 = April 15, 1982

Saying dates:

USUAL WRITTEN FORM	USUAL SPOKEN FORM
January 1	January first/the first of January
March 2	March second/the second of March
May 3	May third/the third of May
June 4	June fourth/the fourth of June
August 5	August fifth/the fifth of August
October 10	October tenth/the tenth of October
November 27	November twenty-seventh/the twenty-seventh of November

appendix 3

Ways of Saying the Time

9:00	It's nine o'clock. It's nine.
9:05	It's nine-oh-five. It's five (minutes) after nine. It's five (minutes) past nine.
9:10	It's nine-ten. It's ten (minutes) after nine. It's ten (minutes) past nine.
9:15	It's nine-fifteen. It's a quarter after nine. It's a quarter past nine.
9:30	It's nine-thirty. It's half past nine.
9:45	It's nine-forty-five. It's a quarter to ten. It's a quarter of ten.
9:50	It's nine-fifty. It's ten (minutes) to ten. It's ten (minutes) of ten.
12:00	It's noon. It's midnight.

a.m. = morning   It's nine a.m.

p.m. = afternoon/evening/night   It's nine p.m.

appendix 4

Irregular Verbs

SIMPLE FORM	SIMPLE PAST	SIMPLE FORM	SIMPLE PAST
be	was, were	eat	ate
become	became	fall	fell
begin	began	feed	fed
bend	bent	feel	felt
bite	bit	fight	fought
blow	blew	find	found
break	broke	fly	flew
bring	brought	forget	forgot
build	built	get	got
buy	bought	give	gave
catch	caught	go	went
choose	chose	grow	grew
come	came	hang	hung
cost	cost	have	had
cut	cut	hear	heard
do	did	hide	hid
draw	drew	hit	hit
drink	drank	hold	held
drive	drove	hurt	hurt

SIMPLE FORM	SIMPLE PAST	SIMPLE FORM	SIMPLE PAST
keep	kept	sing	sang
know	knew	sit	sat
leave	left	sleep	slept
lend	lent	speak	spoke
lose	lost	spend	spent
make	made	stand	stood
meet	met	steal	stole
pay	paid	swim	swam
put	put	take	took
read	read	teach	taught
ride	rode	tear	tore
ring	rang	tell	told
run	ran	think	thought
say	said	throw	threw
see	saw	understand	understood
sell	sold	wake up	woke up
send	sent	wear	wore
shake	shook	win	won
shut	shut	write	wrote

Index